Spaces in Migration

Spaces in Migration
Postcards of a Revolution

Edited by
Glenda Garelli, Federica Sossi
and Martina Tazzioli

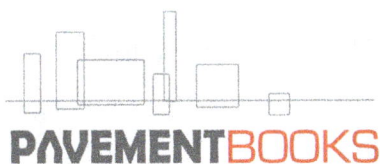

PAVEMENTBOOKS

Pavement Books
London, UK
www.pavementbooks.com

Spaces in Migration: Postcards of a Revolution

First published 2013 © Wafa Abida, Paola Gandolfi, Glenda Garelli, Lucio Guarinoni, Robby Habans, Issam Heni, Federica Sossi, Martina Tazzioli

Cover Image based on a detail from the 'Spaces in Migration' Map by Robby Habans (2013). Reproduced with permission from the artist.

Parts of the text reproduced with permission from the original Italian publication, F. Sossi (ed.), *Spazi in migrazione. Cartoline di una rivoluzione* (Verona: Ombre Corte, 2012).

British Library Cataloguing in Publication Data.

A catalogue record for this book is available from the British Library.

ISBN: 978-0-9571470-1-0

Contents

Acknowledgments

This book comes out of two years of discovery, marvel, research, and political engagement spanning the two shores of the Mediterranean, and which for us started with the Tunisian revolution and with the upheavals of European spaces that Tunisian migrants brought about. We would like to thank all the people who have shared these past two years with us and who have been the protagonists or the narrators of these discoveries, marvels, and engagements.

Quoting Issam Heni from one of the interviews in the book, we would like to start with a 'tribute to the anonymous people' who made a revolution and to thank those, among these 'anonymous people', who shook European space as they exerted this newly conquered freedom as a freedom of movement. In the meantime, some of them ceased to be anonymous to us as we met them in Tunisia or in the spaces of their 'insistences' in European countries. It would be too long to list all their names here but to them goes all our gratitude. Likewise, we want to thank all the refugees and 'rejected' refugees of Choucha camp, those we met, those we interviewed, and those with whom we have only crossed paths and exchanged a few words.

A special thank you goes to the mothers and the families, the fathers, the sisters, the brothers, the wives, and the grandmothers of missing Tunisian migrants and to the feminist collective Le Venticinqueundici. We thank them together – Tunisian migrants' mothers and families and the collective Le Venticinqueundici – since we have been living our political engagement with them.

Particular thanks also go to: Karima Elhilali, Walid Fellah, Bohren Abichou, Amidou-Karim-Refus Soley, Patrizia Safira Mancini, Hamadi Zribi, Ouejdane Mejri, Omeyya Seddik, Hassan Boubakri, Swanie Potot, Nejib Abidi, Kais Zriba, Marta Bellingreri, Ramzi Bettaieb, Debora Del

Pistoia, Hajji Mounir, Francesca Zampagni, Abderraouf Abidi, Yahya Dridi, Bright Samson, Fatma Hizi, Mariem Hizi, Rim Hizi, Khaled Hizi and their friends in Kasserine.

We owe additional thanks to Sophie Fuggle at Pavement Books for her dedication and editorial wisdom. Thank you also to Sara Tracey and Nicholas Gledhill for revising some of the essays in this volume. Finally, we want to thank the publisher Ombre Corte for granting us the right to translate and republish parts of the book *Spazi in migrazione. Cartoline di una rivoluzione* (2012), which this volume partially draws upon.

Notes on Contributors

A.A has been living in Bergamo since he arrived in Italy in April 2011. After a long job search, he was hired in a pizzeria and is now converting his residence permit for humanitarian reason into a work permit.

Wafa Abida is a Tunisian student in Paris. Since May 2011 she has been participating in the struggle of Tunisian *harraga* in Paris.

Paola Gandolfi teaches at the University of Bergamo. Her anthropological research focuses on transnational migrations between Maghreb and Europe and on cultural change processes in Morocco (and Tunisia). Her recent publications include *La sfida dell'educazione nel Marocco contemporaneo* (Città Aperta, 2010) and *Rivolte in atto* (Mimesis, 2012).

Glenda Garelli is a doctoral candidate at the University of Illinois, Chicago where she works on a spatial inquiry of the European Union, focusing on migrations' contested spaces. At UIC she also teaches a course on cinema, migrations, and the urban. She is part of the editorial board of www.storiemigranti.org.

Lucio Guarinoni studies Social Theater at the University of Torino. He lives in Bergamo where he works as a playwright and director with intercultural acting companies.

Issam Heni is 36 years old, has a degree from a commercial school, and works for the Ministry of Education in Tunisia. He is a blogger and a photographer and lives in 'Cité Ennour,' in Sidi Bouzid.

Robby Habans is a PhD candidate in Urban Planning and Policy at the University of Illinois at Chicago and an experienced cartographic and information designer. His dissertation research examines the changing relationship between biomedicine and urban development policy in the United States.

K., S., Y. are three men from the Ivory Coast we met at Choucha camp in July 2012 when they were part of the 'rejected refugees' group. In July 2013, the Tunisian government granted – or at least officially declared it would grant - rejected refugees the possibility to stay on Tunisian territory. We use their initials as we could not ask K. S. Y. if they wanted their names to appear on the pages of this book.

Chiheb Khlifi is a Tunisian who left from Sfax to get to Italy. He lived in France, in Switzerland and is now back in Italy where he has some friends and takes part in theater workshops.

Federica Sossi teaches Aesthetics at the University of Bergamo, Italy. She coordinates the website storiemigranti.org and has written several books on migrations: *Autobiografie negate. Immigrati nei Lager del presente* (2002), *Storie migranti. Viaggio tra i nuovi confini* (2005), *Migrare. Spazi di confinamento e strategie di esistenza* (2007).

Adel Souei was a mechanic in Tunisia, the country he left in the spring of 2011 to go to Europe. He made it to Belgium where he married Fabienne, with whom he lives.

Martina Tazzioli has an MA in Philosophy from the University of Pisa and has just completed her Phd in Politics at Goldsmiths College. She is part of the editorial board *Materialifoucaultiani* Journal. Her publications include *Politiche di verità: Foucault e la critica del neoliberalismo* (Verona: Ombre Corte, 2011).

Foreward
FEDERICA SOSSI

December 17, 2010 – January 14, 2011. These dates have been fixed as constituting the beginning and accomplishment of a revolution which took the world by surprise, opening up a sudden and peculiar spatial upheaval of the Maghreb and Mashreq region.

Mohamed Bouazizi's gesture was an extreme one. Setting himself on fire in front of a local government building to protest the confiscation of his street vendor's wares by the police. Immediately following this act, squares and streets started to fill up, from Tunisia to Tahrir square, to Sana'a, to Tripoli and to Damascus. The revolutions that originated were revolutions against political dictatorships and against dictatorship over people's lives, against the way poverty was rendered invisible and against the unbearableness of existence. These revolutionary struggles staged an unprecedented capacity for common action based on a logic of 'spatial takeover'.

Such existences decided to stand up and be counted, taking over streets, squares, kasbas, medinas, filling them with their lives and with words, slogans, murals, meetings, assemblies, banners, dreams and desires. These were not virtual revolutions; they were indeed revolutions in all senses, which did not target the sites of power except to address them with a single word, '*dégage*,' a command to clear out and liberate space, a demand to take space back, returning to such space the full presence of one's existences. In the kasba and in the squares people eat, struggle, sleep, dream, and make decisions about how to keep fighting.

In kiosks around Tunis, a new postcard took the place of those depicting a Tunisia framed through images of seaside and beaches occupied by the bodies of tourists. A postcard of the revolution, bearing the slogan: '*Révolution, 14 janvier 2011*,' and featuring faces of men, women, children, the young, middle-aged and old alike, looking out from between military tanks and next to colorful walls.

A space in upheaval where bodies and existences took up their freedom, the freedom to be, to go, to be noticed at last. They did so forming an uncontainable movement, from Tunis to Cairo, from Maghreb to Mashreq.

From Tunisia to Europe. Yes. The 'Arab Revolutions' and, particularly, the one sparked in Tunisia have not followed just one direction in their 'spatial takeover'. They have also managed to fill, with existences and bodies, a series of European spaces: streets, islands, stations, parks, from Lampedusa to Paris, crossing the sea with an unexpected and sudden capacity to unify two shores and two continents, hence erasing centuries of history, acting on and performing their 'natural' proximity. This is another postcard from the Tunisian kasbas: from Tunis to Zarzis, through small towns and villages inland, the image of a Tunisia made of existences, the existences of predominantly young men, pouring onto the shorelines to fully act out the freedom they had seized, as a freedom of movement. This was not so much a dream of Europe, or maybe it was partly that, but more than anything it was the irresistible enactment of freedom, the following of desires, taking over space thoroughly and swamping those borders that had been designating that space as 'elsewhere'.

These practices transgressed those mobile, visible, invisible, sea and land frontiers which current government policies on human movement have been distributing everywhere, enacting a reconfiguration of lives as confined lives.

In the months that followed January 14, 2011, the world became familiar with the postcard of a Tunisian Lampedusa. This postcard was indeed produced by the practice of rendering border as spectacle, an art which, Italian ministers, European commissioners, governmental and intra-governmental agents along with operators in charge of delivering the story of humanitarian practices over confined lives, had been refining via migration policies over the years. In this case, however, their practice and custom was upstaged by these transgressive bodies which added a new twist to the narrative. And after the sea, after the island, and after the first confinements in old and new places of detention, came the flights, the riots, the acts of self-harm required to reiterate that freedom, to locate one's desire in those European railway stations, streets, tracks, parks and gardens, to locate it amid the revelation that Europe did not mean freedom and that 'democracy' was limited, imprisoning, and not so very different from that dictatorship over lives and desires so well-known on the other Mediterranean shore.

This is another Tunisian postcard, after the one of Mohamed Bouazizi's body ablaze and the one reading, '*Révolution, 14 janvier 2011*,' but, unlike the latter, it is not sold in the kiosks of Tunis, Milan, Paris, or Vintimiglia. Yet, it pervades the streets of Europe, redesigning their spaces with bold strokes produced by the realization that European space is both too similar and too close to the space Tunisian migrants had left.

Finally, two more postcards, one widely circulated, the other more clandestine. 'Ni police, ni charité. Un lieu pour s'organiser' ['No police, no charity. We want a place where we can organize'] is the message appearing on May 1, 2011 in Paris, on the windows of a building at 51 Avenue Simon Bolivar, in the neighborhood of Belleville. It was the banner chosen by the *Collectif des tunisiens de Lampedusa à Paris* [The Collective of Tunisians from Lampedusa in Paris], a group of 250 Tunisians, who moved to that building from the Parc de la Villette – their abode after Lampedusa Island, after the Italian railway stations, after the small square in Ventimiglia and the perilous paths taken from Italy to France. With that designation this group sought to break down the political, cultural, existential frontiers that divide up spaces into national territories and mark our lives in terms of belonging and citizenship.

'*Révolution, 1 mai 2011, avenue Simon Bolivar*' [Revolution, May 1, 2011, avenue Simon Bolivar] constituted the headline for that day, a possible slogan to put on a postcard sold in kiosks around the world, rewriting the revolution once again, this time with the nomination of multiple locations and belongings as its starting point. Between May and July, 2011 the summer of their revolution took place between the hills of Belleville, in occupied buildings, non-publicized squats, in reclaimed *foyers* [hostels], in French-Tunisian sites which became homes, between avenue Simon Bolivar, the rue de la Fontaine-au-roi gymnasium, rue Bourdon, rue Bichat, and the villa on rue Botzaris, former residence of the Tunisian police, between the 19th and 21st Parisian arrondissements, from one side of the Parc Buttes Chaumont to the other, encountering evictions, expulsions, and re-occupations. It is a postcard that is easy to reconstruct simply by looking at the websites where words and images belonging to this movement have been deposited. A postcard, or indeed a set of postcards, depicting the many other Lampedusas in Paris is much harder to reconstruct. It is more secret, less publicized, more silently claimed given the natural necessities of such existences, lives which exist and persist in space. A postcard from Porte de la Villette, from Plaine Saint-Denis, from the lines of the soup kitchen, from the squats in abandoned houses, from unlikely abodes at the side of gas stations, in the rooms of some Tunisian association or other where a coffee, maybe a blanket might be provided. In these places migrants were forced to reorganize the space in migration of their desire for freedom, here rendered as a body which could not be accounted for, which could not stand up and be counted, a body that government policies on mobility cannot recognize.

Yet this is also a revolution: this turning of a space into one's own within a regime of invisibility, employing strategies of existence and insistence in order to locate a political presence in the folds of silence and imperceptibility. In November 2011, Martina Tazzioli and I were in Paris looking for someone from the *Collectif des tunisiens de Lampedusa à Paris*, with the idea of also trying to find the words with which to draw the image of this final postcard. However, this postcard escapes verbal articulation. As we searched in underground stations, in the rooms of associations, looking around places furnished with abandoned mattresses or in squats with no heating, Tunisians in Paris, all of whom had travelled through Lampedusa, failed to understand precisely who we were looking for. They did not understand since they all now considered themselves 'Tunisians from Lampedusa in Paris,' beyond the organized and hyper-visible web presence of political activists.

Spaces in Migration. Postcards of a Revolution is an attempt to rearticulate some of the images of what happened starting from December 17, 2010, sketching a necessarily fragmented story, a series of postcards, and piecing together the fragments of before and after, following the spaces in migration of this revolution, pausing at the threshold of some of the spaces where it continues. The book does not aim to tell the story of the Tunisian revolution or of the 'Arab Springs' nor does it claim to conduct an analysis of these. Rather, it constitutes a sketchbook, a set of snapshots, a series of postcards - short descriptions tracing the contours of the spatial upheaval of the Tunisian revolution from within the very spaces where its authors are located.

I. Spaces in Migration

Spaces in Migration, Daily Life in Revolution
PAOLA GANDOLFI

Translated from Italian by Kate Townsend

Introduction

For years in Tunisia, an increasing number of protests occurred at a local level but never received any acknowledgment from the mainstream media. For a long time they were considered unimportant, for although the political context of Tunisia was headed by an authoritarian *Rais* [leader], at the same time society was still partially open, characterized by an important diaspora and animated by opposition strategies, underground yet nevertheless present.

The development of an uprising against the establishment started to become truly visible with the occupation of streets and public spaces. In comparison with other Arab revolutions, where the intensification of protests was obstructed by the use of extreme violence (as occurred in Libya and Syria), what developed in Tunisia (and similarly in Egypt), once protests had flooded many areas of the country, was the progressive formation of a space for action and national struggle, created by the occupation of Avenue Bourghiba, located in front of the Ministry of Internal Affairs, the de facto seat of power and therefore the strongest symbolic expression of the regime.

The uprising was confirmed through the participation of those who joined the *rue*, a space for local protest throughout various regions of Tunisia, and Avenue Bourguiba, a space for national protest. I shall therefore start from this event in particular in order to propose a course of analysis for the contemporary context of Tunisia as well as some paths for reflection on recent revolutionary dynamics.[1]

The reappropriation of public spaces and the hybridization of spaces for political action

The appropriation of public space (the most visible example being the main street of the capital, the symbolic site of centralized power) came about as a result of a new and unprecedented inter-classist and inter-generational alliance (which unfortunately since the days of the revolution seems to have almost disappeared and now calls for new political efforts). The subsequent appropriation of the kasba of Tunis, another governmental site par excellence, formalized a break with the past and paradigms that had for so long forged political imaginary. It is important to underscore the fact that 'for the theologians or for the classical Arab thinkers the "multitude," has, for a long time, been nothing more than a source of disorder. In order to grasp this acceptation, one must consider the overtones ascribed to it: *ghawgha* [noise, cacophony], or *dahma* [shadows]'[2] – as if from the street, from the crowd, comes nothing other than *fitna*: disorder, discord, chaos; as if anything (even violence and repression) were better than *fitna*. The revolution in Tunisia brought about an historic retraction of the doctrine on *fitna* and this, in time, will have repercussions on the legitimacy of state power. The protest movements were organized and enacted collectively, publicly voicing sentiments which, until recently, had been expressed only in hushed tones among individuals or small groups. Now, together, they were able to make unanimous demands. Collective action, however slow and unprecedented, arose from sporadic individual or heavily minority struggles.

The revolution ushered in a multitude from the street that reappropriated space in an original way. For this reason, many socio-political analyses have highlighted how necessary and important it is to protect the street even now, in the successive phase of the revolution, because without the 'street' and the dialectic surrounding it, the revolution cannot be fully realized. Today, remaining in the street (or in the square) is essentially a very minor component of youth (who are not associated

---

[1] Due to the rapid and complex evolution of events in Tunisia, I would like to point out that the original text in Italian was published in June 2012.

[2] M. Tozy, 'De bon usage de la monarchie', *La revue*, 11 (2011), p.58.

with the labor movement and other social and political realities). Yet the exceptional nature of the revolution once also attracted the unemployed, workers, students, manual laborers, intellectuals, and artists, all united in the same struggle.

In order to understand where the Arab revolutions originated, it is necessary to retrace the gradual occupation of spaces and identify all the areas that were gradually transformed into private spaces during the last few years in Maghreb, owned and operated by businessmen who invested, for example, in the new creation of newspapers, radio stations, or other enterprises. We may recall that some years ago Michel Camau spoke of a progressive 'hybridization du politique.' According to Camau it was necessary to discuss 'authoritarian democracies and democratic authoritarianisms,' but his statements received a dismal reaction from the research community.[3] By the early 2000s and increasingly in 2008 and 2009 the first studies on media in the Arab world were published,[4] and they clearly showed how in the early 2000s the spaces once run by standard news networks that had been present for years were slowly becoming occupied, allowing for what attentive observers have called a hybridization between forms of political action and forms of political expression. Supporting this was a slow and almost invisible occupation of public spaces which, over time, had a significant impact on the collective. Meanwhile, other forms of daily political action were coming into play at an individual level.

Moving between marginal spaces: racing through the interstices

Course à Ikhobza (a colloquial expression in Tunisian dialect that could be translated as 'the bread race') is the expression Hamza Meddeb has used to describe the daily anxiety that the majority of the youth population felt during the years and months leading up to the revolution. Through

---

[3] M. Camau and G. Massardier, *Démocraties et autoritarismes. Fragmentation et hybridization des régimes* (Paris: Karthala, 2009). See also S. Ben Nefissa and B. Destremau (eds), *Protestations sociales, révolutions civiles. Transformations du politique dans la Méditerranée arabe, Revue Tiers Monde*, Hors Série 2 (2011). For an analysis of the specific Tunisian context, refer to: M. Camau and V. Geisser, *Le syndrome autoritaire. Politique en Tunisie de Bourguiba à Ben Ali* (Paris: Les Presses de Sciences Po, 2003).

[4] Cf. K. Mohsen Finan (dir.), *Les médias en Méditerranée. Nouveaux médias, monde arabe et relations internationales*, (Arles: Actes Sud, 2009).

field research, he revealed that the youth had adopted many survival tactics. Faced with an authoritarian, clientelist, corrupt power, they tried to 'implant themselves in the interstices, in the minimal margins left open by power,'[5] clearly hoping to 'play the power' [*jouer le pouvoir*],[6] making a power play by strategically embedding themselves into the interstices of the informal economy, for example, using creativity and inventiveness. In this context, Meddeb identified a youth capable of reacting, rather than succumbing, prepared to recreate the minimal spaces left free from authoritarian rule. It was a youth that appeared ready and willing to reinvent the most marginal spaces available to them. But if on one hand the most excluded and marginalized were the first to 'race' to invent spaces of action for 'the bread race,' on the other hand, after a while, many other young people chose their own personal '*course à Ikhobza*' by migrating. Still, altogether the focus was on a race, a take-off: the system had forced them to take on precarious work and they reacted with various races for survival.

The first example of a race that started as individual and grew to become collective occurred in Gafsa in 2008, when (as all the socio-political analyses have now pointed out) an intense protest movement arose during a worker recruitment campaign for the phosphate mines, contesting the results, evaluation procedures, and patronage of job applications.

The recurring aim of the 'bread race' in the months and years preceding the revolution was to put a stop to political violence in daily life, to eradicate the indecency and immorality of power. From this angle, perhaps we can easily see a connection between this 'everyday' race that marked the years and months preceding the revolution and the outcome of the last elections, measuring it based on how it was perceived by many as a sort of return to 'morality' and 'decency.' According to this perspective, with parties incapable of producing a message that was direct, clear, and fully shared by the heterogeneous 'street,' a hypothesis for interpreting electoral voting behavior could be thus formulated: in the absence of valid alternatives, would the religious party perhaps have been one of the few parties capable of guaranteeing morality, non-corruption, and justice?[7]

---

[5] H. Meddeb, 'L'ambivalence de la course à "el khobza". Obéir et se révolter en Tunisie', *Politique Africaine*, 121 (2011), pp.35-54.

[6] M. de Certeau, *L'invention du quotidien. Arts de faire* (Paris: Gallimard, 1980).

[7] The result of the elections was, according to Hamit Bozarslan, 'moral and conservative,' that is, people voted within the parameters of religion, moral order, and the maintenance of order. From the contribution of H. Bozarslan at the international

The greatest desire of the people in the aftermath of the revolution was to break away from the clientelism and corruption of the former government. Field research, carried out by Meddeb after the revolution, shows how the key factors at play at the time of the electoral campaign should be interpreted as a call from the common people for dignity and recognition. In fact, many voters admitted to having supported the candidates who claimed to be 'the most clean,' the most upstanding. In this light, not only did the Islamist party *Nahda* speak a language (at all times) close to the people, it also very likely in some way represented a 'clean' model, that is, it seemed 'morally palatable.' From this point of view, Moncef Marzouki also naturally represented a 'clean' model citizen, a spokesman for those who had been marginalized and excluded during the years of dictatorship and thus he similarly offered the possibility of a clean break with the past. In this sense, those chosen by the Tunisians in the last elections tended to embody decency and 'clearness,' contrasting and diverging from the 'dirtiness' and opacity that had ruined them during the previous long years. In the days leading up to the political elections, cartoons and even jokes about some of the many candidates circulated. In one of the most common, a gentleman, asked by a friend for his opinion about a certain candidate, responds: 'I was with him in prison when we were under Ben Ali, *il est propre*' [he is a good person, he is 'clean']. It is therefore as if references to dignity and morals had recaptured concrete spaces and permeated the collective mindset. Similarly, historians who opposed the regime (Islamists and defenders of human rights) occupied spaces of action, spaces that had become in some way mobile and open: spaces, indeed, to be reappropriated and, above all, spaces to be reinvented.

The fragmentation of mobilization and the inversion of centers and peripheries

It is difficult to generate a macro explanation for revolutionary processes. Transitology, research on the processes of political transition, should be re-examined and continuously discussed. Furthermore, the Tunisian revolution and other Arab revolutions have inverted the center-periphery order. The outskirts of the capital have become the fulcrum of the

conference '*R-évolution arabes*', Università Ca' Foscari di Venezia, February 24, 2012, Venice. Further reflection on revolutionary and post-revolutionary processes can be found in: H. Bozarslan, G. Bataillon and C. Jaffrelot, *Passions révolutionnaires: Amérique latine, Moyen-Orient, Inde* (Paris: Éditions de EHESS, 2011).

revolts while the outlying urban centers and suburban peripheries have often anticipated and accompanied the protest that unfolded in the capital. In Tunisia, marginal spaces played a central role not only on January 5, 2008 but also on other occasions in the two or three years that preceded December 2010. Not only should the 'spaces in migration' which marked the initially subdued revolutionary movement of the interior of the country be carefully retraced, but we should also examine the fragmentation of protest mobilization. Who reappropriated these spaces spread across national territory? Youth, workers, the unemployed, unionists, activists, bloggers, Islamists, left-wing representatives, military kids, lawyers, some party representatives dissenting from the leadership of their parties, and many others. In Tunisia the protest movement started in the periphery well before arriving at the center of the capital. Once concentrated in Tunis, in reality it was composed of multiple points of protest, all fragmented.[8] Everywhere, peripheral spaces became the center of the first demonstrations; marginal spaces throughout national territory became protest hotspots.[9]

What has prevailed for decades in Tunisia, as Emir ben Ayad has pointed out, is the political stratagem of 'divide and conquer' which exacerbated regionalism among Tunisians to such an extent that those

---

[8] We can further analyze the fragmentation of protest mobilization in the current revolts and Arab revolutions by citing a few significant events. In Morocco, the February 20, 2011 demonstration, first declared in Casablanca and Rabat, immediately spread to 80 locations throughout the entire country: separate spaces all part of a single protest. It is important to remember that an important dislocation of the protest subsists in Syria, despite the conditions being completely different from Tunisia and Morocco, and that at the end of February 2012, protest sites totaled 567 (from the contribution of Caroline Donati, 'Syrie: Dynamique de la contestation et ressources du mouvement révolutionnaire', at the international conference 'Révolutions arabes'). With further regards to the Syrian case, refer to: C.Donati, *L'Exception syrienne: entre modernisation et résistance* (Paris: La Découverte, 2009).

[9] Although each country has its own unique history, a similar event occurred in Morocco at the beginning of the first mass demonstrations when a significant protest was held in Sidi Ifni following a period of hire in which 8,000 people competed for eight job openings. This event had an important influence on the vacillation of central power and the shift from political protest to social protest. Thus, even in Morocco the protest movement was not an urban phenomenon but rather exploded earlier in isolated, or secondary, regions. Concerning both Morocco and Tunisia, another discourse on geographical displacement might be developed with respect to the role that the Maghreban diaspora played, likewise considering how and to what degree expats contributed in part (at times even partially coordinated) by launching protest movements over the internet.

from the North considered themselves better than those from the South and the rivalry between the big cities (Tunis, Sousse, Sfax) has endured. In Ayad's opinion, all this suddenly disappeared between December 2010 and January 2011.[10] In the course of two sit-ins in the kasba of Tunis, almost every city was represented by youth so exasperated by unemployment and hunger that they occupied government territory in order to make their voices heard so that actions might be taken which would restore a little human dignity to their lives. The union of these people managed to overthrow the government twice. According to Ayad, the revolutionary process and the first and second occupation of the kasba resoundingly showed this fact: that the representation of Tunisia as a modern, Western country constructed around its capital and its big cities was, for a long time, disconnected from the rest of the country.[11]

Moreover, in recent days, the inhabitants of Kasserine and other minor centers, where the first Tunisian protests were born, contested the legitimacy of the three Tunisian presidents (Hamadi Jebali, president of the government, Moncef Marzouki, president of the republic, and Mustapha Ben Jafaar, president of the assembly) to such a degree that they were forced to abandon their posts. It was an extremely bold gesture that shows how the relations between central power and marginalized regions remain persistent and fundamental. In this sense, according to Mohammed Kerrou, 'the revolution is not over yet.'[12] Tunisian protest mobilization has called attention back to the relations between centers and peripheries, real and symbolic, allowing spaces, which for years were considered marginal, to emerge, discarding the uni-directionality of movement in the management of power from center to peripheries and imposing the question of a present where the relation between dominant and marginal spaces implies an impressive transitivity and circularity. We must consider not only the unprecedented movement between peripheries and center, but also new in-between spaces (to apply the expression of Homi Bhabha to another context),[13] spaces and practices of mobilization that are an

---

[10] E.Ben Ayed, 'Luttes pour la liberté et la dignité. Témoignage postrévolutionnaire d'un photographe tunisien', *Archivio Antropologico Mediterraneo*, XI, XII, 13:2 (2011), p.55.

[11] Ibid., p.56.

[12] M. Kerrou, 'La révolution tunisienne n'est pas terminée', *Jeune Afrique*, 2662 (2012), p.45.

[13] H. Bhabha, *The Location of Culture* (London: Routledge, 1994).

expression of the contemporaneous and simultaneous interplay between the center and the peripheries.

'Burning': from the '*harraga*'[14] youth to the immolated unemployed

In the framework of these unprecedented spaces of daily action and practices capable of dwelling within, surpassing, or even 'burning' the borders between the centers and peripheries, an attentive look should be cast upon the youth who stand at the margins, the borders, the peripheries. In these past months we have found ourselves before an escalation of the methods of 'burning' – passing from burning 'oneself' and 'one's personal documents,' and 'burning one's life,' ready to leave everything behind and risk it all in order to start fresh somewhere new (considering the *harraga* that secretly cross borders in order to reach Europe), to a veritable immolation of youth in Tunisia. Mohamed Bouazizi lit himself on fire on December 17, 2010 at Sidi Bouzid: he was not, unfortunately, the first young man to commit such an act, but he became an instant symbol of a direct and heartfelt protest that acquired, in the course of very little time, an unpredictable form and force. The video of the immolation of Mohamed Bouazizi, which circulated on the web and shocked viewers, contributed to rendering this extreme act all the more visible and communal. Within a short period of time, youth, adults, students, workers, everyone identified themselves with this young man who, in the spirit of desperation and protest, set himself on fire and, due to the severity of the cuts and burns, soon afterwards died in the hospital.

Thus, burning – inherently an act of immediacy, extreme risk, and deliberate transportation into a state and condition of total 'otherness,' being prepared to lose everything – underwent a social evolution. In addition to the 'burning' of young migrants, an act of desperation and altogether a search for release and rebirth, there was the 'burning' of other youth who were willing to take their own lives in order to expose the misery of their own extreme condition in exchange for a freedom impregnated with tragic fatality. It was a trajectory of people so humiliated and marginalized, considered bodies without names, without history,

---

[14] Literally, 'harga' means 'to burn' and 'harraga' in the Maghreb indicates 'those who burn', meaning both young people who 'burn' frontiers as they migrate across the Mediterranean sea and those who are ready to burn their documents (but also their past and eventually their lives) in order to reach Europe.

without dignity, that they took strength in showing their disgrace publicly, thereby deliberately choosing to have no name, no history, and no future.

This was yet another inversion of order, a movement that spread from the margins to the center of the scene, from daily humiliation and annihilation to the attainment of an important position, a public space, and acknowledgment.

Perhaps, at another level, we can consider another form of movement between the periphery and the center, a transition from the periphery to the center, and a reinvention of the peripheries as new centers: a fearless *course à Ikhboza*, a daily and patient strategy of occupying the marginal spaces which at a certain point, however, becomes merely a race – not to search for bread but rather an unstoppable and lethal hurtle, no longer towards survival but towards death.

It is with this need to pass from the *course à Ikhboza* to burning oneself, in this form of ultimate protest, in this fragile interstice, that events have developed from an individual to a collective history and that individuals have felt empathy and at the same time shock, growing ever more in solidarity and united by the urgency to take a stand and act.

But what is the point of this process, this disconcerting movement? Not only before and during the revolution were there various cases of youth immolation, but in the later phase of the revolution they unfortunately became a regular phenomenon in the internal regions of the country, those most peripheral, indeed, marginalized. It was a genuine cry of desperation from people who longed to attract attention to the catastrophic economic situation of their homelands. The difference, with respect to the suicide of Mohamed Bouazizi (as Mohamed Kerrou affirms) is that today it is not only youth but also fathers and mothers of families who ignite themselves. 'Therefore this is not the rejection but the continuity of the revolution, following the same logic of destruction. And if immediate solutions are not sought, if no one listens to these disinherited people from the interior of Tunisia, the situation will explode.'[15]

The history of an ongoing, multifaceted revolution is narrated by the circular movement between real and symbolic centers and peripheries.

In the same vein, the union organizer Adnan Haji cited a 'total absence of the state in the marginal zones, still left, without any prefect or police, in a condition of total insecurity.'[16] In his opinion, whoever is in government

---

[15] M.Kerrou, *La révolutionne tunisienne n'est pas terminée*, p.45.

[16] Contributed by Adnan Hajj at the 'Cinquième Rencontre européenne d'analyse

should quickly sit down at the table to talk with citizens, workers, and students, otherwise no substantial change will follow after the revolution. During a seminar on the revolutions, he firmly criticised the Tunisian government for wanting to reassure everyone, especially Europeans and capitalists, except for the Tunisian people. In his view, in this phase, a lack of dialogue and serious negotiation with the citizens would be deleterious and could degenerate into violence.[17]

It is evident that after a revolution, founded on the mobility of people and spaces, topples political uni-directionality, a phase of dialogue between peripheral and dominant spaces remains necessary and urgent. In this phase, it is necessary to continuously focus on the spaces and the social and political actors who have managed to move from the margins to elsewhere, albeit sometimes a close elsewhere.

Activists who migrated into Europe, lawyers who migrated into the streets

It is important to recall some of these trajectories as an example. The lawyer Redda Raddaoui, one of the first supporters of the trade unionists in Gafsa, Kasserine, and Jendouba, has repeatedly pointed out, with statistics at hand, how much corruption in Tunisia had absorbed all the wealth of the country and how neither state nor law exist, rather there is a mere division between families close to power and the rest of the population. During the reign of Ben Ali, judges had never in fact had any real authority, rather, those who truly held power, as everyone knows, were the Minister of the Interior and the police. In this context, for a long time militant activists could seek refuge only within the structure of civil society and social movements in Europe. Perhaps the first attempt to hold a public meeting of the opposition groups, which for the first time resulted in some cooperation between the left and the Islamists, was at the *Sommet de l'Information* (2005). Afterwards, during the turning point of the revolt in Gafsa, when corruption was denounced on October 5, 2008, the first negotiations with power were launched through long sessions of discussion. However, at the end of the negotiation process, the demands

---

des sociétés politiques' *Printemps arabes: mythe et fictions*, CERI, Sciences-Po, Paris, February 3, 2012.

[17] Concerning possible escalations, in Algeria the last extreme act after the *harraga* and after immolated youth (and there were many in Algeria) was to burn electoral voting cards.

of the trade unionists and workers were not accepted and mass arrests, already sufficiently reported elsewhere, were executed through the use of violence and torture. The account of Redda Reddaoui regarding these events is worth citing: 'We realized very clearly, for the first time, that our role as lawyers was not to sit in the tribunals but to go out into the street, among the people.'[18] It was almost a 'declaration of migration' of lawyers: magistrates relocated from the tribunals to the squares, entire tribunals migrated into the streets. It was a continuous localization and de-localization, mobility in daily practice, which requires new tools for interpreting reality.

From overturning spaces to questioning traditional analyses

The recent Arab revolutions, in primis the Tunisian revolution, sparked a dilemma for traditional models of analysis used to study Arab reality. Without a doubt, the revolutions challenged the culturalist interpretation which attempted to explain Arab reality by reducing it to exceptionalism.[19] Above all, the Arab revolutions have relegated the role of Islam in the contemporary Arab-Islamic societies, for it is not in the name of Islam that they were conceived and born. Although it may be too early to draw any conclusions, some initial analyses can be proposed. First of all, we must overcome the failure of political science to produce a convincing argument on the supposed 'resistance' to any democratic change. Explanations and approaches based on 'tribal organization,'[20] religion,[21] or patriarchy,[22] have revealed their limitations. Meanwhile the predictions of demographers, who forecasted a youth revolution[23] and a women's movement concerning

---

[18] Contributed by Redda Reddaoui at the 'Cinquième Rencontre européenne d'analyse des sociétés politiques'.

[19] Cf. S. Huntington, *The clash of civilizations and the remaking of world order* (New York, NY: Simon & Schuster, 1996).

[20] Cf. E. Gellner, *Les saints de l'Atlas* (Paris: Editions Bouchene, 2003).

[21] Cf. B. Lewis, *Le pouvoir et la foi: questions d'islam en Europe et au Moyen-Orient* (Paris: Odile Jacob, 2011).

[22] Cf. H. Sharabi, *Neopatriarchy: A Theory of Distorted Change in Arab Society* (Oxford: Oxford University Press, 1988).

[23] Cf. Y. Courbage and E. Todd, 'Révolution culturelle au Maroc: le sens d'une transition démographique', *Revue Marocaine de Sciences politique et sociale*, 1:2 (2010-2011), pp.27-45; Y. Courbage and E. Todd, *A Convergence of Civilisations: The Transformation of Muslim Societies Around the World* (New York, NY: Columbia University Press, 2011); P. Fargues, *Générations arabes: l'alchimie du nombre* (Paris:

changes in family structure due to fundamental education and birth control initiatives, have been correct. Expert formulas, however, regarding transition processes (which worked well enough in other contexts) have not been successful in the Arab countries, and yet the notion of Arab exceptionalism has for a long time been encouraged and confirmed.

The proclamation of the end of 'political' Islam,[24] partially eclipsed by the events of September 11, 2001 and global media spotlighting Al Qaeda and the international 'jihadist' figure, have complicated the historical background. In such an environment, commentators and observers of the Arab revolutions have oscillated between excessive feelings of empathy and scepticism.

In reality, the events of these past months constrain us, as researchers and academics, to reassess these societies within the matrix of national boundaries and global capitalism.[25] Moreover, if all the most recent conferences and international seminars on the revolutions have one *refrain* it is to re-evaluate the unique characteristics of each Arab country and the historical authenticity of each national situation.

In Tunisia the revolution should be described as both a political and social revolution, for the revolutionary dynamics, as we have seen, were born in a peripheral, secondary space. Even before Sidi Bouzid, they were born in Kasserine, in Jandouba, in the provincial spaces of minor regions.

Tunisia was the first 'authoritarian republic' to gradually embrace a revolutionary process well before December 2010.[26] In attempting to understand exactly what happened, we may need to reconsider the figure of the militant. For years in Tunisia, activists and intellectuals alike fought for the conquest and defence of human rights, and to a great extent they have been the 'porteurs' of revolutionary issues. With this in mind, the boundaries of academic research might as well go up in flames since scholars have not adequately investigated anything other than the

---

Librairie A. Fayard, 2000).

[24] O. Roy, *L'Echec de l'Islam politique* (Paris: Seuil, 1992); G. Kepel, *Jihad: expansion et déclin de l'islamisme* (Paris: Gallimard, [2000] 2003).

[25] From the introduction by François Bayart at 'Cinquième Rencontre européenne d'analyse des sociétés politiques'.

[26] The contributions of Michel Camau and Sarah Ben Nefissa provide a good tool for understanding the dynamics and combinations between authoritarian and democratic enclaves. Cf. Camau M., Massardier G., *Démocraties et autoritarismes fragmentation et hybridations des régimes* (Paris: Karthala, 2009); Ben Nefissa S., Destremau B. (dir.), 'Protestations sociales, révolutions civiles. Transformations du politique dans la Méditerranée arabe', *Tiers Monde*, Hors Série (2011).

authoritarianism of the system, neglecting the hidden fissures created within it in the past years.[27]

The social movement of 2008 condemned a political system that was economically fuelled by injustice and subordination. Such a movement caused a crisis for the implicitly legitimate class structure, norms, and values. The level of discontent, no longer reducible to a purely material dimension, reached breaking point. In order to understand the complexity of the social movements, we must look at several processes that were set in motion. First and foremost, through daily norms and practices a social movement reveals a different perception of legitimacy and political order and produces a sense of conflict that allows normally hidden actors to come to the surface. Even in a situation where the social contract appears to be consolidated, there are actors who distance themselves and refuse the imposed legitimacy and norms that are at the heart of social life. In this sense, despite the speed and shock of the intensity of the revolutionary process, we know all too well that what happened in December 2010 cannot be viewed as a spontaneous act. Rather, it is the consequence of a slow, underground process, and thus behind the immobility, obedience, and consensus, nevertheless rests a comprehensive logic of economic, social, and moral rationale which provokes antagonism. Maybe it is best to use this concept as a new point of departure so that we can exclude the 'total virginity' of a situation of action, awareness, and protest. In this light, so to speak, we can open the discussion for socio-political and socio-cultural readings that focus on militancy, rejection, and civil disobedience. And, above all, there is now an autonomous frame of reference for new ideas regarding justice, dignity, and the notion of a new political order. Today, common analysis seeks to understand what degree of durability the protests and demonstrations possessed during the sporadic movements that occurred prior to the explosion of events in 2011. But perhaps it is again worth emphasizing that, for a long time, such an analysis was neither promoted nor subsidized.

Maurizio Gribaldi discusses a conflict of interests between the two faces of the state: one privileging order and hierarchy, the other created at a social level and functioning as a part of daily life in the community.[28] The

---

[27] Cf.K. Mohsen Finan, P. Vermeren, 'La France ne se donne pas les moyens de connaitre le Maghreb', *L'Express*, February 2, 2011. Available: http://www.lexpress. fr/actualite/monde/afrique/la-france-nese-donne-pas-les-moyens-de-connaitre-le-maghreb_958019.html. Date Accessed: 30 August 2013.

[28] M. Gribaudi, M. Riot-Sarcey, *1848, la révolution oubliée* (Paris: La Découverte,

second view petitions authority, which produces inequalities and derives from political order. In the context of Tunisia, the authorities regularly and systematically used violence which was not only physical but also relative to the social norms of the time, a mass violence enacted with respect to (Foucauldian) legitimacy. Therefore, the violent conflict not only produced absolute disorder but it may have possessed another type of coherence. Today, as we are finally beginning to examine all this, we find ourselves before a political quagmire, hearing babble describing a type of conflict that could lead to more violence. With this, we must return to an analysis of the complexity of the social movement in relation to politics. We must recreate new ways of thinking about reality, beginning with accurate ethnographies and serious fieldwork where the point of view of internal researchers will become increasingly pertinent.[29]

Only by starting from this premise can we become fully aware of mobility as an increasingly intrinsic part of contemporary Tunisian reality - a sort of mobility which, before being observed and described from the outside, must be narrated and deciphered by its own protagonists.

Migrating Words

Accompanying the migration and occupation of spaces, during the later stages of the revolution in Tunisia, a migration of words, that is, the free movement of speech occupied every public and private space. For anyone who lived in Tunisia during the reign of Ben Ali, it was a surprising and intense novelty to see how anyone on the street, at home, in cafes, in taxis would talk about politics, plans for society, and how best 'to protect' the revolution, how to organize daily life. Likewise, now anyone could venture out to recreate their own space, even beginning with a small physical area (there were cafes that moved their chairs into the square or even to the edge of a flowerbed at a street intersection, citizens who placed their chairs outside in order to sit freely on the street and chat with their neighbors, and a thousand other similar situations). The days and months following

---

2009); M. Gribaudi, *Espaces, temporalités, stratifications. Exercices sur les réseaux sociaux* (Paris: Editions de l'EHESS, 1999).

[29] Cf. P. Gandolfi, 'Etnografie e lavori sul campo in Maghreb e in Marocco: prima e dopo le "rivoluzioni"', *Archivio Antropologico Mediterraneo*, XI, XII, 13:2 (2011), pp.89-103; P. Gandolfi, 'Quali diritti? Il diritto di trasgredire e il diritto di re-inventare la propria storia. Frammenti di storie e di inedite rivoluzioni in Maghreb', *Deportate, esuli, profughe*, 18-19 (2012), pp.245-256.

January 14, 2011 were animated above all by a climate of continuous public debate (between friends, neighbors, and also among strangers).

Political revolutions often translate into semantic revolutions, but even prior to the rearrangement of words, we can perhaps first discuss a 'migration' of words. In fact, not only did renaming space, as was the case with several streets and squares (one of the very first collective moves after January 14, 2011 was to dismantle the street signs of many roads named *7 novembre* – the date of Ben Ali's accession to power – with the intention of then renaming them *January 14* or *Revolution Street* or simply leaving them unmarked), happen immediately and almost instinctively (precisely because it was the symbol of the liberty that was won), but also at a deeper level, the lexical stakes were often set very high. The greatest debate animating the post-revolutionary weeks and months centered on moral liberty and the definition and designation of the Tunisian state as secular and laic or Islamic. In the long and heated discussion surrounding the constitutional text - especially Article 1 - there was an extraordinary 'mobility' of words. Tried and true words migrated towards the right or the left, following the direction of a conservative or progressive judiciary, or following the perspective of one business plan or another. Inside of this complex framework of analysis, the 'mobility' of semantic choices moreover revealed pragmatic, theological, and opportunist attitudes. In the months after the revolution, a wave of words flowed from the street to political parties and vice versa, essentially revealing two demands from the population: the demand for a secular state and the demand for an Islamic one. In the end, the political parties chiefly responded by proposing a laic state with Islamic reference (understood at a cultural level, wherein the major reference for civil policy is recognized as Islamic). Now, in Tunisia, secular powers can claim historical tradition and they could probably garner consensus around this for a new public space, even if everything is still in the process of being developed and defined.

Can a consensus possibly be reached regarding the fact that religion is a statute and faith a private matter? What is certain is that Islam and Islamism now challenge the social sciences, requiring us to use new approaches in order to interpret societies. Perhaps well before choosing new words and new concepts, we should seriously and consciously choose where those words should migrate. In Tunisia, and elsewhere, a vast and complicated process of reinvention and re-occupation of politics and democracy is underway. Many subjects are open for discussion: the denial of youth and others within the concept of leadership is surely one of the most recurring topics. With this purpose in mind, we have been able to observe the trajectory of current protest movements against political organization and criticism of the leadership. This trajectory has shifted from one side of the Mediterranean to the other, and beyond (in public forums created by the *Indignados* protest in Spain, and Occupy Wall Street in the U.S. and in other places, to provide just a few of many examples).

In this delicate phase of political reinvention, the intergenerational dialogue and action that was surprisingly and exceptionally maintained throughout the course of the revolutionary process deserves a greater amount of attention. Now, with rare exception, in the later phase of the revolution, particularly during the electoral campaign, youth and younger adolescents have been using languages that are often more distant.[30] On the topic of languages and generations, it is important to remember how the youth, throughout the course of the revolution, were able to express their concerns in a simple and direct manner, managing to communicate with anyone. The slogans accompanying the revolution were imbued with an extraordinary sense of immediacy and fury that sought to reclaim something very essential, elsewhere taken for granted: dignity, freedom, and the right to work.

Words of condemnation or hope appeared everywhere – on the walls, on the street, on the web. Neither sophisticated strategies nor a revival of old revolutionary cultures were involved; they were slogans containing very simple, even naïve, concepts. The most common '*dégage*' [*irhel*] is an example of these, and many others could be cited as well.[31] Words that were mouthed in silence for years now migrated onto the facades of impervious government buildings and onto the walls lining every different street, gaining visibility which amplified their volume. The words moved from physical space into cyberspace and vice versa, one often complimenting the other. The tag '*Merci le people! Merci Facebook!*' (appearing on the building of the Bank of Tunis, located on the Habib Thameur street of the capital) showcased at least two currents in this vast movement of words: one which moved from the private walls of houses to walls among the most visible and communal public spaces (the city walls) and

---

[30] Concerning the Tunisian gerontocracy, cf. M. Kilani, 'Une expérience de la révolution tunisienne. Réflexions recueillies par Gabriella D'Agostino', *Archivio Antropologico Mediterraneo*, XI, XII, 13:2 (2011), p.75.

[31] See also the booklet on the Tunisian revolution. V. Bettaieb, *Dégage, La révolution tunisienne* (Tunis: Éditions du Patrimoine/Paris: Editions du Layeur, 2011).

another which originated from the very first spaces of action and protest, surpassed censorship, and was launched into cyberspace. Thus, the words were clandestinely in migration, transmitted across an assiduous counter-information operation perpetrated through the internet, blogs, and social networks. Words and images allowed for that critical leap from '*dégage*' to '*engage*' and they involved many young internet users and cyber-activists. The latter are labeled as such precisely because they are 'on the ground' – as Leena Ben Mhenni explains, discussing her own personal experience – they take risks, they photograph, they interview, they document, and immediately afterwards they connect to the internet by means of the USB key or by some improvised connection point and they create posts on the web about everything they have seen, heard, recorded, and filmed so that anyone might discover it, uncensored and in the most brief amount of time possible.[32] The images, words, and fragments of stories, moving in sequence with all the immediacy, synthesis, and clarity that information has when circulated on the web, contributed to the definition of a circular movement of words and images that allowed real-time web documentation and produced a novel method of expressing oneself, communicating, and informing, all that being an integral part of the revolutionary process.

Voices from a young part of Tunisian society articulated energy, decision, and motivation and expressed their own interpretations of reality, their own testimonials, their own memories, through new forms of collective memory. Their narratives challenge us to think of the internet as a possible tool 'for the exercise of citizenship'[33] and to also reexamine the role of diasporas and transnational networks.

Local and disaporic imaginary

To what extent had words and images already migrated long before the revolution, even on the web and in contemporary media? Even in Tunisia, how many of the individual and collective hopes and dreams had long been nurtured by ideas, values, thoughts, words, and images which had originated from multiple 'elsewheres'? Many studies have discussed how new media in the Arab world has created a public sphere very different from that of the past. Likewise, the multiplication and privatization of

---

[32] L. Ben Mhenni, *Tunisian Girl, Blogueuse pour un printemps arabe* (Barcelona: Indigène Editions, 2011).

[33] Ibid., p.126.

mass media has also had an effect on the daily practices connected with social relations. Widespread behavioral patterns have created an enlivened sense of community and public life, confirming the existence of a renewed public sphere and the vital influence of civil society – also on a trans-national scale. Within the scope of Arab mass media, we need only recall how *Al Jazeera* was defined as a sort of 'rebellious and ambiguous mirror of the Arab world'[34] and a sort of 'counter-power' in Arab space. It was a media source that some considered capable of 'opening the realm of possibility' for citizens from the Arab-Islamic world.[35]

All this recalls how mass media production and new means of technology contributed to creating alternative spaces of information and had an influence on the reformulation of guiding norms and values. Mass media, granting the possibility of electronic communication, and the liberalization of markets, now open to transnational enterprises, equally contributed to reducing distances and favored such complex interconnections that even political culture was affected by these mutations. Hence, the nature of the local sphere in a globalized and de-territorialized world must be questioned.[36] The response to these situations and questions is largely shaped by the role imagination plays in social life, considering the fact that people increasingly view their own existence through the prism of possible lives and worlds offered by the diverse media images that circulate across the globe. 'Imagination as a social exercise is filtered through the image, the imagined, and the imaginary.'[37]

Since the complexity of global cultural flows is a constituent element of cultural globalization, national identity is constructed through a local and disaporic imaginary and becomes a sort of 'imagined world' where cultural material crosses national borders and renders identities fluid. In the era of globalization it becomes possible to question the compromise between what an individual imagines and what social reality actually allows. It is thus possible to imagine one's life according to the 'electronic

---

[34] O. Lamloum, *Al-Jazira, miroir rebel et ambigu du monde arabe* (Paris: La Décou-verte, 2004).

[35] Ibid.

[36] Cf. A. Appadurai, *Modernity at Large*, Minnesota, MN: University of Minnesota, 1996); L. Basch, N. Glick Schiller and C. Szanton-Blanc (eds.), *Nations Unbound: Transnational Projects, Postcolonial Predicaments and Deterritorialized Nation-States* (New York, NY: Gordon and Breach, 1994).

[37] P. Gandolfi, *La sfida dell'educazione nel Marocco contemporaneo. Complessità e criticità dall'altra sponda del Mediterraneo* (Troina: Città Aperta, 2010), p.185.

landscapes'[38] in which we form relations. This could forge a 'rhizomatic'[39] and schizophrenic sense of belonging and favor the development of ambivalences (impulses and repulsions) toward various group identities. Beyond the conjectures (and without entering too specifically into the active and intentional role of the Tunisian diaspora with regards to the revolutionary process), we can consider the extent to which the Tunisian population (especially the youth) had already incorporated mobility, de-territorialization, border-crossing, and a dose of both local and disaporic imagination into their daily lives.

Upon closer inspection, one of the settings in which such mobility of imagination was most tangible was the informal expression of youth both through the web and social networks and through artistic and cultural production. Despite however long this production had been subdued and pushed entirely underground – demonstrating just how alive and active it already was once it came up to the surface in a striking way during the revolution – it is worthy of observation. Often youth production, above all in music, initiated a discourse on identity. From the songs emerged a strong sense of belonging and a love for one's country, yet they also contained a strong indictment of all those who had vilified the country and the government. To consider a final point, the ultimate sign of this movement was and is the expression, of almost all groups, in their mother tongue. This provides a strong testimony of a process undergoing rapid development, as if it were 'a sort of language belonging to those who were more or less left abandoned at the margins of the process of globalization, a means of expression in a language reinvented by simple, incisive, direct words and concepts, nearly broadcasting their presence on the national and international scene.'[40] It is the response to a process of globalization concentrated on financial flows and international markets, pronounced with words and languages that are, first and foremost, local expressions.

It comes as no coincidence that occasional ethnographic investigations of these youth movements in the Arab have called this kids the interpreters of a sort of 'revolution' that was may already be underway: Mark Levine has worked on the subject of young Muslims and Western pop culture, investigating the results and contradictions of the crossroads between Western influences, Arab-Muslim culture and local cultures in other Arab

---

[38] A. Appadurai, *Modernity at Large*.

[39] G. Deleuze and F. Guattari, *Rhizome* (Paris: Les Éditions de Minuit, 1976).

[40] P. Gandolfi, *La sfida dell'educazione nel Marocco contemporaneo*, p. 134.

countries.[41] Now, even in Tunisia the analysis of the contemporary music scene paints an original picture, a fluctuating movement between tradition and a desire for freedom, between religion and a desire for change, which already existed in the past months and years. If before it was confined to playing in basements without being heard or seen, in the post-revolution era it has hosted live performances, singing all its complaints, doubts, and hopes without limits and without censorship.[42]

Conclusions

On the one hand the Tunisian revolution brought attention to multidirectional movements between centers and peripheries, occupied and reinvented spaces, a hybridization of forms of political expression in everyday life. On the other hand, it challenges us regarding the individual or collective practices that describe a multitude which is heterogeneous and deeply nourished by both local and diasporic imaginaries. Many questions can be posed about the development of a society like that of Tunisia, which in its specificity and complexity has been ushered into a phase of post-revolution. How will it be possible to secure a new plan for society where the 'various singularities that make up the "multitude" will genuinely be involved'?[43] 'How is dignity to be upheld' in the name of that which the Tunisian people have fought for?[44] Meanwhile a break has occurred at a marginal level between reality and its representation. To summarize, with the Tunisian revolution, reality prevailed over representations (both those created by the regime and those from outside perspectives) that wanted the country to stay rigid, monolithic, and unitary. A population emerged at the center of different trajectories and contradictions, spaces and words in 'continuous migration.' This mobility of people, ideas, images, and imaginary unhinges any fixed representation. From here unfolds a difficult and delicate course that, in order to make sense, must begin from something unprecedented. Given such a state of complexity, it is hard to understand how many outside views can hold so many certainties.

---

[41] M. Levine, *Heavy Metal Islam* (New York, NY: Random House, 2008).

[42] Numerous Tunisian rap groups, from cities both big and small, took the spotlight after the revolution.

[43] M. Kilani, *Une expérience de la révolution tunisienne*, p.76

[44] Ibid.

A Tribute to the Anonymous People
AN INTERVIEW WITH ISSAM HENI

Interviewed by Glenda Garelli, Federica Sossi, and Martina Tazzioli
Sidi Bouzid, July 2012

Q: Did you speak with many others journalists or we are the first to interview you?

I: Yes, I've spoken many times with journalists. I also participated in some conferences with other bloggers. So to introduce myself, I've been a blogger since 2006. I have a blog in Tunisian, in French and in dialectical Arabic. It is a form of expression now common in Tunisian blogs: using ordinary language to communicate, we speak Arabic but in an ordinary way, as an ordinary language. And in this blog I talked about the political and economic situation in the country and it was systematically censored by the Tunisian Internet agency. This agency uses a very expensive American system that is based on keywords –like Ben Ali, his family and keywords related to specific arguments – and you should not use those words if you don't want to be censored. Elsewhere in Tunisia Facebook pages or blogs were blocked and disappeared. Instead, censored blogs continued to function out of Tunisia. This agency organizes access to the Internet in Tunisia. It is an agency that is simultaneously part of the Ministry of the Interior and the Ministry of Communication. And if problems occur, on the page an image appears indicating that the page does not exist. Every time that a page or a website is censored you receive a false message saying 'the page does not exist' and the message '*Erreur 404*' appears. Actually, it was a false message. Also Facebook was censored for more than a month. After the international meeting on communication that took place in Tunisia in

2005, in which we talked about the future of the Internet, many criticisms were directed towards Tunisia about the freedom of speech and expression, free access to the Internet and therefore the analysis on Internet was less constricted. It was a world event, in some senses, but Tunisian activists took a position against that meeting. But *reporters sans frontières* and many associations of activists that work in this domain were against the decision to organize it in Tunisia, since Tunisia was classified among the most repressive countries concerning the Internet. The Internet in Tunisia was not like in Europe or in the US. There were no websites or international press. There were no French newspapers. It was limited to the exchange of images and some videogames. There was heavy repression concerning public affairs. Before 2005 there were very few people that had a blog - there were just around ten blogs. These blogs were blogs only about gossip or about new technologies, such as new mobile phones or other technology stuff. But then dozen of blogs were born, using a Tunisian dialect, and that talked about the Tunisian political and social context. And the Tunisian dialect escapes censorship. And thus it became something of a phenomenon.

Q: But why did it escape censorship?

I: Because it does not have a determined orthography. You can write it with Latin or Arabic letters, and in this way it was possible to escape censorship. Only if a blogger was very well known he could be tracked, otherwise he escaped the automatic filters. And so hundreds of blogs were opened. All those blogs were in Tunisian dialect. I was censored in 2008, that is two years later. After 2008, Tunisian authorities started to recognize the importance of this form of expression.

Q: But what I don't understand is this: did the Tunisian dialect elude censorship because you had some codes with which to say things like 'Ben Ali,' 'Leila Trabelsi,' 'regime,' or 'dictatorship' - and so you invented these devices to express yourself? Or did it elude censorship as it was based on the classic Arabic language?

I: No, it was first of all because dialectical Tunisian language is not written in a correct way; but also because we used indirect words to speak. For instance, it was enough to say 'him' to refer to Ben Ali, or other times we used the expression 'the big patron.' So, we used these words but we understood each other very well.

Q: And, in order to talk about Leila Trabelsi was it enough to say 'her'?

I: No, sometimes we used words like 'the belle,' 'the princess,' 'the hairdresser'. We used an indirect style. We acquired a savoir-faire when faced with censorship. It was quite predictable to work out under what conditions one could be censored. And every time that censorship took place, it was enough to go back to the last three things posted to understand why one was censored. Often when the style was too direct one was censored. It was sufficient to pronounce the name of Ben Ali or to write about real facts to get censored. For instance I remember that in 2009, on November 7, the date when Ben Ali came to power, a journalist wrote about that as a supreme form of religion, it alluded to the pilgrimage to La Mecca, where people make seven tours of the stone. In the Islamic religion there are the seven deadly sins, and he made a connection between the November 7 and the number seven of the Islamic religion and ultimately his blog was censored.

Q: And so when someone has a blog censored, could he/she continue the activity somewhere else?

I: Yes, with the proxy it was possible. But only in order to stay abreast of what was happening in the world. If your blog was censored you could still actually post, but nobody did that, since users were eminently Tunisian.

Q: But I want to understand better: if a Tunisian who lives in France knows your blog, and then the blog is censored, but you continue to post, could he/she see what you post?

I: Yes, it could be censored. But if it was on a free platform it could be censored but consequently only the access from within Tunisia was blocked. But the problem was that a blog blocked for users in Tunisia lost its efficacy. And so we tried to transfer all the material to another blog, creating a third blog. But then someone ends up with 20 or 30 blogs. And when the access was blocked, it was transferred to another blog. We also developed more extreme forms of 'blogging'. For instance, there was something like a political exile: you could offer another blogger the access to your blog in order to post on his/her blog. In Arabic we call it *alloujoy iftiradhi*, namely cyber-exile. So, we offered exile to our blog to those who were censored. We use that strategy among us: before being censored I offered my friends the possibility to post on my blog. This is also quite widespread in Egypt. Other strategies consisted in spending sleepiness nights on the web: we fixed a data, we produced some logos to post on all blogs for organizing a kind of virtual campaign. The first time that we made a big campaign was in May 2010, against 'Ammar 404'.[1] It was the first time in which Tunisian bloggers decided to shed their anonymity, without using pseudonyms, and surface on the real world. And that day we decided to set a demonstration in Tunis and to dress in white t-shirts. The meeting was fixed in the front of the Ministry of Telecommunication and Technology. But finally almost everyone who wore a white t-shirts was harrassed by the police.

Q: But for you this day was an event which was a precursor to the revolution?

I: For me it was a sign speaking indirectly. It was a sort of heroism, and in 2010 we gained some ground. We started to post some dossiers, real dossiers on corruption by the Trabelsi family. We started to organize ourselves in various ways. The two bloggers who organized the event went to the Ministry of the Interior to demand the end of the censorship and authorisation for a demonstration. One of them was forced to post on his blog a video asking the Tunisian bloggers not to participate in the demonstration; but this video was obviously coerced. However, in the end they succeeded in coming out intact. Do you know Zouhair Yahyaoui? He is the first Tunisian blogger, he was arrested in 2002 and tortured and then he came out of prison and died, on the May 13, 2005 and after the revolution that day is celebrated as the day for the freedom of the Internet. His pseudonym was Ettounsi (The Tunisian). He was savagely tortured. May 13 is now a national holiday in Tunisia. At that time he did not have a blog, he posted on the forum Tunezine. Before Facebook, at that time there were the forums. The remembrance of Zouhair terrified the Tunisian internautes. When we saw that the two persons who went to the Ministry of the Interior to organize the demonstration of Ammar, Slim Amamou

---

[1] 'Ammar' is an Arabic proper name. It is the common name for the ATI (Agence tunisienne de l'internet).

(who became a secretary of state in the first transitory government after the fall of Ben Ali) came out intact from that experience, we interpreted that as a sign of the weakness of the regime, since they were not tortured but only arrested and then released and returned to their ordinary activities.

Q: So, was it a sign of weakness of the regime?

I: Yes, because before the regime did not tolerate actions like that. Before it would have entailed 10 years of prison, maybe deaths and torture. Before they did not tolerate these kind of gestures. Instead, that time, things went differently. They were held for only 48 hours. The day before the demo they posted some videos suggesting Tunisians should not join the demonstration, but obviously it was the police who forced them. If you want now I can tell you about the revolution.

Q: Yes.

I: What changed during the revolution is that Facebook became the real information media in Tunisia. Nobody had any trust in the official press and newscasts. Instead, Facebook, in some way had what Tunisians were looking for: information on the events, the discourses on the family of Ben Ali and on corruption. After the 'Ammar day', the majority of Facebook pages, focusing on interests in music, sport, games and photo sharing, realized that Internet in Tunisia was not similar to other places. And consequently the majority of Facebook's users supported this cause. As far as people are concerned, censorship was the main theme at the core of the debate on Facebook. And thus, since the first events in Sidi Bouzid, a series of photos taken with the mobile phones was posted. For instance, I took some photos with the mobile phone because I could not go out with the camera, since the police were filming the demonstrations from the roofs and other sites. And it was too risky to show a camera. I had been in Avenue Bourguiba since the day after the immolation of Mohamed Bouazizi. And since that time onwards I've never stopped. I tried to take images in a discrete way, but there were terrible clashes with the police. I took some photos of the repression and I also made some videos but filming very badly. And when I watch those videos today, they are crudely made. I posted them on Facebook, and then I found them on *Al Jazeera* news. I don't know how this was possible.

Q: So, you posted them on the afternoon of the 18th and in the evening of the same day they were on *Al Jazeera*, right?

I: Yes, they were on *Al Jazeera* news, and on Sunday again. This was before we organized ourselves as bloggers. In fact, then we organized ourselves, we built various more or less professional networks, also with some friends of ours in the U.S., such as for instance Tarek Kahlaoui. I don't know if you know him. He was also a blogger, he was professor at the University of Rutgers in the U.S., he teaches history of the Middle East, and now he is the director of the Tunisian Institute of Strategic Studies, he came back after the revolution but at that time he was a blogger.

Q: But which Institute?

I: The Institute of Strategic Studies is connected with the presidency of the Republic, and that sets strategies on Tunisia in the long run.

Q: Is it connected to the Presidency of the Republic?

I: Yes, mostly concerning the orientations of the country at any level - political, social, economic - both in the long and in the medium term. We created a Facebook page and we call it 'Press agency of the Tunisian street,' the street in the sense of public space. It was more difficult to block Facebook than the blogs. Indeed, Facebook could be blocked only page by page. For instance, this page was blocked three times, and every time we had to restart. I remember that one night there were 30,000 visitors. Tunisians were hardened by official news. This Facebook page was a page of Tunisians living here and of Tunisian living abroad. We filmed everything we were doing, and then we posted it for our friends abroad. We were worried that Tunisian authorities could find us, and it was quite predictable that there would be some arrests.

Q: And did you post only in Tunisian or also in English and in French?

I: Only in Tunisian because it was for our friends. But we had some contacts, our friend Tarek had some contacts with *Al Jazeera* and also in Qatar. Because he wrote articles in many Arab newspapers and quite often he spoke on *Al Jazeera* newscast about the events of the Arab world, Tarek transferred abroad what was happening in Sidi Bouzid.

Q: Concerning your codes of access in Facebook, did you have the impression that it was easier to elude censorship than before?

I: No. The group Anonymous alerted Facebook in order to protect those who had a Facebook account in Tunisia. In this way the Tunisian Internet Agency (ATI) could not control them as much as before. I remember that after the outbreak of the revolution there were dozens of people filming what was happening in Sidi Bouzid, in Kasserine and in Thala.

Q: We asked you that question because a blogger from Tunis told us that at that time he got the impression that it was quite easy to elude censorship. And that after the revolution, when medias said that the U.S. supported some Tunisian bloggers in order to facilitate the Tunisian revolution, he made a connection with what happened on Facebook in January.

I: Yes, many people say that the U.S. facilitated the revolution in Libya and that they provided some weapons. But frankly speaking I don't find it strange that a blogger from Tunis could have said that about the Tunisian revolution because they didn't know what the revolution really was and its causes. Here, in Sidi Bouzid, you see the poverty, all these young graduated people who are unemployed. We were sure that one day these things would happen. On December 17 and 18, and during the days which followed when we went into the streets, there were no Americans with weapons, I didn't see any American Marines, there were the people from Sidi Bouzid like us. I know the majority of the people and they were very angry. Before, when I met some people, they told me 'how could this be ok?' All of us were angry. But in Tunis things were different. It was quite easy to find a job, life was good there. For this reason the conspiracy theory finds its place in the minds of the people from Tunis. They had no idea about the reality here in Sidi Bouzid, and so they didn't know the real causes of the revolution. For them Ben Ali was a dictator, persecuting freedom and his opponents. For them it was only a question of freedom, basic freedom, and that's all. Instead, we could not survive; I have been unemployed for a long time. I'm 35 and I only had the opportunity to work for a few years. And I was still living with my family. You see, all the people are in the same condition. This is everybody's problem; if you go here in the neighbourhood you see the poverty in the houses.

Q: What you are saying is interesting, because it is often said that the revolution became political only later; as if the becoming political of the revolution is a nobler element than concerns other claims. Instead, you are saying that the being political of the revolution was precisely what you were describing.

I: Yes, the revolution became political only later, in the beginning it was not political. The first days we didn't demand the fall of Ben Ali, rather it was because Mohamed Bouazizi set himself on fire due to the unemployment, and here everybody knows that. Here I have some friends who are 40 and who have never found a job, graduated in humanities, in philosophy or economics. In Sidi Bouzid it's normal that a family can encounter these problems, and knows these conditions with all the psychological consequences this condition entails. When you are 40 and you can neither go out with a girl nor get married, and you still live with your parents, it's unbearable. Instead, people in Tunis don't know this. For them Tunisia stops in the poor neighbourhoods of Tunis, but they are not comparable with the conditions of this zone. In Tunis there are better conditions. If I take you with me, you can see the differences, also at the level of infrastructure, some houses have no water, when you go to the hospital there are young people who die. In the governmental statistics at the time of Ben Ali it was marked that Tunisia is a developed country in the medical domain and all the rest. But instead we are an African country, like Chad or Somalia. Here it's frequent that those giving birth could die, due to the lack of means and medical resources. Personally I was really disappointed when on January 15, or maybe it was January 17 or 18, we started to see political leaders coming from abroad and talking about the new form of Tunisia, debating if they would adopt the parliamentary or the presidential regime. For me this was not the real issue. For me and for my friends anyone could govern the country and we would not care about that, insofar as he/she respects the claims of the people of December 17. For us the problem was our dignity, we want to live with dignity, we do not care about politicians, about Ben Ali and all the rest. The problem was that the situation in Sidi Bouzid

34

should have changed for the better. In the beginning the problem was not the fall of Ben Ali, but after the massacres, when we saw what happened in Kasserine and in Menzel Bouzaiane, the deaths, Ben Ali could not remain any more. But in the beginning it was about living in a correct way.

Q: So what you are saying is very interesting, because it's true that everybody says that in the beginning the revolution was social and then political. But simultaneously it seems to me that you are saying that when the revolution became political it was also the moment in which your claims started to be betrayed. And you also argued that your claims were political insofar as they were social, and not the other way around. It seems to me that you are saying that you do not care about political government, the problem is your life and what you can do in your life.

I: Yes, the problem was also that Ben Ali favoured some cities on the coast, and he pushed to the margins all the western regions and now it's the same thing. The beginning of the revolution was something very spontaneous, and then from a certain moment onwards, the union organizers of the UGTT and the teacher members of the UGTT started to organize the protests also with slogans like 'a job is a right, band of thieves'. It was the first time in Tunisia that something was said against Ben Ali and against his family. But we did not say 'Ben Ali *dégage*,' we started to say that only around 12th or 13th January. '*Dégage*' appeared only in the last three days, here in the beginning we did not know '*dégage*,' we talked about a band of thieves and we claimed the right to work. But I'm not questioning the importance of '*dégage*,' because I'm not a supporter of the regime, it was not possible that Tunisia was still governed by a dictator who used bullets against its population, before we had not seen something similar happening against Tunisians and so it could not be tolerated any more.

Q: But in Gafsa something had already happened.

I: In 2008? No, in Gafsa it was different. There were two victims and the Tunisians were not aware of this because at that time Facebook was not used. Instead, I remember the night of January 6 or 7, the first video put on the web was about the hospital of Kasserine: there were people with their heads completely broken, and bearing marks of the bullets in their bodies. And the women and children who were crying. It was like a country at war. And so Tunisian did not tolerate that. In Gafsa two people were killed, one by weapons and one by electricity. He was doing a sit-in in a power plant of the phosphate company. And then I don't know if the director of the company or a functionary of the army reactivated the electricity and so he died. But at that time Tunisians didn't know about what happened in Gafsa.

Q: We don't want to accuse you of being a supporter of Ben Ali. We want say that often in the media discourses there is a stark opposition between the social and the political, with the latter considered as the noblest and most important one. While you are contending that the social aspect was important and that the political dimension betrayed that, and that it is not true, the social dimension is more important than the political one. When, after the fall of Ben Ali, politicians started to discuss the form of the political regime, they were already betraying the social issue.

I: Yes, also now one hears politicians saying that this social crisis is temporary and they are discussing what Tunisians need in the next hundred years; they say that we need a new constitution but for us it's not like that.

Q: And for you, as a blogger, what was the role played by Facebook? Since in the European debate it was emphasized a lot. Was it a simple means of communication or not? And what role did the bloggers play? Did they organize the demonstrations or did they spread news?

I: No, here we spread the news, while in Egypt or in Syria the bloggers promoted demonstrations. They announced the demonstration and then they posted it on Facebook. In Tunisia we posted images and news for other Tunisians, and in this way the world could know what was happening here. Many people did that, not only the bloggers. And about this I would like to pay tribute to the anonymous people who posted the news on Facebook. Without them, bloggers would have nothing to share and post. The anonymous people created the content of the news, they put their lives at risk, in fact there were real bullets. Because without Facebook they would have stifled everything. Like in Gafsa, for instance, where more violent protests occurred than here in Sidi Bouzid, on December 17. But Tunisians were not aware of was happening there, and Ben Ali made some quick decisions: after the repressions he sent some entrepreneurs from his family who had created supermarkets and two big markets, and funded the University of Gafsa; they created a radio and all that benefited the residents of Gafsa. In this way Ben Ali succeeded in managing the situation.

Q: But did the government create the university on that occasion?

I: No, but Ben Ali gave some funds to the university to develop it, and in a similar way he improved the road which connects Gafsa to Tunis. Thus, he invested money to tame the people in Gafsa, and he succeeded. Instead, in Sidi Bouzid with Facebook and the first images, the protests spread to Regueb, Menzel Bouzaied and in other places of the region of Sidi Bouzid, and then in Sfax, in Kasserine and in other Tunisian cities. Facebook enabled events to be spread and the protests became against Ben Ali. In the beginning he reacted as he did in Gafsa, reinforcing the police - people talk about 6,000 - 10,000 policemen. I saw many police buses and those of the army. So, he reacted like he did in Gafsa, since he thought it would be possible to tame the protests with an iron hand, with repression. But things were taken out of his hands, because in other regions there were not some many policemen. He also used real bullets but not even that was of use for him.

Q: And now?

I: We still wait; I'm quite pessimistic for our region. Before we used to say that Ben Ali was the cause of our poverty, but now that Ben Ali has gone we are still in the same condition, nothing has improved. Many people are thinking of moving, and restarting their lives in Sousse, Tunisi, Sfax, Nabeul and all the cities of the coast.

Q: Coming back to the previous discussion, in Europe we brought a lot of attention to Tunisian bloggers, depicting them as blogger-stars. What do you think about that? Namely, what do you think that despite the many anonymous people who posted on the web after the revolution some bloggers became so famous?

I: I understand what you are saying. I know what the people of Sidi Bouzid and of the inner regions of Tunisia did, without expecting any reward. We were not paid, we did that for our country. For all of us, the bloggers who became stars were considered the three musketeers of the revolution, as they were called in France on Canal plus: Lina Ben Mhenni, Aziz Amami, Slim Amamou. They participated in a broadcast on *Canal Plus* and they were introduced as the three musketeers. But I don't want to talk about them, I'm not able to judge their contribution to the revolution; in this case maybe I can refer to a conspiracy theory, because these people were then invited to go to the U.S.

Q: But, according to you what is the relationship between conspiracy theory and the revolution?

I: Maybe the U.S. realized that in this space, here in Tunisia, there was a new spirit that was starting to spread; and maybe they wanted to control it or to set foot here. These young people were invited for a stay in the U.S. or in Sweden by a governmental agency, Freedom House. Eight months before the revolution I was contacted by a Tunisian blogger who told me that a foreign agency was interested in providing us with technical devices in order to dodge censorship through the satellites. But I replied that I was not interested and that I didn't get the usefulness of satellites, I'm just a blogger. And this was in early 2010, and so I did not continue this exchange. I told them that I was not interested and that's all. Instead, those young bloggers left for internships in the U.S. and in Jordan and in other places around the world. I don't want to support the conspiracy theories but they became the stars of the revolution, I don't' know whether or not it was a coincidence.

Q: But while the life of these blogger-stars changed after the revolution - because they are invited to many conferences in Europe - did your life change as well?

I: Not at all. I work and I'm paid 300 euros. I stay here in Sidi Bouzid, yes, some Italian friends came here before the elections and they invited me to a festival in Bologna, but I've been refused the visa, I participated in a Skype conference in Montreal. But my life has not changed. I simply stopped smoking, that's all.

Q: Have you been contacted by any European associations in order to do some projects?

I: No.

Q: We are interested in this because the European Union is funding many projects by Tunisian associations and we know some Italian and European associations that are making these connections with Tunisian associations. But what we notice is that, except the 'stars,' European associations do not meet the others, the anonymous remain anonymous, while they create a sort of elite with the Tunisian stars and the others remain what they were before the revolution.

I: Yes, I understand. Maybe this is because this elite offers to the Americans and to the Europeans what they are looking for, namely a progressive elite; and they try to demonstrate that Tunisia is an integralist or salafist country while they support freedom of women etc. But also here we are for the freedom of women...I saw Lina Ben Mhenni on Swiss TV with Tariq Ramadan, and she was talking about the present situation in Tunisia, saying that the conquests of women are in danger and that bearded people harass persons in the street, but this is not true. Yes, there is an increase in Salafit but it's not as terrible as she depicts. But for the European ear it's good to hear this, and thinking to come for helping Tunisian women. And these bloggers sing this song well. But concerning Salafists, this is another question. Here in Sidi Bouzid there are many of them, but it's not so serious a phenomenon.

Q: What is quite strange is that all these people who became the stars in western media and who sing the song that Europe wants to hear, are the same who have also been invited by European activists. We are not journalists but we are politically involved in Europe and in Italy and those people were also invited to our meetings. And so we are at the same level of the media, and it's the mainstream thought of Obama and the U.S.

I: Yes, you think yourselves to be alternative people but you are not.

Q: We try to be alternative, but we are not able to be. Activists contact Lina as the true revolutionary and the media contact her as the icon of the revolution.

I: Yes, but also in Jordan and in Egypt it is more or less the same, there are people who were invited to every part of the world. It has become a kind of trade.

Q: It's striking that that we speak the same language as the commercial scene. And also when we speak of the revolution in a different way, we reproduce if not the same at least very similar prejudices. We almost speak the same language, and consequently it is a misunderstanding.

I: Sometimes I think that the West generally loves seeing these stars and speaking of the Tunisian revolution as the 'Facebook revolution', because it is a sort of cultural success; and this digital culture which started in the U.S., in Europe and in Japan, that, is considered in the West as able to change countries without the use of force - as if it was possible to change the regime with Facebook. Before it was necessary to make an attack, with bombs and parachutists, while now, according to the West, this is would not be necessary any more, and this would be a success.

'Here and There Are the Same.'
The Upheavals of Spaces and Narratives
FEDERICA SOSSI

1. May 1, 2011: 'The President of the European Executive, Jose Manuel Barroso, responds to the letter from the Italian Prime Minister Berlusconi and that of the French President Sarkozy that "the temporary reinstatement" according to the "well established" criteria of the internal borders between the EU Countries that are part of the Schengen agreement "is one of the possible options" to reinforce the agreement that abolishes the internal frontiers of the European Union. The European Commission will present some propositions moving in this direction soon.' (TgCom)

It is indisputable that when it comes to producing a press release a certain art is required, namely the gift of extreme synthesis which can only be learnt by those having mastered the craft. Thus, on reading this statement one might be inclined to think that those who wrote it were lacking this craft, or had simply omitted to exercise it here. But this is not the case. The idea of reinforcing the Schengen agreement on free circulation through the temporary reinstatement of the frontiers is exactly what Barroso had argued, according to the same art of contradiction and illogical enunciations that became customary in 2011.

This illogical, pervasive art has dominated the scene of migration control policies since when, following the revolutions and the uprisings movements in the Maghreb, and most of all during the aftermath of the Tunisian revolution, Tunisian migrants left for Europe pursuing the only possibility permitted to them by the policies of the European Union, sidestepping the frontiers and burning their indefinite irradiations. For several months, from the end of January until the summer, during the rapid and unexpected succession of the events, politicians followed hot on the heels by journalists were forced to learn another modality of reportage in line with the customary logic of their policies, developing a different narrative, which no longer took the form of a coherent narration but a disconnected and contradictory one, in which the rhetoric of illogicality was sovereign. Closing the borders in order to open them, reinstating controls to abolish them, was just one of the many examples of this new narrative through which politicians and journalists tried to find again the habit of the politics of control and the consuetude of its legitimizing discourse.

Indeed, both the politics of control and the legitimizing discourse stopped working according to the usual schema, and while the logic of control continued to provide a backdrop to increasingly inventive and improvised practices, the structure of the narrative which legitimized them was completely broken, running the risk of constituting nothing but a distorted mirror of their unsustainability. The result was a horizon with huge disconnects between differences practices, as well as between practices and the discourses legitimizing them. Due to the anxiety to control, there was a delirium in the making of 'closed borders open' and of 'clandestine migrants' protected by humanitarian measures with residence permits that were not meant for staying.

2. May 2, 2011: 'At midnight on May 1, The Collective of Tunisians from Lampedusa in Paris occupies a building that is the property of the municipality of Paris at 51 Avenue Simon Bolivar, in the XIXth *arrondissement.*' In fact, if we want to understand the disconnect here, we should avoid reverting to the number of arrivals which simply risks affirming and reproducing existing techniques of control along with new, improvised forms. The 'biblical exodus', that never happened, was indeed one of the images used when in February the arrivals on the Island of Lampedusa began, following an automatic reproduction of the usual narrative of invasion, that, over the past few years, has been staging a place of the spectacle, some actors and background actors - the migrants - who usually disappeared just after the images of their arrival. An 'earthquake', a 'wake', a 'human tsunami': these were the other images evoked by the 'traffic wardens' in charge of human traffic, long accustomed to translating this into the language of natural disaster, referring to people in terms of 'avalanches', 'wakes', 'flows', 'floods', 'natural catastrophes', where a few others would search to see the faces and bodies of men, women and

children who had left, arrived and sometimes drowned. This 'natural' dimension which steals and deprives human events of action, decision, choice and desire, attributes such events to a different, independent, and definitively inscrutable, force. At the same time, this terminology enables the production of a defensive 'we,' in need of protection when faced with this unavoidable 'flow of the elements'.

However, this time the spectacle had lasted for too long to remain credible. Already after just a few weeks the residents of the Island of Lampedusa started to give the first signs of its possible failure. Moreover, on stage the number of supporting actors intentionally left there to create the scene of the invasion risked blocking everything. The surplus of bodies with respect to the places available made it possible for the migrants coming from Tunisia to assume center stage. They were no longer extras but actors, no longer bodies to manage but subjects to talk with; human beings in possession of speech when confronted by the journalists who, as usual, hastened to the island to get front row seats; subjects with whom the habitants of Lampedusa were able to exchange experiences. Most of all, these were people of all ages who, just weeks before, had been involved in the insurgent and revolutionary moment that by that point was crossing the entire space of the Maghreb and Mashreq. Therefore, these were subjects that as well as demanding the right to speak before the journalists had brought with them a speech and an action largely exceeding the horizon of the 'wretched on the boats,' 'escaping refugees' - thus breaking with the script and the plot which tries to contain them within this storyline.

3. 'The Arab danger. Democrats disembark in Europe': this was the title of a French cartoon that circulated the web during those days. Indeed, this is exactly what happened. Neither wretched nor refugees, they arrived in Lampedusa in late January and then in February and in March. Little by little, they eventually became wretched while the Italian Minister of the Interior Roberto Maroni 'used' them in order to keep them on the island, staging the drama of a non-temporary residence and transforming the island into a detention center to evoke both to his electors and to the allied European States the risk of the invasion, anticipating votes from the former and funds from the latter. At the same time, backstage, a possible change to the still restrictive politics of asylum was at stake, carried on through the opening of a 'hosting center' in Mineo, in the province of Catania. The center, which was presented as 'the solidarity village,' worked

as a big container into which both the asylum seekers scattered across Italy and the Tunisian migrants disappeared. Already at that time, in mid February 2011, it was not unusual to come across the same complacency amongst journalists, ignorant to the differences and inclined to perpetuate confusion and who, perhaps grasping the meaning of Maroni's snares, started to write using the usual language of desperation to refer to the Tunisian migrants.

To add to the confusion, during the days which followed, the insurgent Libyans and, Italy's lifelong friend, Gaddafi - with the war he was making on his population - came to the rescue. Then, from there, from the Libyan beaches, refugees could effectively escape, most of these being refugees coming from the Horn of Africa, imprisoned for two years in Libyan concentration camps, by the 'pushing back' policies inaugurated by Italy in May 2009. Indeed, none of the European member States seemed to possess the shred of humanity required to imagine this evacuation of undesirable human beings along with Libya's own citizens in its rush to go to war, the war of the 'Willings'. But this is precisely what happened and the consequences are well known. Bodies at sea, listed as dead people as they emerge from between the waves, or considered to have disappeared when the sea leaves no trace of them. Yet, in the middle of all this, there were still Tunisians, still alive, besides those who died or 'disappeared' and who, like all dead people, could be left to their own destiny or, as with all missing persons, could be left to that half grief that migration policies allow to their families, as has been the case when families call Italian authorities hoping to come across a trace of a missing person.

Nevertheless, those democratic, living people did indeed arrive in Europe. And they arrived after getting rid, at least in Tunisia, of the *space of elsewhere* where they could be relegated again. Democratic and alive. Democratic, alive and in search of democracy, as many of them argued expressing the desire to return to Tunisia some months later, once the process of democratization had been accomplished. In the meantime, they wanted somewhere to stay. Democratic, alive and in search for democracy and, this time, with a dictatorial space burning behind them along with the frontiers of Europe. For this reason, they were there with that huge demand, inconceivable for the European States: bodies that persist and that highlight, simply by remaining, the *space of suspension* that migration control policies had assigned to migrants at large, before addressing them. Indeed, according to the European Union they should have agreed to remain suspended in space, since Italy gave them the 'permit to move out,' while the other EU member states rejected the idea of a stay on their territories.

4. May 2, 2011: 'At midnight on May 1, the Collective of Tunisians from Lampedusa in Paris occupies a building that is the property of the municipality of Paris at 51 Avenue Simon Bolivar, in the XIXth arrondissement.' Reflecting on such a statement, it might appear to be a statement that shares the same rhetoric of non-logicality with those enunciated by a politics of control. Not so much a tale but the simple description of an action. In this respect it was not so very different from the many statements made by the 'sans papiers' or the 'refugees' who over the years have occupied a similar place, in the attempt to exceed the horizon of suspension that was established and intended for them. But what is odd about the above sentence, erasing every trace of illogicality, is the who that constitutes the subject of the enunciation. A collective of Tunisians: there is nothing strange in that. In fact, it was the persistence of a collective identification with the place of origin and national citizenship. The persistence of what other comparable collective identifications constituting the 'identities of arrival' - and for this reason 'suspended identities' defined in terms of a lack, a 'without' [sans] – had over the years succeeded in exceeding. So, let's start again: a collective of Tunisians from Lampedusa. And once again: it was a collective of Tunisians from Lampedusa in Paris. In other words, this was precisely what they wrote in their statement without any commas to signal a pause or interruption: 'the Collective of Tunisians from Lampedusa in Paris.' This statement was without doubt the description of an action; and at the same time, the action consisted of the occupation of a place which exceeded the horizon of suspension. But the fact that a collective identification with a place of origin and with national citizenship drags along with it two places of two nation-states through the operation of identification, suggests the transformation of the action into some sort of revolution.

Before the eviction and the arrests which ensued, here, at 51 Avenue Simon Bolivar, in the XIXth *arrondissement*, the 'Collective of Tunisians from Lampedusa in Paris' proclaimed, through its public statement, that 'here and there are the same'. They evoked three nation-states in order to designate a collective of equal persons, three nation-states, two continents intertwined with the places of their journeys and stays; in order to narrate a collective of equal persons which enact an occupation but, simultaneously, an act which revolutionizes that space; a space which, the politics of migration control as well as their legitimizing narratives had plotted for the last ten years, defining, tracing and shaping our perception of it.

5. 'Here and there are the same': this claim was already being uttered by Tunisian migrants as soon as they arrived in Lampedusa, when they were not yet 'Tunisians from Lampedusa in Paris'. And when the customary discursive regime tried to silence them having recourse to the naturalizing words.

Firstly a 'wave,' and then a 'tsunami.' But a 'human' tsunami. Indeed, this was the sign that the silencing action produced by naturalization was starting to be lacerated from within, evidently swamped by a tidal wave composed of human bodies, mainly males and young people, who spoke without being asked to do so. Sure, it was not a long and clearly articulated discourse, a tale, a narration, that the single components of that wave seemed able to produce on being probed by those sent to verify that they really possessed the qualities of human beings. The language of this strange wave made of human beings was a language of gestures, more than of voices; but a clear and indisputable language, since it was its own sheer presence that spoke, precluding the necessity for many words. The wave was here and it said so, in a simple way, precisely by being there. Moreover, since the wave was formed only of human beings, these human beings - the young and not-so-young - were here and they said that, in a simple way, by being there. Here but where? Here, in Lampedusa, in Italy; someone, a few of them, in the days soon after the first arrivals already appeared in France, or in any case here, in Europe. On February 13, 2011 during a TV broadcast one of the EU Ministers of the Interior reminded us, somewhat concerned, that it was a question of a distance of 70 kilometers, invoking the support of the other member States of the 'here.' '70 kilometers,' Maroni repeated 'the same distance that there is between Milan and Bergamo,' clearly accustomed to tracing everything back to his own myopic and local gaze, even the so-called 'natural' events of those proportions, as he might also do an earthquake. Yet, 70 kilometers is 50 minutes by train, if we are talking about the ground covered between Milan and Bergamo. Instead, in the case of Tunisia and Lampedusa, several hours of navigation apart, it was the places of departure and arrival of those human beings that frightened the Minister. Here and there are in part the same, as two cities of the same region and of the same state, nothing more, nothing less. Their departures and their arrivals told us this with such clarity that even the Minister was aware and anguished about this.

First, it was a certainty, in the delirium of the 'biblical exodus' and of the sizeable difference in the numbers with which governmental actors tried to corroborate this. The certainty of the short distance, less than an hour by train, or a few hours navigation. Then, the other certainties and the various consequences that every one of us might work out. In order to cover that distance someone goes to the train station, buys a ticket, gets on the train, reads the newspaper or enjoys the dull landscape of the Po valley, arriving an hour later at the railway station in Bergamo. In order to cover the same distance, someone else took to the street, resisted in the squares, destroyed buildings, fought against the police, aided one's own friends, cried '*horria*' [freedom] and had already mastered a body language which could be understood without a translator: 'here and there are the same'.

6. 'Here and there are the same' was already at that point, around mid-February, a revolution. Not just one but infinite burned frontiers. 'Here and there are the same' was before the events taking place during those months, already a certainty that the *harraga* from Maghreb had carried with them for years, tearing out their ID cards and burning the distances marked by the more or less visible frontiers that the European states put into play in order to hamper their journeys.[1] Over the years, other *harraga* left, undertaking increasingly dangerous journeys, not only due to the greater distances being crossed but also because of the increases in the mobile deployment of the European borders, which scattered multiple obstacles onto their paths. In the last decade we have become accustomed to this, coming to perceive this as something natural – a 'natural event' along with the European policies introduced to fight immigration and the wars we have been forced to fight – even when it results in the deaths of those left in the street.

But after the revolutions in the Maghreb and the first arrivals of Tunisian migrants in Lampedusa, 'here and there are the same' has become something more overwhelming, due to the evidence through which it was told and shown via that language of bodies and of their presences. A

---

[1] For a definition of '*harraga*,' see footnote 14 of Paola Gandolfi 'Spaces in Migration, Daily Life in Revolution' (this collection).

language that, beyond not needing a translation, seemed not even to need a narrative, because it was a productive language. And what was burning was not just the frontiers and the obstacles distributed everywhere over the years by migration policies, waging war against migrants, but also those centuries-old frontiers which are structured by linguistic, cultural, economic and military plots. Through those frontiers, the short distance of 70 or less kilometers - depending on the locations from which one looks at it - was transformed by the 'naturalness' of a 'we' and a 'they', articulated now and again from a distance which was nonetheless abyssal. 'Here and there are the same' was their Spring. A Spring acted out as much through the rapidity of their movements as it was through the 'demand', the results of which were inconceivable for the politics of control, to move in absolute freedom. They acted with the frontiers of the elsewhere burning behind them, the frontier of the 'here' burnt en-route, enacting the 'proximity' in the light of the sun, needless of partnerships and pacts, regardless of visas and politics of quota, disrespectful of the 'good order of migrations' and practicing only the disorder of a spatial confusion. A confusion not only of the 'here and there' but also of the remaining national borders that interweave the space of the European Union. Lampedusa stands for Europe, Italy stands for France, and this is in the last a 'very European' practice that we owe them.

And to be aware that 'here and there are the same' was already another revolution, as overwhelming as the Tunisian revolution and the revolution of Tahrir square, it was enough to read one of many analyses from 'here' that, with a naturalness customary, suggested representations of what was happening *now*, evoking once again the abyssal distance, this time with recourse to temporality. '1848 of the Arab world', '1989 of Maghreb', phrases which recurred time and again in editorials. It seems a strange tactic to resort to history precisely to forget history, both the history of there and the history of here, keeping quiet *en passant* both the anticolonial struggles of 'there' and the walls and the pervasive post-89 frontiers of 'here'. But, most of all, there were just the tutors of the 'internal' European order who made us perceive that, running from one summit to the other. This was less a case of their more or less veiled support or the delays with which they distanced themselves from those dictators who were falling and not even with their economic and political complicities, but rather through the deployment of forces of various kinds, that they were hastily trying to position between the 70 kilometers that the young

Tunisians arriving in Lampedusa had reduced to a short distance, their 'natural' distance.

7. 'The Collective of Tunisians from Lampedusa in Paris on May 1st at midnight occupies a building that is property of the municipality of Paris at 51 Avenue Simon Bolivar, in the XIXth *arrondissement*': in May 2011 this was the narrative through which the revolution was continued and accentuated. This happened despite the policies of the different member states of the European Union, which had become increasingly inventive during those three months, in order to tighten the sovereign law of control. One of the main inventions was devised by the Italian Minister of the Interior, Roberto Maroni, who in early April, using a kind of magic wand, conjured up a decree called 'humanitarian measures for temporary protection': as a result of which, some Tunisian migrants were given both a temporary resident permit and a permit for travelling.

However, the Italian Minister was aiming not so much for the laminated card –namely, the temporary permit – but for the travel permit, in the hope that all the Tunisian migrants would move away, to stay in other member States, as the decree itself suggested, recalling explicitly the free circulation within the European space. Nevertheless, Maroni's fantasy did not take into account the background history underpinning anti-immigration policies, enacted by the European Union: common policies as long as there was a *space of the elsewhere* in which humans might be banished, expelled, transformed into non-humans.

For this reason, over the years aggressive policies opposing immigration, could not but transform themselves (as has happened) into a politics of externalization: this was with the consequent supported by the dictators who were demanded, from time to time, to provide, through both military and policy, forms of control over their territory, in order to transform and maintain it as a *space of the elsewhere*. 'Everywhere but not in Europe': this was the rhetoric and the action that, for more than a decade, was perpetuated by the European member states, following Frontex, their vanguard, and its philosophy: acting before the frontier, preventing the arrivals, pushing back the bodies before their passage.

For this reason, in early 2011, due to the absence of the *space of the before*, put in motion by the upheaval produced by the revolutionary insurrections, while the key concepts for a new philosophy were still lacking, 'corridors of bounce' were improvised, between the old frontiers of Europe; a sort of extemporary trial of the principle of non-contradiction:

'neither here nor there,' or better, 'neither here, nor here,' to the extent that both 'here' and 'there' inevitably referred to the states of the European Union.

However, focusing more closely on this it is possible to recognise fissures emerging over the years, during the time of the politics of externalization. Especially at sea, when the member states regularly accused each other of non-compliance in rescuing people in international waters; and also within territorial waters, where the army of Frontex was deployed with its cooperation missions, in more or less vast search and rescue (SAR) zones as well as in the territorial waters of North African states transformed into European waters with a wave of the magic wand usually in the form of economic exchange.

But in these instances, the non-rescued persons, due to the negligence on the part of both states, died and, as it is well known, dead people do not speak; for this reason even diplomatic furores and mutual complaints about equally mutual responsibilities, could be buried at sea. Beyond the initial accusatory utterances against the other state - which were necessary to provide the appearance of a modicum of humanity in the face of the dead along with those still alive, left floating for days in tuna cages – deep down Ministers, their deputies, spokespersons and functionaries knew full well the reality. All guilty with the complicity of non-compliance. Rescues sent with delays of hours or even days after the SOS was sent by the boats in distress at sea, in the hope that it was up to the other state in its own territory to rescue and take charge of the bodies found alive. All were guilty and therefore, it was better to ignore it, and to forget the initial accusatory tones through a handshake and a renewed goodwill in the face of the 'supreme law' and its fight against human beings.

8. This supreme law had a space and a narrative. First of all, it had space. A mobile space, sustained by a state-of-the-art war logic, even in relation to the new forms of war, more or less humanitarian or permanent, inaugurated around the mid Nineties and after September 11, 2001. A moving war, in the attempt to lead and control people's mobility, never explicitly declared and based on a preventative logic, in which frontiers, borders, seas, national territories and the territories of other states were subsumed, into a sort of indistinct space; in that space the main task was to stop, block, manage and divert - beyond any law, norm and international treaty - the people who crossed it. A subterranean and silent war, that

during the most extreme moments was soon masked by an multitude of euphemisms aimed at clouding the action of militarized agencies or of preferably non-European armies, which were asked to cooperate by the European Union and its member States. Indeed, sometimes migrants were shot without waiting to die at the hands of shipwrecks; but then, there were the narrative inventions that intertwined with such action, transforming it into an act of defence. The result was an indistinct and continuously expanding space: thus, a space that could not be illustrated, despite attempts made by the legitimizing narratives to graphically depict it through geographic maps formed of innumerable arrows, all heading for Europe. No longer a varied delimitation of 'here' and 'there' - as it was during the colonial epoch - but a 'here' under threat from actors located at infinite points around the globe, while in the realm of politics, there were treaties, agreements and pacts which irradiated the necessary mobility of controls, giving rise, from time to time and from context to context, to unprecedented forms of sovereignty: *Spainmauritania, Eusenegal, Italylibya*.

Mixed sovereignties, a real bugbear for the political tradition of the nation-state, through which experimental forms of citizenship without territory were undertaken creating, as was the case in Senegal, *stateless-citizens* suspended in a space of elsewhere and even in their countries of origin, even before migrating. Mixed sovereignties through which inventing the possibility of *a space of elsewhere*, in which to warehouse the suspended bodies, adding to the spaces elsewhere in the European Union - increasingly mobile camps and 'tight' to the subjects - the territories of States out of the European Union. Mixed sovereignties almost always enacted through forms of neo-colonial invasion in the state territories of other continents, but sometimes also conjugated through the externalization of national territorial zones, or the undoing of the sovereignty of those actions of control, aimed at once again re-marking the space of sovereignty.

Here, let's take just two examples, both emblematic of these paradoxical forms of conjugation. The first example: Lampedusa, the extraterritorial island *par excellence*, since it is there, over recent years, that practices of detention of migrants were enacted, notwithstanding even the regulations established by the double track put in place throughout the camps. It was also not by chance that, in the first months of 2011, Lampedusa became a camp-island also for its residents, confined in a space to be shared with the migrants. The second example pertains to how after the ratification of the agreement with Libya, patrolling guard ships with mixed Italian-Libyan crews but with rules of engagement establishing that the Italian military corps, *Guardia di Finanza*, would technically 'shape and train' the Libyan crew, yet at the same time possessed no possibility of intervening in the action. This was the case even when, without the need of any 'training,' Libyans shot Italian fishermen, in September 2010. Also for this reason, perhaps, the image of 'Fortress Europe,' as impressive as it might seem, was not fully appropriate in evoking what was happening: not only because such an image is incapable of accounting for the porosity of the borders and of the continuous crossings which occur, but also because it relegates Europe to an illusionary fixity, giving the idea of a space not corroded by that unavoidable erosion of sovereignty generated by the politics of control.

But beyond the space there was its narration. A 'grand narrative,' with an infinity of words poured into the real and virtual public spaces by men and women, by executors of order, by journalists and by researchers, before long becoming common parlance giving shape to a new perception of humanity.

South towards North, Africa towards Europe, regular and irregular migrants, 'all the misery of the world,' invasion, clandestine migrants, disembarkations, flows, floods, biblical exodus, illegal or clandestine *emigration*, nomads, abusive camps, false asylum seekers: these are the rallying-cries, variably articulated, of this narration. Not a tale of migrations and not even a tale of the effective spaces of people's movements but a toolkit of expressions through which the horizon of a new partition of humanity is designated. In this sense, that tale was not so very different, in its structure, from the colonial tale which accompanied and legitimized colonial practices. 'We narrate the others': a discourse able to perform as much the 'we' as 'the others,' in this case according to the plot of a defensive barrier, necessary for producing the 'we' that requires protection from the assault of 'the others.'

The effect was a kind of paranoid blinding in the face of reality. A last order of non-perception: 600,000 or more people who crossed the Tunisian border with Libya within a few months, in contrast to the 25,000 Tunisian migrants who arrived in Lampedusa or in other places in Sicily.

9. 'The Collective of Tunisians from Lampedusa in Paris on May 1st at midnight occupies a building that is property of the municipality of Paris at 51 Avenue Simon Bolivar, in the XIXth *arrondissement*.' It is a story that undermines the 'grand narrative' and its silencing logic, bringing it back to the past. It was not only a collective speech, as it had been in other cases – in the '*sans papiers*' movements or among the 'African workers in Rosarno' in Italy, or even in the statements released by the detainees in different detention centers after their revolts or their hunger strikes, tales of a 'we' emerging as a subplot out of a grand narrative, assuming its 'othering' identifications, reversing their semantic function.

Discursive practices that over the years appeared within the horizon of dominant forms of narration, producing figures of a 'we narrate ourselves' that diverged from the alternative between, on the one hand, being narrated as 'others' to be silenced, or, on the other hand, *being narrated* as a more human 'I' or 'we'. In this last case, it was a question of paradoxical first-persons, halved first-persons, more often singular but sometimes also plural, created by the innumerable tales that little by little, tried to oppose the dominant logic, however impossible dismantling its structure might be. Good tales to counter the bad 'grand narrative,' that, nevertheless, in turn run the risk of silencing the 'others' of which they tell the story. 'We, the African workers in Rosarno,' 'we the *sans-papiers*,' 'we, the detainees from Corelli/Vincennes/Lukavica...,' these were small fissures produced within the layers of silence, direct speeches. However, they were internal to that horizon of division that seemed impossible to undermine. Instead, 'The Collective of Tunisian migrants from Lampedusa in Paris' breaks that division, producing a 'we' which represents a complete rupture of the 'othering' narrative logic which supported and legitimized the practices of control.

A confusion of the spaces, until now possible to identify as three nation-states and two continents, which merged into a 'we' that fragments the fiction of a space of elsewhere of European politics supported or tolerated, from time to time, by the different African watchdogs of the elsewhere. 'Here Tunisia, Italy, France' is the first effect of their narration, the performance of another space just as non-representable as the space of the mobile and expanding frontiers of the politics of control, but in which, differently from that space, 'here and there' are precisely the same. Not only a spring of space but also of concepts: this was the second effect of their nomination, the ability to cause the concepts of the political tradition to '*dégage*'. One among others, the concept of 'citizenship', through which subjects are routinely still captured into nation-states or in spaces belonging to broader communities. Also in this case the act of nomination has a performative function. Three spaces, three states and two continents combined as a unique nomination, irrespective of any logic of citizenship, insofar as it confuses the national belonging with the belonging to the places in which people have passed through or want to stay, an island and a town, Italy and France, Europe and, in the end, Tunisia itself, all swamped by a collective which is anarchic with respect to the nation-state logics of belonging as well as to the old and the new captures made by citizenship. To the *Tunisianlampedusaparis* who changed the stakes of any possible identification, responded the refrain of the same, reiterations of the practices of control by now incapable of identifying the 'space of elsewhere' that are not 'here', and producing dystonic narrations with respect to their legitimizing function. 'Open borders in order to be closed', 'resident permits for not staying', inventive and fantastic practices and *illogic narrations* that, in running after the 'Tunisian from Lampedusa in Paris' brought here the space of elsewhere. In this way, they generated 'clandestine tourists' and 'migrant European citizens', residents of that *suspended space*, the only one possible produced by a frontier which was enforced in order to be abolished. A similar event happened on April 17 in Ventimiglia with the cancellation of trains ordered by the French government to prevent migrants crossing the border. No more theatres of the South, with their spectacular arousals of images of the invasion, but rather 'theatres of identification' in which 'we are all clandestine migrants'.

And while the 'Collective of Tunisians from Lampedusa in Paris' was evicted from all the buildings it occupied, leaving in their statements on the web the postcard of their upheaval of spaces, other *tunisianlampedusaparis* continue silently to sidestep the space traced by the government of migration and by migration controls, swiping Lampedusa, Tunisia and Paris itself in their infinite urban squats. At the same time, their travel companions, *tunisialampedusaparis* or *tunisialampedusamarseille, milan, rome, brussels, zurich, berlin* who returned to Tunisia, following the same patterns of delusion or repatriated by the politics of control, contend in turn that 'here and there are the same'.

February, 2012.

There Were Moments of Joy
AN INTERVIEW WITH WAFA ABIDA

Interviewed by Federica Sossi and Martina Tazzioli
February 2012

Q: We know you arrived in Paris some months before the start of the Tunisian revolution. How did you experience that moment from a distance?

W: I lived it glued to the TV. Social networks, especially Facebook, hugely contributed to an almost immediate diffusion of what was going on in Tunisia. The news about the uprisings, the fights and the attacks against the headquarters of the Constitutional Democratic Rally (RCD) and against other institutional buildings had been arriving unceasingly from everywhere across Tunisia. With a lot of anger and bitterness, I witnessed from far away those outbursts of anger and rage that we had awaited for such a long time. Being away, though, allowed me to look at events with a necessary distance. The same distance that enabled us, together with some comrade-students living in France and especially in Paris, to think of self-organizing ourselves in order to bring the claims chanted in the streets of Tunisia, to France and elsewhere. The form of this political organization was inspired by organizational forms created in Tunisia during the actions. By action I mean the occupations of the kasba, the sit-in and the neighbourhood committees. The 'Front de Libération Populaire de la Tunisie' was conceived as a horizontal structure, organized in sectorial and/or regional independent committees coordinating their actions through the network (not as an Internet network but with the structure of a network). In practice, The Front was a gathering of individuals whose perspective consisted in carrying on the struggle up to the event of the revolution and to the coming to power by the people, that was one of the street claims: 'power to the people.'

Q: Your experience of crossing the spaces and the distance between Tunisia and France required a lot of time and many bureaucratic practices. Instead, just after the revolution, the distance between these two spaces was burnt very quickly by some young people, almost all men. Do you think that there is a connection between these two experiences or not?

W: I started to answer this question by email, saying that it seems to be quite incoherent trying to associate these two experiences.

Q: Why?

W: Because I came here to France with a specific status, as a foreign student; and, ultimately, although I had to pass through different administrative apparatuses, such as 'Campus France,' the demand for a visa to the embassy didn't fall under the same logic and need as that of migrants. Because my arrival in France is situated within a students' program while, on the basis of the discussions that I had with migrants, I believe that their project is instead linked to the hope for a better life; and this hope is strongly associated with all the images conveyed by European media and by Europe itself, as a rich country, a country in which one could fully benefit from one's own freedom, and so on and so forth. And then, there is the hope of finding a job, earning more, helping one's own family in Tunisia, living freely, and practicing one's own freedom. This is the reason why these two experiences do not correspond to one other. Besides, as far as I'm concerned, on coming to France I never thought I was entering a paradise: I've never associated France with the image of a paradise or with the image of a country where it is possible to fully benefit from one's own freedom but, as I told you before, I came within the frame of a specific project of study. And on the basis of a very specific status.

Q: But don't you see a connection between the fact that students who want to go to France need to follow such a complicated bureaucratic pattern and that the journey for those who want to go to France to

work, with the imaginary that you mentioned, is very complicated too?
W: All these bureaucratic apparatuses such as 'Campus France' were created in 2003. And, ultimately, these apparatuses which are promoted under
the logic of a better quality of studies in France, are instead apparatuses
of privilege. Yes, there is a form of elitism that circulates within these apparatuses: in Tunisia not everyone can go to France to study, not everyone can afford it, most of all from an economic standpoint, that is from
the point of view of social class, because you need to pay for your visa
application, you need to pay for the bureaucratic process with 'Campus
France', you need to prove you have a certain amount of money saved for
the duration of your stay in France. So from this point of view, it is a very
selective procedure, you must have parents who can afford it or you must
have some national fellowships, otherwise you cannot have access to studies in France. Besides, you need to prove you have eleven millions dinars
in Tunisia, more than five thousand Euros, a very large amount; before
leaving you must prove you have this amount of money in a reserved bank
account. And in Tunisia it is a considerable amount of money.

**Q: What do you think about student mobility fellowships and the Eras-
mus projects that have been recently increased by the European Union
and in collaboration with IOM? Since, as you say, on the one side there
is facilitation for some people to leave and on the other side others are
encouraged to stay. Do you think that it is a kind of twofold logic?**

W: I wouldn't say that it is a question of a twofold logic; rather, I would
say that this element in turn is part of a selective logic, because these fellowships that are granted to Tunisian students are granted for doctoral
degrees. I don't know how the procedure works in this case, but I know
that they are not granted to everyone and that they are very selective, up-
per-level bursaries.

**Q: But precisely for this reason I would like to go back to the previous
question, why do you say 'this is a very tricky question'? Do you say this
because you perceive in it a European gaze, a European projection on
your experience, yours for instance? Is this idea of selection something
that is about all Tunisia and all people who can arrive in France or anywhere in the EU from Tunisia?**

W: I think that this concerns all foreigners. I know that procedures for European students are not at all the same as procedures for students coming from the Maghreb or any Arab country.

Q: Yes, but I am interested in understanding why you said that our question seemed 'to be quite incoherent trying to associate these two experiences.' Now it looks as if we are somehow associating the two experiences. So I ask you: did this question sound like a question asked by a European person and that it would never have been asked by a person coming from somewhere else, say from Tunisia, because Tunisians would not make this connection between you and a person who is trying to get on a boat to leave?

W: Maybe yes, in the sense that for you I am a foreign student and someone may be a foreign migrant, so we are both foreigners to you. Yes, in this sense it seemed to me a question raised by a European person, but frankly speaking this is not what I thought reading your question. Indeed, as I told you before, I don't come from the same social and cultural milieu as a Tunisian migrant, we have neither the same projects nor the same perspectives. From my point of view, as a Tunisian, these two projects, these two practices do not echo each other, they are not connected to one another.

Q: Why and how did you get in touch with migrants who came in Paris?

W: Some comrades and I were at the May 1 rally with migrants. At the end of the march, with the *harraga*[1] and with some people supportive of their struggle, we divided into small groups to go to the office of the CIP (*Coordination des intermittentes et précaires*) where some of them had found shelter after confrontations with the police which took place after a demonstration migrants organized after the April 29 raids at the Stalingrad métro station. At the CIP, a place I didn't know before and where I didn't know anyone, we found about 150-200 people.

Q: You did not know these people from before?

W: No, I didn't.

---

[1] For a definition of '*harraga*,' see footnote 14 of Paola Gandolfi 'Spaces in Migration, Daily Life in Revolution' (this collection).

Q: But did you know that these Tunisian migrants were in Paris?

W: Yes, I knew they had arrived but I met them for the first time at the May 1 rally.

Q: And did you know anything about the problems people faced trying to cross the border between Italy and France?

W: Not in a detailed way. I understood these things better during the occupation, when I got to know them and talked with them.

Q: And what did you think when you saw the images of Lampedusa, if you even saw them?

W: I didn't know what was going on and I didn't have any interlocutor who could explain the situation to me. But in an instinctive way I was quite aware of the political stakes in place between the two governments, how Italy was chasing Tunisian migrants away from its territory by releasing the temporary permit to move them into to France and that this was a matter of political games.

Q: Did you follow the closure of the borders at the border post between the Italian city of Ventimiglia and France? Before May 1, the border between France and Italy got closed, when Italian and French associations had organized the 'dignity train' event to travel with people who were crossing the border. Did you know about this?

W: No, I didn't.

Q: I was curious about that to understand what was visible in France about those events to people like you living there

W: I was not aware of that.

Q: Did you go to Port de la Villette, where Tunisian migrants found a 'parking' place themselves?

W: No. I had heard about what was happening there. But the first time that

I met the *harraga* was at the demonstration of the May 1 and then at the headquarters of the CIP.

Q: But why did you go to the demonstration on May 1?

W: I knew that the organization that I mentioned to you at the beginning was thinking about what kind of action could be done in support of *harraga*. There were many debates among us about a possible occupation, so we decided to start by taking part in the May 1 rally and then this continued with the occupations. But in parallel we were also following what was going on in Tunisia and were retrieving and translating texts from the occupations in Tunisia. So the first encounter with *harraga* was at the May 1 rally.

Q: You also took part in the Avenue Simon Bolivar occupations and in other occupations as well. Could you tell us about that? How did the idea of the occupation come about and what was, in your opinion, the significance of these occupations?

W: The idea of the occupation was already in the wind when we arrived at the CIP after the May 1 rally. As I told you before, we had already discussed that and we had found some possible places, like the building in Avenue Bolivar. And up against the criminality of the French state, *harraga* were resolved to take by force what they considered to be entitled to: namely, their dignity. To the extent that some of them witnessed and participated in the events which took place in Tunisia starting from December 2010 and faced possible death crossing the Mediterranean, the Tunisians from Lampedusa in Paris decided to act in a direct way. At the CIP there was a first assembly with the *harraga* and their supporters, and we told them that we had found a place, explaining that, in the case that we occupied it, evictions could take place etc. Then, the Tunisians met on their own and discussed it: they decided to occupy the building that evening and so we all went there together.

Q: May I point one thing out? Before you had talked about *harraga* while now, when you mentioned that they discussed this on their own, you called them 'Tunisians'. Is it because at that moment you were not Tunisian anymore?

W: Maybe … it's true. Ok, you are right: *harraga* met on their own.

Q: No I didn't mean it that way, it was just to understand how you situated yourself as a Tunisian considering that they were Tunisians as well. Since you were in another context didn't you feel a Tunisian as well?

W: Maybe, but I don't care much about nationality.

Q: In the interviews that we did at the squat-café in Rue Charenton, some Tunisians who have been living in France for a long time and who took part in the occupations of May and June 2011, told us that in their opinion the real force of the Tunisian migrants was at Parc de la Villette, when they were all together; and that, to the contrary, the occupations weakened their force. What do you think about that?

W: It is a complex issue. I believe that through the Avenue Bolivar occupation and the others which followed, squatters succeeded in establishing a certain relation of force with the municipality of Paris. Besides, although the number of people is an important element, it cannot be the parameter. Occupations were part of a declared struggle. It's true that migrants' massive presence at the Parc de la Villette enabled them to maintain the space as theirs for longer; and that space was a kind of anchoring point, but that did not preserve them from raids and attacks by the French police. Besides, the occupation is a radical political action with open claims, somehow in continuity with the upheaval in Tunisia. The café was not a squat and it was not opened according to the logic of a squat. It was a venue obtained by FTCR (Féderation des Tunisiens pour une Citoyenneté des Deux Rives) thanks to the agreements with the municipality of Paris, with a contract of six months.

Q: What was the relationship between Tunisian migrants and French activists in the context of the occupation movement?

W: French activists were people in solidarity with the struggle of the *harraga*, according to an idea of international solidarity that today seems to be necessary considering what is happening everywhere in the world. That relationship between activists and migrants was essentially one of comradeship in the context of that struggle. During the occupations Tunisians, the *harraga*, were somehow astonished by all the French support they got; they were astonished that there were even French people who didn't have accommodation, a job etc. For this reason we, and I in particular, explained to them that although I'm a Tunisian, I have the documents and accommodation, I'm here because I find it legitimate and necessary to struggle for the freedom of circulation. In the beginning Tunisians were a bit skeptical about this support and for this reason we spent a lot of time discussing this with them, explaining that what brought us together in that moment was the idea of the freedom of circulation; and the idea that their presence in France was a legitimate presence because everyone should have the right to circulate and to live with dignity. Finally, there was the idea that nothing could legitimize the treatment that they received.

Q: And what did they say about this, about this explanation? I am interested in the fact that you as a Tunisian – as you are a Tunisian anyway – explained to a group of Tunisians something that I have often been asked about during struggles with *sans-papiers* or asylum seekers in Italy. When people got to know me, some would ask me: 'why are you involved in these struggles?' And they didn't believe that I could be involved in those struggles without any personal interests. Ultimately, in my opinion they were convinced that actually Italian people had some kind of self-interest when involved in those struggles, in the sense that maybe they thought that we were paid by some association; so they were suspicious about us and I was wondering if they moved past this position with you.

W: Actually, my case was very specific since I was the translator during the occupations so there was already a relationship of trust. I discussed things a lot with them explaining that some of the people who were there had been struggling for years for free circulation, residence permits and freedom for all; and that the arrival of Tunisian migrants on French territory was in continuity with a struggle that they had been carrying out for years. And, although at different levels, they understood that point: this enabled us to establish a clear relationship. When they understood that those people had a home, a job and food, and that they were not in the same condition but despite that they stayed there day and night, meeting with them etc, this made it possible to establish a relationship between the *harraga* migrants and the supporting group in the struggle.

Q: But in my opinion it was also a quite complicated question, since on the one hand I believe that the suspicion on the part of the *sans-papiers* or the asylum seekers towards European militant groups or the Italian ones (since I know the struggles that took place in Italy better) stem from the fact that these persons often come from places of dictatorship, in which there are neither the associative milieu nor struggles of this kind, and so they ask themselves: why do all these people struggle with us? But on the other hand, the European associative milieu often has its own interests in these struggles, since associations are interested in building a name for themselves; in fact, associations function according to a mechanism where they seek out projects which lead to sources of funding for that association, and in this sense it's true that there is an element of self-interest. Besides, even though you are not necessarily part of an association, a collective or a committee, you have an interest in suggesting or deciding what they should do and to stand up in place of the migrant or to tell them 'it would be better to do this or that.' In my opinion this is a very complicated issue.

W: Yes, it is quite complicated. People who participated in the occupations, and above all in the occupations in Rue Bolivar and in Rue Botzaris, were not members of associations. They were people who knew each other and who met during the sans-papiers struggles, people who struggled together. Besides, *harraga* who were at the Parc de la Villette became closer to certain associations and their problem was that these associations were inside the squat, while at La Villette associations had a lot of money but only provided some food. So *harraga* saw a difference between the people who occupied buildings with them and members of associations who managed to get some funding, mostly from the municipality of Paris, funding which Tunisian migrants never saw. Those associations did not really engage with them in mobilizations, that is in actions of struggle, and thus on the part of the Tunisian migrants there were many critical discourses directed towards these associations.

Q: May I insist on this problem? I know associations always have some degree of self-interest. I participated in certain struggles while not belonging to any association. I belonged to groups supporting riots with-

in the detention centres, in the squats and then we started a struggle together with migrants, for instance. But in this way of struggling together, from my point of view, as an Italian person who is neither an *harraga*, nor an asylum seeker, there is always a 'squat side' so to speak, the position of a group thinking 'I'm interested in struggling against detention centers, so if I intercede when there is a riot within a detention centre I try to make this riot stronger' so in this way, in the end, this association has some interest.

W: I don't believe that the interest is ultimately the same; maybe the word 'interest' is problematic, because these people - who anyway I didn't know from before - actually had been struggling against detention centers for a long time and joined the struggles of the *harraga* because they also followed what was happening in Tunisia as revolutionary people. They tried several different actions, wrote different things and circulated many flyers. The interest for me was more in the relationship of force - as the presence of so many Tunisians all together and being in Paris from a revolutionary context became the strength of a struggle that had been there for long time. It was not out of a charitable humanitarian spirit that people joined that struggle, but because of an ongoing struggle; and what happened with Tunisian migrants reignited and carried on this ongoing struggle in a stronger way.

Q: Do you think that within the French modality of struggle, when one refers to freedom, it is the same freedom that is thought of and put into action by Tunisian migrants? It seems to me that in France there is the problem of human rights, universalism etc., and I don't know if the meaning of freedom is the same.

W: I believe that when *harraga* talk about their freedom they do that within the frame of three essential claims: documents, work and accommodation. They formulate a clear discourse, so I don't think that they have the same idea of freedom as we do, since they came out from a dictatorship, they came out of a dictatorial government; and consequently the meaning of the word freedom cannot be the same as for a French person living in a 'democratic' state, in the state of the human rights etc. And, after all, one thing that was only at stake in migrants' comments was: 'but is this France? Is this the country of human rights? Is it really this the way that people are treated in the country of human rights?' These were their comments all the time. This means that they all came with the image of the French state, maybe an idealist one, as the state of human rights, freedom etc.; and instead they were confronted with the reality of marginalization, alienation, discrimination and disdain. So there was actually a big disillusion and this element was very important in making them join the struggle. It cannot be the same thing: what a French person understands as freedom is not the same as a Tunisian *harraga* or as a Tunisian.

Q: I agree with you. But in this way isn't there the risk that French activists come to redefine the struggle in order to redefine migrants' practice of freedom according to their idea, superimposing in this way their model of freedom onto migrants' practices?

W: No, I don't think so, because in the end the reality of the situation with the Tunisians is there; and *harraga* react to a concrete situation. I don't know if this answers your question.

Q: How did you feel being a woman within a movement formed mostly of men?

W: There were many women, most of all among supporters; and as I told you before, since I was the Tunisian translator, I had a certain relationship of trust with *harraga* and a relationship of reciprocal respect. Therefore, it was a mutual relation of struggle.

Q: But were there some women among the *harraga*?

W: No, during the occupations there were not women.

Q: Were you the only Tunisian woman or were there also other Tunisian women?

W: No, every now and then some Tunisian women stopped by, but I was the only Tunisian woman that was constantly present during the occupations. Indeed, many Tunisian women passed by there, but it was a relationship of familiarity because there was the possibility of speaking in the Tunisian language and of better understanding each other, and consequently it was a relationship of respect.

Q: And how did you feel being sort of in-between, that is you were an activist but also a Tunisian person? Were there moments during which you could have also criticized French activists or, to the contrary, you could have taken a distance from Tunisian *harraga* as non-activists?

W: As I told you before I didn't know anybody beforehand, and so I tried to actually keep a distance in order to have a more objective gaze and if I had some criticisms I brought that out during the assembly. I took the right to take the floor and speak my opinion.

Q: But has there ever been instances when the fact of being a woman in a mainly masculine context became a problem and you thought 'how boring, they are all men!'?

W: No, I never found myself in such a situation with Tunisian *harraga*. There were instead other minor problems... for instance, during the occupations someone circulated the idea that I was part of a political party and that I was there for political reasons; another time some of them told that since I was always wearing a skirt I had to be Jewish. There have been things like this but nothing more than that.

Q: But what is the relationship between the skirt and the fact of being Jewish?

W: I don't know, from what I understood it seems that only Jewish women wear skirts, but I didn't know about that.

Q: Me neither.

W: Yes, it's quite odd. I laughed for a moment, but then nothing more.

Q: Could you describe how these moments of political decision took place? For instance, we liked the way in which the collective often referred to itself as: 'the Collective of Tunisian migrants from Lampedusa in Paris'...we liked it a lot because we think that it is very relevant for many reasons. How did they choose that name?

W: When I met the movement of *harraga* during the occupations the collective was already there. From what I understood talking with some of them, the collective was already in place in Lampedusa and it travelled to Paris with Tunisian migrants, insofar as people who were part of the collective had moved to Paris. Political decisions at the times of the occupations were taken in a collegial way, during long-lasting assemblies when it was predominantly *harraga* speaking, since they were the most interested and the most exposed to risks.

Q: Sorry, I don't understand: you are saying that you think that the collective of the Tunisian *harraga* was already formed in Lampedusa?

W: Yes, this is what I've been told by some *harraga*. Yes, they explained to me that this collective was formed in Lampedusa.

Q: And so, they decided to name themselves the 'Collective of Tunisians from Lampedusa in Paris' because...

W: Because they arrived in Paris.

Q: And what do you think of this name?

W: I think that it is a very territorial and reductive name, since this collective included Tunisian migrants coming from Lampedusa at the same time; and there are many Tunisians who arrived later and who did not necessarily arrive at Lampedusa. And consequently, this collective was managed by a narrow number of *harraga*, if compared with the larger group of *harraga* who arrived in Paris.

Q: There had been Tunisian migrants who did not arrive at Lampedusa but not many because at that time the journey to Italy through Lampedusa was the only one that could be done by boat. So when you say that there were many other migrants who came to the squat, I think that almost all of them must have gone through Lampedusa too, even if they did not arrive at the same time.

W: Yes, but they did not arrive at the same time.

Q: I like this name a lot, because through it Tunisian migrants define themselves as 'Tunisians' and they manage to match two continents; they succeed in naming their own identity without naming any state: only as Tunisians they name a state while as far as Europe is concerned, they do not name the states but the places they went through and not as the terri-

tory of a state; they name Lampedusa not as an Italian place and Paris not as a French place.

W: I believe that all this is part of the logic of migration, that in any case is a crossing, an experience of places.

Q: In the early days of the Avenue Simon Bolivar occupation, Tunisian migrants released a series of public statements and you took part in that experience. Could you tell us about it? Those occupations have been 'articulated' by others (for instance the group Les Intermittents du spectacle). Was this a problem at the time? And later, at least in terms of what could be followed at a distance or on the Internet, this experience started to be narrated exclusively by others and not by the protagonists. What happened exactly? And how was the migrant word interrupted?

W: The statements Tunisian migrants released were shared collectively and these moments were not so much for discussing the content but for sharing it with the assembly of the occupants. Tunisians said with their words what they needed to communicate. It seems to me that the struggle was collective, between *harraga* and people in solidarity with them. In practice I was the translator. Concerning other statements, the collective of Les Intermittents du Spectacle wrote many texts that have been posted on Indymedia and other places. But this fact didn't raise many problems, because even if these were statements released by Les Intermittents du Spectacle these statements were anonymous and described what was going on, reproducing what Tunisian migrants had said; so in that moment this didn't raise any problem. Then the occupations, and mostly the occupation of the school in Rue de la Fontaine-au-roi, were infiltrated by certain political parties, mainly Tunisian and Muslim parties; and the relationship of struggle that we had managed to establish during previous occupations through the assemblies and *harraga* speaking etc., then little by little started to get lost because there were people coming and speaking in place of migrants. Besides, during the assemblies, while we were discussing together what decisions to make regarding the municipality of Paris, Muslim associations came with sacks full of sandwiches, since the *harraga* were hungry; so suddenly the concentration was lost. For this reason, we lost the relationship we had with them before. Some people started to leave and I left at some point as well, because the situation was unmanageable and it could not go on that way. I think that it started from the moment that *harraga* collective statements stopped.

Q: Do you think these occupations by Tunisian *harraga* were different from other forms of occupation? And, in your view, did they give rise to an unusual form of political action?

W: I'm not sure I fully understand the sense of your question because I know that in Paris there have been many occupations by the *sans-papiers*, many squats were opened and then continued functioning; and I think that the main difference in comparison with the other occupations made by the Tunisian *harraga* is they referred directly to the insurrectional situation in Tunisia, to a different political context; I think that this was the main difference in comparison with the other occupations made by Tunisians.

Q: What do you mean when you say that these occupations referred to the revolutionary context?

W: For instance, Delanoë, the mayor of Paris, referred to the Tunisian revolution and the French government and Sarkozy did too. They revised their position declaring their support to the insurrectional uprising in Tunisia, the uprising of Tunisian people. For this reason, there was as a link with the occupations by Tunisian *harraga*. It was a politically thorny affair, I believe; and I'm not able to elaborate a more detailed point of view, but for instance I think that it created troubles for the government and for Delanoë as well with respect to the Tunisian government, the Tunisian political context and the international context.

Q: And what about migrants? What I saw about Tunisian migrations is that their migrations have been very different, since Tunisians said something like 'we are here and we have the right to stay here, I have the right to migrate in the same way as I made a revolution as a person who has the right to be free in Tunisia, now I am here with the same desire to speak, to take the space, to squat, to have a place'. In this I saw something new.

W: Yes, it's true because Tunisian *harraga* signed their statements as 'the sons of the revolution'; so they thought 'I am here and I am here to stay.' And that's why, as I stated also before, they were determined to take by force what they considered to be something that was theirs by right. First of all, because of the insurrectional experience in Tunisia, and then also because of the experience of crossing by boat, since they risked their lives in Tunisia and also to come to France.

Q: Do you see a relationship between revolution and migration concerning what happened to Tunisian migrants?

W: Yes, I believe that there is a relationship but I think that *harraga* may answer better than I could.

Q: In your opinion, what is the meaning of all these experiences, and particularly what did they mean for Tunisian migrants who were the protagonists?

W: It is precisely what we said before. This is an important point in relation to what happened in Tunisia and to the insurrectional movement, since it made Tunisian migrants confident about the possibility of getting certain things; and in some sense, in some continuity with this logic, Tunisian migrants said 'by being united we can succeed in obtaining what we demand,' that is to say documents, accommodation and, essentially, our dignity. I think that this was a strong point among Tunisian *harraga*.

Q: How do you understand the expression 'being united'?

W: It refers to the idea that 'all of us are *harraga*, all of us came by boat crossing, we are all from the same country, from the same insurrectional political context and being united and struggling all together we can obtain some things. And as in Tunisia we succeeded in chasing Ben Ali out and to be part of this quote unquote revolutionary process.' It's in this sense that I understand the expression.

Q: What was the meaning of this experience for you, your subjective experience?

W: For me it meant give a quite satisfactory answer in relation to what I can do…against this world system. And there were also joyful moments, even if there were many tensions, many risks but it was a joyful moment; actually, having the possibility to take part in the struggle of Tunisian *harraga* was somehow as if I participated in what happened in Tunisia. Because, in my view, what happened in Tunisia is not an insurrection against the dictator but rather an insurrection against a system. And ultimately, what Tunisian migrants underwent in Paris, is a manifestation of all the political stakes of this capitalist system; for me they were very strong and insurrectional moments. Well, they were not insurrectional about dignity, because also in the word dignity there is an invocation, a claim to return to the freedom of an individual, of a human being; and *harraga* are more and more marginalized and thrashed. In my view, what happened in Tunisia and what happened here were part of a broader logic of ideas concerning the freedom of everybody and the freedom of circulation… For me this is what it meant.

Q: Do you think this movement won or lost?

W: I don't know. It depends on what you mean by winning. In the sense that yes, it's true they didn't obtain the documents, they did not obtain accommodation but I think that the mere fact that they have managed at some point to establish a very strong relation of force with the French government and the municipality of Paris, was a success in itself. As far as concrete things are concerned, there were no answers and thus from that point of view it could be argued that this movement has failed; but it has failed because it is a movement and a struggle that didn't go on and in this sense, yes, maybe it has failed. Maybe the biggest failure was that we did not succeed in keeping up this relation of struggle; or better, that *harraga* did not succeed in maintaining this relation among themselves and for themselves, and in this sense it failed.

Q: Why didn't they manage to maintain this relation of struggle?

W: For many reasons, since at some point the movement was infiltrated by FTCR and by political parties. Secondly, these people did not come to struggle, rather they came here with specific reasons and specific expectations. And then, by constantly seeing all these people who went back to Tunisia and that the Tunisian government was giving out documents to go back to Tunisia - in the sense that it gave the documents to those who didn't have a passport... because this is what happened - *harraga* scattered and a dynamic was lost, there was no longer that dynamic of struggle.

Q: Are you still in touch with some of them?

W: Yes

Q: Are they in Paris now, or did they return to Tunisia?

W: They are in Paris

Q: What do they do?

W: They work

Q: So, they found jobs?

W: Yes, they work, some of them are in squats, others live in rented places.

Q: In the beginning, there were around 250 people involved in the occupations. Do you know by chance how many of these people have gone back to Tunisia, how many are still in France and how many people found a job?

W: No. There are about ten *harraga* that I come across from time to time and they took different paths.

Q: And what do they say about the squats?

W: These are places opened by the *harraga* themselves, who manage to keep these places collectively; but I've never been in one of these squats and I don't really know what happens there, I heard only some echoes but I haven't seen them for long time, I only have some news.

Q: May I ask you two more questions?

W: Just one, because I have to go.

Q: The name that you always use is '*harraga*,' while in Tunisia we often found people talking about migrants calling them 'clandestine migrants.' I imagine the reason why you prefer the name '*harraga*,' so I won't ask you about this, it would be a stupid question. But what struck me is that migrants themselves use the adjective 'clandestine.' In the sense that you are 'clandestine' in relation to a country where you cannot enter. And what struck me was to see that also in Tunisia people talk about 'clandestine migrants' about Tunisians who maybe are still in Tunisia even if they may be planning to leave as migrants. Could you tell me why there is such an idea? Why this adjective 'clandestine'?

W: A clandestine migrant is one who lives outside of the law and he/she is a clandestine migrant because he/she enters a territory without a visa; and in Tunisia a clandestine migrant is a person who lives outside of the law. I cannot say much more than this.

Q: Because for me it's quite odd. First of all because I don't like the expression 'clandestine migrant' at all and I thought that it would only be used in Italy and in Europe. But in Tunisia I realized that some people use it talking about friends who are willing to leave and so I asked myself: did this depend on the fact that there is a law against illegal emigration?

W: Yes, it is a crime.

Q: But has something changed after the revolution about the way in which people think of 'illegal' emigration and immigration

W: I don't know. I will go to Tunisia in four days and I will see. The last few times I went to Tunisia I didn't enter into a discussion about *harraga*, I didn't talk about that, so I really don't know.

Q: Thanks a lot.

Schengen Intermittences:
The On/Off Switch of Free Circulation
Glenda Garelli

When some Tunisians decided to 'put into play' their revolution by leaving for Europe, the northern shore of the Mediterranean tempered its enthusiasm for jasmines and springs and reacted by staging a crisis. Cries of 'invasion', 'human tsunami', and 'biblical exodus' accompanied confinement practices at Lampedusa island, states of emergency declared in newly-invented geographies, push-back agreements, prison boats, and 'humanitarian' tent camps.

Focusing on the intra-European mobility of Tunisian migrants at the Italy-France frontier in the aftermath of the revolution, this paper reflects on the conflict that this crossing - a successful, failed, or even just imagined crossing - opened in the Schengen Area.[1] A radical conflict, indeed, as it involved the spatial dispositive which founded the Area, i.e., the removal of checks at the EU internal borders, and the free circulation regime of the single market. Whereas both Italy and France shared the objective of keeping Tunisian migrants away from their respective national territories, each country deployed rather different EU territorialities for internal borders, speaking also to the elasticity of Schengen *governance*. On the one hand, Italy granted a temporary humanitarian permit allowing intra-Schengen free circulation to migrants 'from North African

---

[1] For an account of this conflict, its stages and its political and institutional implications, see S. Carrera, E. Guild, M. Merlino and J. Parkin, 'A Race against Solidarity: The Schengen Regime and the Franco-Italian Affair', *CESP Liberty and Security in Europe Working Paper*, April 29, 2011. Available: http://www.ceps.eu/book/race-against-solidarity-schengen-regime-and-franco-italian-affair. Date Accessed: September 1, 2013.

countries'[2] having arrived before April 5, 2011; on the other hand, France organized border patrols at the frontier with Italy pushing Tunisian migrants back. When the European Commission finally intervened in this conflict, it enlisted yet another territorial rule, i.e., the Europeanization of the decision mechanism with which to interrupt the Schengen Area's principle of free circulation.

Engaging with Tunisian migrants' contested crossing of the Schengen Area, this paper aims to develop an approach to conflicts of territoriality spurred by mobility. Instead of looking for a normative resolution to establish which was the appropriate border management practice among those deployed by Italy, France, the European Commission, I am interested in tracing the *traversability* of the Schengen Area, the traversability that emerges within this very normative disagreement. Which spaces and times of circulation were produced by Tunisian migrants crossing Europe and by member states responding to this crossing? And more specifically, what are the spatio-temporal coordinates along which Tunisian migrants' crossing of Schengenland get organized (and disorganized)?

Methodologically, my aim is to de-border critical policy studies, shifting it onto the terrain of 'existence strategies,'[3] a de-bordering of the study of policies onto the always-contested terrain of existences, those existences which organize themselves from within the very tangles produced by such policies. The paper develops an approach for studying a space of free circulation produced by policy, as Schengen is, from the vantage point of its migrant crossings. Is it possible to move beyond the mere scrutiny of migration policy captures which, as often occurs within the tradition of Governmentality Studies, ends up distancing these very crossings and the contested politics they put in motion? And how do we avoid producing an apology for crossing, as certain contributions to Border Studies and frontier ethnographies tend to do, fixing migrants to their encounter with transnational borders? Finally, how does one account for the enduring production and reproduction of the Schengen Area without reducing this to the institutional discourse of membership enlargement, focusing instead on the spaces that migrants contest and produce while crossing the Schengen Area?

The idea of using spatio-temporal coordinates as a method to study 'the

---

[2] Consiglio dei Ministri, 'Decreto del presidente del Consiglio dei ministri', February 12, 2011.

[3] F. Sossi, *Spazi di confinamento e strategie di esistenza* (Milan: Il Saggiatore, 2006).

Schengen Area as traversed' is an answer to these questions. It involves first of all an attempt to map the Area of free circulation from within the spaces and the times deployed to organize and disorganize the migrant existences crossing it. Moreover, the use of spatio-temporal coordinates allows the study of the constitutive logic of the Area - i.e., the free circulation at internal borders - without essentializing this logic. Instead, this approach forces the temporalities and spatialities of migration - those that migrants enact, receive, and mobilize while crossing the Area - into the frictionless space and instantaneous time of the EU single market.

1. Tunisians in Europe: Crossing Schengen

'Schengen?' asked a young Tunisian man, interrogating the Italian researcher interviewing him in Ventimiglia, at Italy's border with France.[4] It was April 9, 2011 and they were talking about the temporary residence permit for humanitarian reasons that he and his friends would be entitled to as they were 'coming from countries of North Africa' torn apart 'by events of a particularly serious nature' and because they had entered Italy before midnight on April 5, 2011 in accordance with the Decree declared by the Italian Prime Minister.[5] The young man came from the city of Gabès, which he had left on a boat directed to Lampedusa Island, which he then left for Crotone, proceeding to Rome, from Rome to Milan, and from Milan to Ventimiglia, which was not his final destination either. As a cosmopolitan of the two shores he knew perfectly well how to perimeter the European space of free circulation: he knew its extension, its borders, and its traversability. But he also knew this European space as a social space, as the space inhabited by some of his friends, relatives, friends of friends and also as a space rich with possible chance encounters to come. When he was asked why he left Milan to come to Ventimiglia, he explained that he was actually headed to France, that it was to France he wanted to go. And when the interview touched on the residence permit he would be eligible for in Italy, he promptly asked his interviewer: 'Schengen?', probing the European traversability that the permit would ultimately either facilitate or preclude for him.

---

[4] F. Sossi, *Tunisia Ventimiglia. Prima intervista, gruppo di uomini tunisni*. Available: http://www.storiemigranti.org/spip.php?article866. Date Accessed: September 1, 2013.

[5] Decreto del Presidente del Consiglio dei ministri, April 5, 2011.

These stories of migration to France or Northern Europe told by Tunisian migrants always come with a long list of Italian names, indicating the detours and forced stops of cross-Schengen mobility standard for Tunisian migrants: 'Lampedusa, Catania, Crotone, Sicily-Milan, Milan-Vardello, Vardello-Milan, Milan-Ventimiglia to go to France.'[6]

Ventimiglia was also the destination of a group of three young Tunisians whom a radio-journalist interviewed on an intercity train from Milan at the end of March 2011. 'They want to know,' the journalist tells listeners, 'where they may find a Western Union in Ventimiglia and how late it will be open as they hope to get there in time to get cash. They have family in France. Yousef's father is in Lyon but Yousef prefers to join his friends in Paris.' The journalist asked whereabouts, in Paris, he would go and he answered: 'I don't know but I have a phone number. My friends will come pick us up.'[7] At the Ventimiglia station another young Tunisian man was very clear on where he did not want to go: 'Pas la France, je n'aime pas ... Italie, Germany, España mais pas la France, je n'aime pas.'[8]

This 'traversed' Europe has been well-illustrated in Lucio Guarinoni's interviews featured in this volume where three Tunisian men tell of their cross-EU stories: Italy as the European docking place after days at sea taking wrong routes; the dream to end up in Belgium or in France; the friends one makes en route; the unexpected offers of hospitality; the offers for jobs in France that don't come through; the return to Bergamo, Italy, to renew the residence permit; the idea of one day 'making a film about this,' 'a film about what people in Tunisia dream of when they dream of going to Europe.'

It is these social spaces, these travel desires, these careful assessment about the radius of one's options, the ground beneath one's feet one starts to feel (or not), the choices as to whom to join in Europe, and the evaluations on where one may or may not cross, that I take as the vantage point from which to study the reorganization of the space and time of 'free circulation' in the Schengen Area in 2011 and 2012.

---

[6] C. Ronzani, Interview of March 30, 2011, in 'Il mattino di Popolare Network,' *Radio Popolare*. http://www.radiopopolare.it.

[7] S. Giacomini, Interview of March 25, 2011, 'Popline', *Radio Popolare*. http://www.radiopopolare.it.

[8] F. Sossi, *Tunisia Ventimiglia. Quinta intervista, uomo tunisino*. Available: http://www.storiemigranti.org/spip.php?article870. Date Accessed: September 2, 2013.

2. Schengen Space: Multiple Regimes of Circulation

Within Schengen, instead, this freedom to leave through which some migrants enacted their revolution, produced a tumultuous dispute with regards to the jurisdiction and the boundaries of their arrival. Where could they stay in Europe? What would be their appropriate status? For how long should they stay?... How do we return them? Where Tunisian migrants were engaging with Europe as a regional bloc, and, upon arrival at Lampedusa and Linosa Islands, imagining a European city - a French, Belgian, or German city - as their final destination, the Schengen Area was rapidly being deregionalized by the contrasting territorialities that Italy, France, and the European Commission were deploying and by the restructuring of Schengen's spatial dispositives upon the mobility of Tunisian migrants crossing the Area.

Schengen-Italy: The Mobility of the Humanitarian and the Injunction to 'Keep Moving!'

In Italy, the Berlusconi government deployed the Schengen regime as an injunction of mobility - as a 'move away from' territoriality or as the order to 'keep moving!' It did so in two ways: mobilizing humanitarian and securitarian instruments, directly implementing their brotherhood, and staging both the temporary international protection instrument (e.g. 'Articolo 20' of the 'Testo unico sull'immigrazione') and the expulsion provision of repatriation agreements.

The context: Tunisian migrants had been arriving at Lampedusa Island for weeks after the outbreak of the Tunisian revolution at the end of December 2010. Most of them fled Lampedusa as well as the various Italian reception sites where they were originally 'hosted' (Manduria tent camps, detention centers in Bologna, Turin, and Rome, the mega processing center for asylum seekers in Mineo, in the province of Catania, to name just a few). They left Italy for other Schengen countries, France in particular - and most had planned Italy as only a transitional place in their travels. As it turned out member states[9] were not going to respond to the call for

---

[9] The only positive answer to Minister Roberto Maroni's request for 'burden sharing' issued to all EU member states came from Romania. On April 17, 2011, Romanian Prime Minister, Traian Basescu, offered to take up to two hundred Tunisian migrants. This offer marks an uncanny geometry of solidarity in the Schengen

'burden sharing'[10] that former Italian Minister of the Interior Maroni and former Italian Prime Minister Berlusconi directed to Schengen signatories on multiple occasions.[11] The Minister of the Interior even invoked candidate countries, saying: 'some countries of the OCSE area like Turkey expect to enter Europe but are not doing anything about these matters.'[12] With this declaration, the Minister attempted to deploy the externalization of European functions to candidate countries as an entry token - this deep-rooted EU practice of externalizing border functions was here being extended to 'humanitarian' reception. The argument soliciting 'burden sharing' from candidate countries was built not only along meritocratic coordinates, i.e., earning entry in the European Union, but also along the usual coordinates of population and 'culture.'[13]

These calls for European cooperation by Italian institutions were supported by careful orchestration, with the staging of dramatic images and alarming statistics, that docufiction which has been narrating Italy to Italians for so many years but that had never caught on outside of Italy. And nor did it this time: the image of a Lampedusa island 'invaded' by migrants was quickly deconstructed by international media which constantly pointed to the smallness of the island ('little tiny island' was the common expression), focusing instead on the reception numbers of other member states at the time of the ex-Yugoslavia wars. When, during a meeting of Mediterranean countries on February 23, 2011, former For-

---

Area: the only country attending to the Schengen 'burden sharing' principle is the country who, despite being a EU member state, has not been promoted to Schengen membership yet.

[10] Article 80 of the *Treaty on the Functioning of the European Union* sets forth the 'principle of solidarity and fair sharing of responsibility, including its financial implications, between the Member States' regarding border checks, asylum and immigration issues.

[11] While in February 2011 the Italian government called for EU help when faced with the arrival of 5,000 Tunisian migrants at Lampedusa island and declared a state of humanitarian emergency on the national territory, Tunisia had instead opened its border with Libya to grant access to those displaced by the Libyan war. On February 27, 2011, for instance, within only 24 hours, 10,000 people entered Tunisia from Libya at the Ras Ajdir border-post.

[12] Camera dei deputati, March 16, 2011.

[13] Answering a Lega Nord interrogation on the arrival of Tunisian migrants in Italy, Maroni stated that Turkey should take in Tunisian migrants and refugees as it is a sparsely populated country unlike Italy 'which is instead densely populated, especially in Padania' and that Turkey has a 'cultural proximity' with the countries of origin of these migrants (March 16, 2011).

eign Affairs Minister Franco Frattini projected, within the 'North Africa Emergency', arrivals between 200,000 and 300,000 and spoke of 'a biblical exodus (sic!), 10 times bigger than the one from Albania in the 1990s', European reproaches quickly came in response. Belgium dismissed the numbers as absurd, whereas Austria and Germany hastily concluded that Italy could and must manage the arrival of 5,000 Tunisian migrants without European intervention. Also the International Organization for Migration (IOM) invited the Italian government to stop using scare tactics and to put these figures in context when, in February 2011, it provided data from the Southern shore of the Mediterranean speaking of 30,000 Libyan war refugees who had been received in Tunisia and Egypt.[14]

It is in this the context that Italy - after a series of heightened negotiations with Tunisia - granted temporary humanitarian protection to some Tunisian migrants.[15] As per the Prime Minister's Decree dated April 5, 2011, citizens from 'Northern Africa countries' who landed in Italy between January 1, 2011 and midnight of April 5, 2011 were eligible for a six months residence permit on humanitarian grounds distributed free of charge.[16] Article 3 of the Decree presented a 'made in Italy' delineation of the Schengen nexus between the humanitarian, mobility, and cooperation: 'the residence permit [...] permits its holder's free circulation [...] in the countries of the European Union in accordance with the Schengen Acquis and [...] with the communitarian law.' The point made about 'free circulation being allowed' was juridically redundant[17] but politically cru-

---

[14] February 24, 2011. Available: http://www.storiemigranti.org/spip.php?article858. Date Accessed: September 2, 2013.

[15] Leading up to the signing of the agreement, Italian politicians' visits to Tunis intensified, suggesting a difficult negotiation among Tunisia and Italy: two times for Prime Minister Silvio Berlusconi (as an official visit), two times for Foreign Affair Minister Franco Frattini and three times for Minister of the Interior Roberto Maroni.

[16] Exclusion criteria are stated in Article 2, paragraph 2 of the Prime Minister Decree dated April 5, 2011: not eligible are those who entered the national territory before January 1 or after April 5, 2011; who belong to one of the categories considered socially dangerous; who have previously been notified of an expulsion order before January 1, 2011; who have been sued or sentenced for a specific set of crimes.

[17] The temporary residence permit for humanitarian protection comes with travel documents [titolo di viaggio]: as with the Schengen normative framework, third country nationals may freely circulate for three months across the Schengen Area if they hold a valid travel document, if they can prove the purpose and conditions of their travel and have sufficient means of support, and if they have not been prohibited to enter through the Schengen information system and if they are not considered

cial, as it clarifies that these permits for Tunisian migrants were in fact 'humanitarian permits to take a hike,' permits to please go![18]

In a way, these permits are the Italian edition of that *mobility of the humanitarian regime* which, in the name of the European space of Freedom, Security, and Justice, produces normative concepts (first asylum country, third safe country, safe origin country, European safe third country), humanitarian military interventions, and 'humanitarian zones' in the countries of the 'neighbourhood,' as EU policymakers call the regions at the southern and eastern borders of the EU. I will return to this last practice towards the end of the essay. But here we see Italy playing out the spatial logic of the humanitarian regime in full force, issuing a residence permit that in fact forces the Europeanization of reception and puts 'protection' in motion, linking asylum status to an erratic figure. This humanitarian territoriality is also inscribed in the appointment of the Civil Protection as managing unit for asylum seekers coming from Magrheb and Mashreq countries, a decision that overlooked the competence of the Agency for asylum seekers and refugees (SPRAR). Among the many embarrassing definitions Italian ministers deployed to name migrations from the countries of the Arab Uprisings, the expression 'human tsunami' indeed spells out a very precise governmental tactic.

France-Schengen: The Suspension of Free Circulation

The suspension of the Schengen free circulation regime that France deployed in 2011 pushing back Tunisian migrants has been at the center of numerous debates about the reintroduction of internal border checks. *The Treaty on the Functioning of the Union* grants this reintroduction as a temporary measure 'in the event of one or more Member States being confronted by an emergency situation characterised by a sudden inflow of nationals of third countries.'[19] The measure has been enforced by different Member States in cases such as marches, political summits and counter-summits, large-scale political and sport events, and in the context of

---

to be a threat to national security.

[18] F. Sossi, *Mentone Ventimiglia: siamo tutti clandestini. Teatri dell'immedesimazione*, April, 2011. In 'Storie Migranti', available at: http://www.storiemigranti.org/spip. php?rubrique122. Date Accessed: September 2, 2013.

[19] Article 78, point 3 of the *Treaty on the Functioning of the European Union*.

new immigration legislation introduced by a particular member state.[20]
In this section I focus on two mechanisms pertaining to the Schengen
border regime that France deployed in 2011 toward Tunisian migrants:
a normative instrument and an economic one. On the normative front,
French politicians engaged early on in profiling Tunisian migrants as 'economic migrants,' thus deriving the illegality of their crossing into France
from their migration status. In an informal note dating February 2011,
the French Police demanded agents to stop 'irregular foreigners of Tunisian nationality,'[21] hence performing a nationaliziation of 'irregularity.'[22]
In fact, as soon as Italy 'regularized' Tunisian migrants arriving before
April 5, 2011, making them eligible for a temporary residence permit,
France implemented yet another mechanism to reject these 'regular' migrants, finally revealing that the free circulation of Tunisian migrants was
not problematic for lack of proper documentation. The new instrument
France deployed was an economic one. In those first days of 2011, in fact,
the French government issued a circular letter to prefects to remind them
of the standards third country nationals need to meet to be granted access to the Schengen free circulation area.[23] The letter particularly insists
on checking that third-country nationals should have 'sufficient funds' for
their stay, i.e., 62 Euros a day (or 31 Euros a day should one be granted
free hospitality).

What France finally staged for Tunisian migrants in those first months

---

[20] Accurate public records of the reintroductions of border checks at internal
borders are not available. A careful reconstruction can be found in the report by S.
Carrera et al., *A Race against Solidarity*, pp.23-24.

[21] This is an informal note of the French police addressing Cannes security forces
and which was publicly circulated by the police union 'SGP Police-Force Ouvrière.'
Available: http://www.davduf.net/La-chasse-officielle-aux-Tunisiens,497.html. Date
Accessed: September 2, 2013.

[22] On the politics of the mechanism of irregularization, see N. De Genova, 'Migrant
"Illegality" and Deportability in Everyday Life,' *Annual Review of Anthropology*,
31 (2002): pp.419-447; S. Mezzadra and B. Neilson, 'Né qui né altrove. Migration,
Detention, Desertion: A Dialogue,' in *borderlands*, 2:1 (2003); V. Squire, *The Con-
tested Politics of Mobility: Borderzones and Irregularity* (London: Routledge, 2011); S.
Mezzadra and B. Neilson, 'Borderscapes of Differential Inclusion: Subjectivity and
Struggles on the Threshold of Justice's Excess,' in É. Balibar, S. Mezzadra, R. Samadd-
ar (eds), *The Borders of Justice* (Philadelphia: Temple University Press, 2012).

[23] France specifies Schengen normative provisions as follows: foreigners may access
the Schengen area for a period of three months, if they hold a valid travel document,
if they hold a valid residence permit, if they have enough financial means, if they
have not entered France in the previous three years, if they are not perceived as a
threat for public order.

of 2011 is a highly securitarian regime, both when it fast-tracked their profiling as irregular economic migrants and also when it monetized access into France for those holding humanitarian permits. It is a variegated space, that of Schengen, where the same people are given international protection on juridical grounds of their vulnerable subjectivity and then pushed back on grounds of their economic vulnerability.

However, this exclusion performed by France, this 'financial push-back,' is in line with the Schengen normative framework: if the Schengen Border Code establishes the removal of border checks for anyone 'irrespective of their nationality,'[24] it also establishes the possibility for member states to verify that third country nationals have 'sufficient means of subsistence, both for the duration of the intended stay and for the return to their country of origin or transit to a third country.'[25]

In fact it was not the first time that France interrupted the Schengen free circulation regime. Here I want to point to a somewhat theatrical precedent. In 2010, France expelled almost 1,000 Roma people: EU citizens from Romania and Bulgaria. In that case, the motivation supporting the expulsion revolved around the irregularity of their housing settlements. When, in July 2010, the French Interior Minister mandated evictions for illegal settlements, he also demanded efficiency and indicated a specific target, i.e., Roma people in illegal settlements. The motivation was somehow an all Schengen-riddle, whereby the Schengen free circulation regime was being interrupted in the name of Schengen: those who live in illegal settlements, French politicians contended, are abusing European free circulation and have to be removed. To this end, France allocated a voucher to disperse to those who would 'voluntarily return' or, to put it more directly, those who would self-deport: 300 Euros for adults and 100 Euros for children. In order to cash in the sum, Roma people would need to register in OSCAR (Outil de Statistiques et de Contrôle de l'Aide au Retour [Tool for Repatriation Aid Statistics and Control Database]).

This episode from 2010 helps situate Tunisian migrants' push-backs in the context of those peripatetic borders through which EU Member States have been following migrants within their national territories over the past few decades: performing ad hoc banishments; switching border dispositives on and off; moving them away from the external perimeter and instead prismatically multiplying them within cities - in public parks,

---

[24] Article 20, *Schengen Border Code*, (CE) n. 562/2006.

[25] Article 4, *Schengen Border Code*.

on buses, in money order operator stores…even in hospitals at times. The 2010 raids and evictions in Roma camps in France as well as the 2011 Tunisian push-back operations speak to this 'urbanization of borders'. Also in the case of Tunisian migrants in 2011, push-back operations didn't only happen at the Mentone-Ventimiglia borderline but also in French cities away from the frontier, producing securitarian raids as well as active resistances across France.[26]

These French enforcement interpretations of the Schengen Border Code produce a segmentation on an economic basis of the right to free circulation across the Schengen Area: Tunisians were irregular migrants with no means of subsistence and Roma people were public land squatters. In both cases, French raids were performed with a rule of efficiency. In 2010, the police were asked to evict 100 camps a month (giving priority to those sheltering Roma people) and in 2011, Foreign Affairs Minister Claude Guéant fixed a minimum target of 28,000 for that year's expulsions, prompting security forces to focus on Tunsian migrants. Whereas in Italy the mode of circulation imposed on Tunisian migrants was disguised as a humanitarian measure, in France it was presented as sheer economic rationality.

EU Schengen: Force and Control over Space

The European Union responded to this controversy over free circulation brought in by Tunisian migrants in the Schengen Area with replies of force. On a regional and trans-regional scale, at a European and Mediterranean level, the EU staged a principle of force in relation to its control over migrant mobility.

Internally, at EU-level, the European Commission proposed a modification to the Schengen Border Code and presented it as a way to 'strengthen the Schengen Area,'[27] stating that during hard times, when Europe has been hit by an economic and financial crisis 'this is not a moment to compromise on our values but rather to strengthen the institutional, political and legal underpinnings of the Schengen system,' as Home Affairs Commissioner Cecilia Malmström put it.[28]

---

[26] On this, see Federica Sossi's essay 'Here and There are the Same', in this volume.

[27] COM(2011) 560 final, September 16, 2011.

[28] C. Malmström, 'Speech for Global Hearing on Refugees and Migrations,' June 5, 2012.

This strengthening consists first of all in the Europeanization of the decision to temporarily reintroduce internal border controls. Presenting the draft, Home Affairs Commissioner Cecilia Malmström, pointed to the inter-governmentality mechanism as the weak spot of a 'key achievement' for European integration, namely free circulation within Schengen. In the proposed change, in fact, the protection of this 'key achievement' was predicated on the centralization of the mechanism for temporarily reintroducing checks at internal borders. In this way, the national prerogative got marginalized to cases of serious threat to public policy or internal security requiring 'immediate action' and even then for a period not exceeding 5 days, after which the Member State should follow the lead of European institutions on how to manage the internal border.[29] While the Commission presented this modification as the response to the Italy-France quarrel over the mobility of Tunisian migrants, the Commission had all along been cultivating the idea of taking on the jurisdiction on temporary interruptions of free circulation at internal borders.[30]

In the context of the Arab Uprisings where the cooperation of EU Member States crystallized on the Southern shore of the Mediterranean (staging 'Willing' combatants and, as I shall illustrate, also numerous neighborhood policies) while it was crushed on the Northern shore, the Commission's intervention also reads as a sort of last ditch effort toward Schengen cooperation. In this last ditch call, however, cooperation is restored only on the securitarian front.

The political document[31] accompanying the proposal for change introduces the issue of interventions at external borders to strengthen, along with free circulation, the compensation game on which Schengen is based, which has been eloquently defined as 'policing in the name of freedom.'[32] In the 'Schengen Governance: Strengthening the Area without Internal

---

[29] The draft allows for a temporary decision to reintroduce border checks at internal borders in the case of a large number of arrivals of third-country-nationals through the external frontier of one of Schengen signatories' states, if this arrival is considered a threat for public order and internal security. States have the prerogative to reintroduce border checks for a maximum of five days and, after that, they have to obtain an extension from the European Commission.

[30] See P. Pallister-Wilkins, 'Playing Politics with Schengen,' Open Democracy, July 16, 2011. Available: http://www.opendemocracy.net/opensecurity/polly-pallister-wilkins/playing-politics-with-schengen. Date Accessed: September 2, 2013.

[31] COM (2011) 561 final, September 16, 2011.

[32] D. Bigo and E. Guild, Controlling Frontiers: Free Movement into and within Europe, (Aldershot: Ashgate, 2005).

Border Control,[33] the European Commission envisions visits to border-zones, with or without warning, in order to verify that the Schengen *acquis* is properly applied. The Modification Draft also mentions the institution of a European-level control mechanism on the workings of single Member States. Moreover, the document expands the role and jurisdiction of the external border agency Frontex, also granting the agency leeway from Member States' control.[34]

The response the EU provided to the Italian invocation of the 'burden sharing' principle in the face of the arrival of Tunisian migrants, was also merely securitarian and resulted in the deployment of the Frontex mission 'Hermes 2011' to patrol the external border along the Sicilian channel and in a financial contribution proposed by the European Commission to the EU External Borders Fund of 52 million Euros for 2012 (against 32 million Euros for the previous year).

But it is on a trans-regional scale that Europe most vehemently expressed its strength, forcing a Euro-Mediterranean appropriation of the developments of the Tunisian revolution and of the Arab Uprisings. In a press release, European Council President Herman Van Rompuy, said: 'Without Europe, there would have been an Arab Spring, but without us there will be no Arab summer!'[35] In 2011, EU policy initiatives and policy mobility heavily targeted the southern Mediterranean shores, pushing the envelope of neighborhood initiatives and policy mobility well beyond the externalization of border enforcement and humanitarian regimes that had been rooting European migration management for years.[36] What started in 2011 was a battle to gain control over the economic space opened up by the Arab revolutions. It was this southern shore of the European single market that the EU started to explicitly articulate as one of the key battle-grounds for European economic prosperity when the Arab Uprisings put in motion the reconfiguration of that economic space and its markups.

This attempt by the EU to appropriate the (economic) spaces put in motion by the Uprisings is an uncanny re-edition of the colonial moder-

---

[33] COM (2011) 561 final, ibid.

[34] This is what Ilkka Laitinen, the Director of the Border Agency Frontex, requested on February 21, 2011. Talking about the Hermes 2011 mission at Lampedusa Island, he demanded for more decisional autonomy for Frontex.

[35] Declaration of June 24, 2011. The press release is available on the European Council website and filed under the title Press: 201, Nr: 29/11.

[36] M. Geiger and A. Pécoud (eds), *The Politics of International Migration Management*, (Basingstoke: Palgrave Macmillan, 2010).

nity and development nexus. The Commission intervened in the neighborhood of the Arab Uprisings with a 'SPRING Programme', putting its signature on that Spring which, in the EU acronym, becomes: Support for Partnership, Reform, and Inclusive Growth. The 'SPRING Programme' is a policy packet aimed at providing 'support for the Southern Neighbourhood countries for democratic transformation, institution building and economic growth in the wake of the Arab Spring.'[37] The Programme consisted of 350 million Euros, between 2011 and 2012, and supported mobility partnerships for 'selective migrations' (e.g. accelerated visas for students, researchers, managers), cultural activities and civil society organizations. The European Commission communications on the neighborhood were on the same page, and possibly even clearer as they framed a 'partnership for democracy and shared prosperity' with the Southern shore[38] and posited a series of EU responses to the evolution of the neighborhood.[39] The European Union even erased the southern shore when, presenting initiatives aimed at reorganizing the mobility of both people and capitals in the countries of the Arab revolutions, it posited a 'Euro-Mediterranean': Euro-Med Partnership, Euro-Med Youth Platform, Euro-Med Industrial Cooperation, Euro-Med Higher Education... These attempts to re-structure Tunisia, Egypt and Libya as euro-Med spaces via European partnership projects speak of the European attempt to forcefully re-claim its dominant role in a neighborhood which radically changed overnight, taking both its neighbours and international observers by surprise.

3. Clockwork Schengen

In the documentary *I nostri anni migliori* [*Our Best Years*], Matteo Calore and Stefano Collizzolli illustrate 'what is left of the Tunisian revolution in the lives of those who have traversed it.'[40] The 'best years' of the documentary's title refer to four temporalities: the time when lives were suspend-

---

[37] Spring Programme Presentation, 'EU Response to the Arab Spring: New Package of Support for North Africa and Middle East'. Available: http://www.enpi-info.eu/mainmed.php?id_type=1&id=26482. Date Accessed: September 2, 2013.

[38] COM(2011) 200 of March 8, 2011.

[39] COM(2011) 303 of May 25, 2011.

[40] M. Calore and S. Collizzolli, *I nostri anni migliori* (Italy: Zalab, 2011) Quotation taken from the film's website. Available: http://inostriannimigliori.wordpress.com/. Date Accessed: September 2, 2013.

ed under Ben Ali regime, the time when Tunisians set the revolution in motion, the time they set about leaving for Europe and, finally, the time during which Europe managed their existences when it 'received' them in 2011. In this section I will focus on this last temporality.

Before delving into the rhythms that Schengen and Italy tried to impose on the crossing of Tunisian migrants, however, I would like to pause on the 'Tunisian' time of departure. What type of time did the decision to leave for Europe in those first months of 2011 constitute for those Tunisians? And what did their time 'in circulation' set in motion? It was a fast-paced time, a time made electric by the sudden possibility the revolution made available, namely the possibility of leaving. With Ben Ali's fall the mechanism which had contained emigration also collapsed, that bilateral mechanism that the Prodi government first, then the Berlusconi government, and finally the Monti government in 2013 sealed with the Tunisian government for many years,[41] no doubt the 'best years' of many people's lives. So it was a time of heady travel projects, travel projects which suddenly became feasible and that some Tunisians indeed decided to embrace, leaving for Europe as fast as possible and at last enacting the notion of a Mediterranean neighborhood, on the proximity of its shores. And this urgency to leave turned out to be forward-looking, if one measures the rapid re-establishment of migration bilateral agreements between Italy and the Tunisian transitional government already signed in April 2011.

But this swift departure was decisively slowed down once these young people landed in Europe where, following disembarking at Lampedusa island, they had intended to leave Italy right away. In this case it was European countries who acted fast, adopting various measures to implement a sort of centrifugal circulation of Tunisian migrants *away from* their territories: away from Italy, away from France, away from Europe.

And velocity is indeed the temporal paradigm of the single market, the objective of the two standardization mechanisms upon which the market is rooted, namely the common currency and the removal of checks at internal borders. But in the same way as the space of free circulation is subject to what in EU policy lingo is called 'a logic of compensation' (compensation between internal free circulation and external border enforcement at the outer EU perimeter), a similar logic also underpins the

---

[41] For a precise account of the Italy - Tunisia agreements, see M. Tazzioli's contribution on *Storie Migranti*. Available: http://www.storiemigranti.org/spip.php?article1004. Date Accessed: September 2, 2013.

temporal dimension of Schengen. Alongside the velocity marking the rhythms of internal markets, other temporalities have been multiplying for migrants in the Schengen Area with the suspension mechanisms, diachronic confinements, and the deceleration of crossings.[42] In this volume, the map *Spaces in Migration* recounts, among other things, these temporalities Europe imposed upon Tunisian migrants and Libyan war refugees crossing into Europe, through temporal borders and the suspension of their lives.

Alongside this bordering rhythm of temporal suspension, there is another rhythm through which Schengen governed Tunisian migrants' mobility across its space in 2011-12. While equally ripe with bordering effects, this rhythm is of a different nature: it is a syncopated rhythm, a time made of interruptions, a time in which duration is marked by expiration dates, a time of *from...to* temporal segments. This is an endlessly interrupted time to the extent that for Tunisian migrants it became impossible to count on any duration beyond that of waiting.

Humanitarian with an Expiration Date

The first dispositive of this syncopated sequencing of Tunisian migrants' temporality in Schengenland is the temporary residence permit granted on humanitarian grounds. Above I discussed the spatial outcomes of this permit and the contrasting territorialities it staged and solicited. Here I discuss its temporal dimension and argue that it works as a kaleidoscope producing diachronic borders.[43]

It is first of all the coupling of qualifiers such as 'humanitarian' and 'temporary' defining the permit ('humanitarian measures for temporary protection') which inserts a paradoxical temporality into the existences

---

[42] Federica Sossi speaks of 'biographies at the border' (*Migrare*, p.34) to describe how Schengen's obsession with borders erases a significant part of migrants' existences through different forms of confinement, control, and suspension. Enrica Rigo devotes a chapter to the 'diachronic borders of Europe' in *Europa di confine. Trasformazioni della cittadinanza nell'Unione allargata* (Rome: Meltemi, 2007), pp.150-5 and analyzes the 'indefinite temporariness' of European migrants' juridical subjectivity within Schengen, their being suspended to pro tempore rights. Sandro Mezzadra and Brett Neilson ('Né qui né altrove') talk of a 'decompression chamber' mechanism that functions at the borders of Europe, performing a deceleration and a selection of migrations and performing the differential inclusion of migrant labor in the single market.

[43] E. Rigo, *Europa di confine*. Ibid.

this document *permits* to stay. On the one hand, eligibility is positioned on the supra-temporal dimension of the humanitarian but on the other hand the practice of dispensing protection is defined as temporary. While the juridical logic is clear (a six months residence permit on humanitarian grounds), the existential articulation that such 'protection' may produce is not: which time could this temporary protection open up? What type of existence might this deadline centered permit enable its 'beneficiaries' to build?

Access and eligibility criteria for this permit were all clearly defined temporally. Vis-à-vis an uncanny vagueness about the spatiality of eligibility ('citizens of Northern Africa countries'), the temporality of eligibility was instead made chronometrically clear. One may have been able to apply for the permit if, coming from a vaguely defined and exoticized 'North Africa,' one had arrived on the Italian national territory within a very precise timeframe, i.e., 'from January 1, 2011 to midnight of April 5, 2011.'[44]

Further stopwatches were mobilized with regards to the permit's application timeframe and release times. Applications were due to the Questura within eight days from the publication in Parliament's Official Journal of the Prime Minister's decree instantiating the protection. These were very improbable deadlines to meet, especially for their addressees. How could Tunisian migrants ever come to know about a publication in the Journal and how could they ever file within such a short timeframe? Why, should eligibility for a humanitarian permit be temporally circumscribed to an application timeframe? Finally, why such a short interval of only eight days? It is highly unlikely that those who were eligible for protection, even if they had somehow become aware of the publication, would be able to mobilize so quickly.

As a matter of fact, among the group of about 24,000 who arrived in Italy by April 5, 2011, only 11,006 permits were granted and, six months later, when the possibility to file for an extension was granted, only 3,052 were prorated and 3,510 converted into work-based residence permits.[45]

---

[44] Decreto del presidente del Consiglio dei ministri, April 5, 2011.

[45] It was very hard to get the exact number of the humanitarian temporary residence permits dispensed in relation to the Prime Minister's Decree of June 5, 2011. While statements by newspapers and politicians made reference to a rounded up figure (11,800), the Interior Ministry and the State Police ignored my requests for clarification. The Civil Protection Press Office, however, promised to work on my request and forwarded me the Interior Ministry Office answer to my question: 'The residence permits released for humanitarian reasons, in line with the Prime Minister

But this chronometric precision through which the decree partitions, on the stroke of midnight, deportability from the right to stay is also not in line with the workings of Italian institutions. The identification of Tunisian migrants, the 'evidence' documenting when they entered Italy, has not always been conducted at the moment of arrival and/or in the place of landing, resulting in misrepresentations of the timing of the moment of entry for potentially eligible beneficiaries.

However, with regards to the moment of release of the permit, the Italian government granted high priority status or 'maximum speed' [*massima celerità*], four days to be precise. It is worth quoting the paragraph on the timing of the permit's dispensation featured on the circular letter sent out by the Interior Ministry aimed at clarifying the implementation standards of the decree. It is the 'urgency' with which mechanisms were implemented in order to make Tunisians circulate that I find interesting here: 'In the perspective of granting maximum rapidity [...], measures have been coordinated with the Ministry of Economic Affairs and Finances and with the Italian Mail System so that the residence titles will be delivered to the Questure from the State Polygraphic and Mint Institute [Istitutio poligrafico e Zecca di stato] within 4 days from the authorization date, via the Postal System special delivery service with packages marked 'PSE URGENTE PT'.[46] (my translation)

If, here, we saw a 'clockwork' temporal schema with provisions for 'maximum rapidity', temporal approximation instead dominated the deportations of all Tunisian migrants who entered Italy after April 5 without a residence and work permit. This institutional tempo for deportations was actually very elusive and, as was denounced by associations for the rights of migrants, abuses were perpetrated, not respecting the timeline for the notification of expulsion orders' that both European and Italian normative systems mandate.[47] An example. During the first repatriation of Tunisian migrants in 2011, Italian authorities deported forty Tunisian migrants who would actually have been eligible for temporary protection. Their arrival was actually recorded on Lampedusa island at 00:25am on

---

Decree's of 05/04/2011 [...], are a total of 11,006; the renewals approved are 3,052; the conversions into work permits are 3,510' (February 15, 2012).

[46] Circolare del Ministero dell'Interno numero 2990, April 8, 2011.

[47] See in particular, the essay by Fulvio Vassallo Paleologo, 'Detenzione arbitraria e respingimenti sommari in Tunisia. Come ai tempi di Ben Ali?', April 22, 2011. Available at: http://www.meltingpot.org/articolo16727.html. Date Accessed: September 2, 2013.

April 6, indicating their arrival in Italian territorial waters by midnight on April 5.[48]

The humanitarian regime under which Italy operated in 2011 was rooted in expirations: very short application timeframes for temporary rights and deportation operations enforced on the basis of temporal vagueness or convenient mistakes.

Short-Term States

But this spatial temporality, this deadline-centered right to space, was most clearly expressed by another migration governance instrument deployed by Italy in 2011: the declarations of states of humanitarian emergency - three in less than six months.[49] The word 'state' clearly describes the multiple ways in which space and time were put into play in these states of humanitarian emergency. Let me start with the asset of time: on the one hand, the emergency becomes the temporal yardstick with which to plot a new territory; on the other hand, a sequence is established, made up of successive 'states of emergency' and their durations (starting day, expiration day, extensions).

But the word 'state' also has a spatial dimension, as it indicates the 'where' of a declared state of humanitarian emergency while, at the same time, also referring to that state's jurisdiction, to that political and normative nexus expressed as territoriality,[50] in this case the territoriality of the humanitarian regime.

I named these declarations of the state of emergency 'short-term states' with the specific intention of indicating the layers woven together within the word 'state' and in order to underline the emergency temporality they instantiated and the governmental leeway this supported. Under emergency and in temporary sites, governance is conducted under a regime

---

[48] See the document by the association 'Fédération des tunisiens pour une citoyenneté des deux rives.' Available at: http://www.citoyensdesdeuxrives.eu/index.php?option=com_content&view=article&id=2178:ftcr-accord-tuniso-italien-sur-les-harragas&catid=102:tous-nos-communiques&Itemid=106. Date Accessed: September 2, 2013.

[49] On February 12, 2011, Italy declared a state of humanitarian emergency in Italy; on April 7, it did the same thing 'on the territory of Northern Africa'; on August 3, it extended it to 'the other countries of the African continent,' each time working through Prime Minister decrees.

[50] N. De Genova and N. Peutz (eds), *The Deportation Regime* (Durham, NC: Duke University Press, 2010, p.11).

of exception and with expiring, always renewable and seldom openly explained, agendas.

In the first declaration of February 12, 2011, when Italy entered a 'state of humanitarian emergency [...] in relation to the exceptional influx of citizens of Northern Africa countries', for instance, the Civil Protection was designated as the unit in charge of the emergency. With this designation, political and social events (such as the upheavals of the Arab Revolutions) are profiled as a natural cataclysm. An uncanny 'humanitarian trespassing' is legitimized by the same logic: the 'state of humanitarian emergency in the territory of North Africa' that Italy subsequently declared on April 6, was in fact hardly rooted in a humanitarian justification. The state of emergency (declared by Italy in 'North Africa') was in fact aimed at 'allowing for efficiently counter the exceptional influx of extracommunitarian citizens on national territory.' With such spatial deferral and jurisdiction hubris, the principle of causality of this declaration vacillates too. The state of humanitarian emergency was declared in Italy, situated in 'North Africa' (first spatial deferral) and aimed to prevent immigration to Italy (second spatial deferral). It is really hard to grasp which causality this humanitarian regime is predicated on: if indeed there is a humanitarian emergency in 'Northern Africa,' which jurisdiction authorizes Italy to mandate 'states of emergency' abroad, hence also instantiating intervention zones under humanitarian label? What is the humanitarian content of the attempt to 'efficiently counter the exceptional influx of extracommunitarian citizens'?

In this *Italian* 'North Africa Emergency' the humanitarian and the securitarian are intertwined intervention principles, deployed in mobile, interchangeable and even invented geographies. The goal that grounded these complicated humanitarian geographies seemed to be that those 'thousands of citizens from Tunisia,'[51] as the decree reads, could indeed be made to circulate swiftly away from Italy: either elsewhere in Europe with a temporary residence permit, or in 'Northern Africa' with exceptional measures implemented to prevent their arrival on the Italian shore, or, should they have in fact landed, to push them back.

4. To Be Continued: 'Spacetime' Interruption Practices

What then are the spatio-temporal coordinates along which Europe governed the crossings of Tunisian migrants? The analysis carried out in this

---

[51] February 12, 2011.

paper points to a sort of condensation mechanism enacting a claustropho-bic and impossible space-time: a space so intensely punctured by temporal deadlines that its ground - the crossing ground - crumbles, and a time that, as continuously synchopated, can be articulated only in the form of an expiration date or, ultimately, a time that, as indefinitely suspended, looms over as peremptory capture. This is in Europe. But Euro-Med spa-tio-temporal coordinates were also mandated in the countries of the Arab Uprisings, with humanitarian states rooted in deferral and in externali-zation and building on the long-established paradigm of 'development', staged in this case as the narrative for reorganizing a 'neighborhood' that the Arab Revolutions put in motion. As such, it is important to keep fol-lowing Tunisians on the Southern shore of the Mediterranean as well as Tunisian migrants in Europe, following the spaces and the times through which they articulate the neighborhood and following the interruptions of that Italian or Euro-mediterranean *spacetime* that they manage to force within its tangles - in parallel, in contraposition, in flight or as a displace-ment.

March 5, 2012

'This is Europe, This is My Europe'
LUCIO GUARINONI

Interviews with A.A., Adel Souei, Chiheb Khlifi

Between September 2011 and March 2012 I conducted research which became part of my undergraduate thesis *Signs: What New Tunisian Harraga Burn and Strengthen*. In that context I interviewed various young people who did the harga and I asked them to tell me their stories.

Adel Souei, who now lives in Belgium, talked with me over Skype. I report our dialogue in full, including the questions and also Fabienne's contribution, the woman he is married to who joined our conversation at some points.

I met A.A. - who asked me not to disclose his name - close to where I work. When I interviewed him he was looking for a job that would allow him to convert his temporary humanitarian residence permit into full residency. At the time of writing he has been hired by a pizzeria and each time I run into him he smiles. He asked me not to record our conversation, but he allowed me to take a few notes and to report his story in writing. I decided to use the first person singular and, where I could not remember his exact words, I did not report the passages. This is what makes his story the shortest in the collection.

I met Chiheb Khlifi right after his arrival in Italy. We are friends and this makes the interview with him different from the others. I asked him to just tell me his story, a story which I had been partially told also because in a way I am part of it. I preferred not to interrupt him and let him put together the pieces which, in our meetings over the course of the year, he had told me as fragments.

Each story has its own specificity emerging from what is said and emerging in the way it is said. This makes each story unique as lived experience is unique. These people are connected not only by their experiences and their common traits but also by their will to turn such experiences into stories delivered to me through words and through those different moments which punctuated the heterogeneity of our encounters. I hope these words may also function as a space of encounter for those who are reading, without forgetting that words come from bodies and to bodies return.

L.G., February 2012

ADEL

Adel: I would like to make a film about this. A film about what people in Tunisia dream of when they dream of going to Europe to change their lives, to look for a job, and a film about the resources and the money that are being pursued in order to pay the owners of boats directed to Europe, a film about those who do not have money and can't go to Europe, and on those mothers who sell their jewellery and valuables to help their kids leave.

As is well known, the problem we had in Tunisia in January 2011 was the fall of the government... We, or better, I wanted to come to Europe because here I have some friends, actually I was in a relationship with a Belgian woman. I had been corresponding with French students since I was very young. Moreover, I also always worked with European, French and German corporations. Well, staying in Tunisia would have meant a big problem, for me, I mean, I would have had a big problem staying there... Tunisia has not stabilized yet; I think it'll take two or three years for this to happen; it's not that I don't love my country, I look at the papers every day trying to understand what is happening, what is changing.

L.G.: So you claim to have had a positive image of Europe before coming. Was this image confirmed when you arrived?

Adel: Listen, I think each of us has their own mentality. As you know many young people arrived in Europe and found themselves on the street, with nothing, and I even heard of someone who did not behave well, someone who was not honest...oh well, this is all stuff I do not like.

Fabienne: Well, you were lucky. Some people arrived in Italy with no money at all, not knowing anyone, with nothing.

Adel: Yes, it is true, as for me I found a wonderful woman.

Fabienne: This is true. Adel had nothing when he arrived and he was wondering how to make it, how to find a job. For someone with no local support, someone you could trust, it is actually hard, maybe impossible, to figure things out and, more than anything, to feel ok. For instance, we did not want to get married right away. It's best to first get to know one another better as it is an important choice: but at some point it became sort of mandatory, do you understand? Even a choice like this, which should have been made considering all sorts of other things, was instead forced by the fact that Adel had to get his papers. It was the only solution. It is very hard to find a job now so this was the only way.

L.G.: I wanted to ask Adel a few more things. First question: where did you arrive in Italy and when did you arrive?

Adel: I arrived in Bergamo right away. Well…do you mean what was it like to arrive in Italy? Well, like for anyone. It was the biggest adventure of my life. I spent three and a half days at sea - it should have been 16 hours but it ended up being three and a half days as we took the wrong route and the boat was damaged. Luckily I have some mechanical skills and I was able to help fix it to avoid taking on too much water. Then we arrived in Italy, even if I did not want to stay there; for me Italy was only a crossing point; why would I want to stay there? If, for instance, I had learned the language necessary to live in Bergamo or other Italian cities, I would have had to stay for at least one year. I circulated my CVs to various job centers but I was told that I would not find anything if I did not speak Italian. Anyway, since I left for Europe I always wanted to go to Belgium.

L.G.: And how did you get to Belgium from Italy?

Adel: When I arrived in Bergamo I made many friends…I didn't have enough money to get to Belgium and so I asked my family to send me some and I also saved until I had enough money to get a ticket from Belgium, the cheapest ticket.

L.G.: Did you have any troubles getting to Belgium?

Adel: A friend of my brother, with whom I talked on the phone, told me he would wait for me in Belgium to help avoid problems with the police. So when I arrived at the airport I found him there waiting for me. I actually thought I would have had problems moving around but this has not been the case. I spent two days at the hostel and then I met Fabienne. And since then everything went fine, 'Amdoullah' [thank God], as I say.

L.G.: Are you aware that some people filmed their trip to Italy with their cell phones and then circulated the videos on the Internet? What do you think about that, do you think it is important to bear witness of those moments?

Adel: If I have a friend who is planning to make the *harraga*,[1] I tell him not to do it. First of all it is very dangerous and also Europe is not as you picture it, it is not paradise as you thought before getting there. I did not eat for three and a half days and after having gone through the Lampedusa first aid centre where my fingerprints were taken, I swiftly ran away because I did not want to stay in Italy, I wanted to arrive in Belgium. Anyway, I did not take any video, it was not a time to take a video and to think about anything else but survival.

But I do believe that bearing witness is important, I just think that during that moment on the boat you don't think about it, you can't have such awareness and make such a choice when your boat is boarding water and you don't know if you will survive the night. What I was talking about is something different, it comes afterwards, when you are calm: one day I thought about making a small film on the thoughts of those planning to reach Europe, on how trips work, on hiding in trucks and turning off cell phones at night, on what happened during my *harraga*.

A.A.

A.A.: When the revolution broke out in Tunisia, I saw everybody leaving, so I asked myself: 'what am I doing here in Tunisia? I will leave too.' So I went to Sfax, the city from where people leave, and I looked for a boat for

---

[1] For a definition of '*harraga*,' see footnote 14 of Paola Gandolfi 'Spaces in Migration, Daily Life in Revolution' (this collection).

Italy. My trip was very long and had many problems: the first time we took the wrong route and after a few hours we were back in Tunisia; a few days later I was told that, with the money I had paid (1,000 dinars, about 500 Euros), I could take another boat to attempt the crossing again. So I left for the second time but the boat had a failure and we came back again after a few hours. The third time we stayed for about 16 hours at sea and when we had almost reached Lampedusa the boat stopped. I noticed a helicopter right away and two boats where we boarded to go to Lampedusa. On the island there were many Tunisians, 7,000 if I recall well, it was really crowded, so we could not stay in the first aid centre. Tents were installed everywhere and we slept and ate there; I remember that people were very nice to us. I stayed there for 9 days and afterwards we were moved to the Bari centre where the situation was very different: people were not nice to us, policemen were everywhere and wanted to know where you were going every time you moved; everybody was very nervous because it was hard to understand what the Italian government wanted to do, if they wanted to repatriate us, it they would give us a permit and for how long. Moreover, after staying 16 days, we were told to go to Foggia and that once there we would be given a ticket to get to whatever place we wanted to go to, so whoever wanted to go to Milan would have gone to Milan and whoever wanted to go to France could go there too. I didn't know where I wanted to go exactly; some people were just crossing Italy to reach other places, maybe to join relatives or friends in Europe but I was travelling with no destination in mind. But when we arrived in Foggia nobody gave us any train ticket. Because I had no money I took the first train without even knowing where it was directed but I was forced to leave the train and this happened again a second time. But by the third time I managed to get to Bologna: it seems like any time I try to go somewhere, I have to try at least three times before actually making it, but in the end I always make it. In Bologna I stayed for a while at the train station and then I decided to go to Milan; I found three policemen on the train: it is absurd how they said completely different things from one another. I remember that one of them was particularly rude and as I was by the restroom he slammed the door several times, hurting me and leaving a mark that stayed for almost a month. Luckily there was a woman among them; I believe she was a *maresciallo*, a chief officer and when she understood I was Tunisian she let me go. From Milan I arrived in Bergamo but I don't know exactly why, I didn't choose to end up here, I simply arrived here and I was brought to the San Vincenzo patronage, where I still live. I don't know how I see this city. Also because for me being here means finding a job in order to be able to turn my residence permit granted on humanitarian grounds into a work permit, because I won't go back to Tunisia before having done something here, I can't go back and say: I did not do anything. For sure I imagined a different Italy, when I was in Tunisia I imagined Italy to be much richer, I imagined better conditions of life; instead when I arrived here I realized that a lot of people are losing their jobs and it is not a place where people are fine: the soup kitchen in the evenings are more and more crowded also with Italians who are homeless and ask for food. The situation is very hard, we are all not doing well, we are not well with this place, not well with ourselves, all in different ways but also in the same way.

CHIHEB

Chiheb: I would like to start by talking about my departure from home. The idea of the *harraga* came about like this: I was spending a lot of time with friends in my city and one day a friend of mine told me that he was about to leave; so I started to think and to reflect deeply and I decided I too would leave. My parents did not agree, they didn't want me to leave on a small boat carrying 80 people with a maximum capacity of 50; my mother rejected this possibility outright, my father tried to talk to me calmly but I had already decided to leave. At nine my friend called me to tell me we would leave from Tunis to go to Sfax, where we would stay for a few days before leaving. I left home without saying goodbye to my family, even if everybody knew I was going to leave. In Sfax we arrived in a house which was a bit far from the sea and we stayed there a few days, and then we moved to another house close to the pier to wait to leave; we stayed for a few more days, enough time for everybody in my neighborhood to ask my family where I was and where my friends Hassan and Mohammed were, discovering that we decided to leave in a *harraga*. On Friday that week we had trouble with the person who had to bring us to the boat, so we had to go back to Tunis, we had to come back, but we met an old man from Sfax who, after a brief discussion, made us change our mind, so we decided to stay, and then leave. We spent the entire day watching TV checking the weather to work out if the sea was calm and the next day, after lunch, the time had come to go. A friend who was with me was scared as he couldn't swim so I went to buy to lifejackets even if I was fine because I am a good swimmer. At night we took a cab and arrived at another house where there were more than 60 people; there we waited for the person who would bring us to the boat to leave: when he arrived there were about 80 of us and we started going out in groups of 20 people, sort of lining up from the house to the pier. We arrived in front of the sea and I saw that the boat was 12 meters by 3 and that it was old, made of ruined wood, and so I thought that in case of a big wave, the boat would have broken and we would have ended up in the sea. During the trip I stayed close to my friends, I had the Koran with me and I was reading a bit from it, some friends were crying but I rested my head on a corner of the boat and stared at the stars. We stayed like that all night, then the day arrived and the trip lasted 5 more hours (17 hours total), and then we saw land: it was Lampedusa.

Close to the island I remember an airplane of the Red Cross flying by; in the meantime we were checking our cell phone coverage to call our family and to tell them we were safe and at some point I saw a military troop coming by and coming close to our boat; some people left with this group, others with a smaller military squad which had come by as well, and we started to dock. On the island nobody told us anything for a very long time, they had given us water to drink but we were hungry, I was hungry but all I could do was wait until some buses came to bring people to the first aid centre. I waited until 11:30 and then I was brought to the Lampedusa first aid centre on the bus. We arrived there after half an hour and we had to wait a bit to let them take our fingerprints and to let them take our pictures to identify us and to give us a 5 Euro phone card to call our family. Before leaving I did not expect there would have been a Centre where they would have put us; I thought that once we arrived on the island, we would have been free to go or to flee to where we wanted to enter Italy; to tell you the truth I saw on TV that on the island there was a Centre but I thought it was a place to get documents before free to go. The Centre was crowded, and it stank everywhere; as soon as I got in I thought things were too dirty and not very sanitary: we looked for a bed and in each bed there were two or more people. We stayed there for 9 days and then people started to get nervous because they did not want to stay there, they wanted to go out and go elsewhere, and everyday a chief police officer would come to tell us that the next day we would be free to go, but it was never true. This is why at the end of the ninth day we started a hunger strike and in the afternoon buses stated to arrive for us. Each of us had a number and police agents started to call us, at times by name but more often by number, so when they called me I took my backpack and I boarded the bus; we arrived to the pier and there was a big boat, there were 1,000-1,200 people and we left, arriving at about 4am in Catania. Even there there were many buses and they did a head count and we arrived at another centre which was in much better shape than the one in Lampedusa. Once we arrived there they took more pictures of us, they asked us to sign some documents, and they gave us a food card: most of us finally called our friends and/or relatives in Italy and France, because many had left to find again the people they knew. We stayed there until the end of the month: during the day at times we went out and we walked to arrive in a small town, Mineo, where we had Internet access; as the Centre was asking for our information in order to give us a residence permit on humanitarian grounds, I gave my information as well: everyday they would show a list of names of people who could take the bus to leave Catania. Finally my day came and I saw that my name was on the list, so I took the residence permit and took a bus to Naples. There were many policemen at the train station and one explained that they were organizing a train just for us; but I went away and took a regular train with other Italians, and I started to talk with people, with a woman and her husband who saw me in bad condition and invited me to go stay with them for a bit, in Ancona, to rest for a bit before leaving. I was happy, it was the first day that I would have not slept outdoors; but then a friend of my brother who lives in Italy called me and invited me to stay with him until my brother arrived: so I decided not to follow the two people from Ancona and I started my trip to Milan. There I did not talk with my borther's friend. We should have met but he told me that he was out of town in Venice, so I thought I would go to Brescia where my brother was living waiting for him to come back and looking for some friends of his. However, when I got there I found a deteriorated situation, with people selling drugs, and I did not like this at all, so I spent the night on a non operating train at the station. When someone woke me up the next morning I realized a train on the next track was about to leave so I got on and arrived in Milan. There I ran into two Tunisian young men who told me nice things about Bergamo, I had heard of this city because my brother's friend had lived there and so I decided to leave without really knowing where I was going. I arrived at sunset, I bought cookies and I stayed in a park where I saw a person sitting on the bench next to me, staring at me, so I offered this man something to eat and he smiled; he told me that he had been living in Bergamo for 35

years and that he had a job and he was fine: he invited me to stay for a
few days with him until I found a better solution. I took part in a march
for Tunisians where there were people helping me and other young guys
just arrived in Bergamo to find a place to stay, that was the day I met D.:
he was an Italian guy who took part in the march but then left leaving his
bike there; so when everybody left I decided to wait until he came back to
get his bike. He arrived and thanked me so we talked for a while. That is
how we became friends, and I met some of his other friends and I started
to find some people I felt good with: I remember that one day I told him
that when I was in Tunis I would always get together with friends to smoke
narghilé, so he organized a gathering with other friends to smoke. This
was the first time since I left that I sat down to smoke with someone. Days
went by, I was fine but it was very hard to find a job because it is a time of
crisis also for Italians so when I met a person who offered me a job in Lyon
I accepted and decided to go with him right away.

The evening before leaving I went out with some friends and I met a
girl, S., who studied in Lyon and she gave me the contact information of
some people she knew and who could help me: I remember I was really
struck by that gesture and felt I had met people who really cared about me,
with whom I was someone for once. I waved goodbye to my new friends
and I took the bus from Lampugnano: I was a bit scared once at the border
as I had heard about this a lot in that period and I knew very well that it
was prohibited to cross the border to go to France. But the trip went well,
nobody said anything or stopped me, so early in the morning I arrived at
the Part Dieu station in Lyon. I stayed for a few days with a friend of S.,
also because the man who promised to give me a job disappeared, I kept
calling him but he was always busy and could not meet with me. I wanted
to find a job because it is very hard to survive in France if you don't have a
job and can't provide for yourself.

I went to check a place offered by the Social Services but it was dirty,
a sort of prison with many sick people and I did not want to stay there:
I looked for a park and I stayed there to live for ten days. I heard from a
friend who did the *harraga* with me and he invited me to stay with him so
I stayed for about two weeks with him but then he asked me to go because
he needed the room. Luckily I met his family, very nice people and I stayed
with one of his relatives during the month of Ramadan. This was important to me, that I was not in the street during that time. I also found a job,
I was selling clothes in a store and at times I would go to markets with a

Turkish man who did not pay me much, but at least I could finally start to save something. At the end of Ramadan I met another Tunisian guy and I went to stay with him: Lyon is a bit like this for me, leaving from one place to another without really knowing why.

Then the time came to come back to Italy to renew my humanitarian permit for another six months: I was happy to have to go back to Bergamo, a city I liked, even if I knew I would lose my place and maybe even my job in Lyon by taking that trip. I thought I needed to stay just for a week but the time was much longer: I had to stay in Italy for almost a month before I got my permit renewed. I came back to France to start my job again but when I came back my boss was not calling me anymore to work and I had lost my place so I was sleeping in the Internet point of an Algerian guy who invited me to stay there, also because it was winter and it was very cold. I did not want to stay, I didn't have anything and my brother, who in the meantime had moved to Switzerland with his girlfriend, invited me to go to stay with him, so I started another trip and I went to visit him. Someone told me that in order have a permit there the only way was to file an asylum claim: I knew I was not eligible as I had a humanitarian permit from Italy but they told me that many Tunisians tried this way to stay in a holding centre until the meeting with the asylum commission, so I filed my asylum claim and went in a center in Bern. Finally I read my name on the list one day, once again my name on a list, and this meant I could leave and go to a centre while I was waiting for my audition with the commission; I took a bus where I met a girl from Tibet and I went with her where we were told to go but the place was not how I imagined it: once again a centre, this time this was a former barracks with huge dormitory rooms and it looked like a prison to me. When we arrived I was the only one who spoke a bit of French and Italian and I translated for everybody, there were many rules, and they told us that we had to wait there for at least three months or maybe more. So I thought I would stay there for a short period of time, and even if my brother was there the only way to get a permit was to say something false and I knew they would not give me the documents, so from the first day I was there I knew I would have to leave. I worked for a few days as a cook and they gave me a little weekly stipend, in the kitchen there was an African guy with me, from Burundi, it was the first time I heard the name of this country! I stayed for three weeks and then I packed and went back to Italy to my friends in Bergamo. This is Europe. This is my Europe.

Migration (in) Crisis and 'People Who Are Not Our Concern'
MARTINA TAZZIOLI

The slippages of the migration crisis, the crisis as a catchword

The two-year period 2011-2012 could be seen as an age of 'Mediterranean crisis' spanning from the edge of Africa - the Libyan war - to countries in Southern Europe. If Europe itself is one of the spaces most overwhelmed and shaken up by the 'crisis' - assumed here as an all-encompassing term, which incorporates economic issues, social/class conflicts, border struggles etc - in this analysis I turn to the Mediterranean space, thus shifting the continental signifier, Europe, towards a more blurred political referent, the Mediterranean - since in this case two overlapping 'crises' can be identified: the 'migration crisis,' in which the 'humanitarian' and the 'security' crisis are in part intertwined and in part segregated, and economic collapse. Concerning the latter, Europe is seen as one of the points of origin from which the crisis proliferated towards other spaces - and, indeed, where the impact has been also more crippling than in Europe itself. Instead, the former, the migration crisis, is figured as a flood coming from the Southern and Eastern shores of the Mediterranean: in this case, the spatial and political upheavals produced by the so-called 'Arab Spring' and branded as the democratic awakening of the Arab countries were very soon stigmatized as social turmoil and as migratory chaos, mostly when the so-much awaited reverberation on the Northern shore actualized into the presence of thousands of migrants on the European soil. And it's precisely through the instabilities produced by these two proclaimed 'crises' that I will explore their interactions and their mutual reinforcements. Focusing on the politics of mobility, I investigate here the ways in which migration agencies have, on the one hand, depoliticized the connections between the European governmental crisis and the crisis of the asylum system, and on the other hand seized the discourse on the crisis as a floating signifier for setting up 'migration in crisis' as an odd compound where different kinds and meanings of crisis collapse into one another and become conflated[1]: the crisis in Libya, the humanitarian crisis at the Tunisian border after almost one million people fled the country with many of them still stranded in refugee camps, the risk of crisis for the European states receiving thousands of migrants, the crisis of the asylum system and finally the crisis of the migrants arriving in Europe only to struggle with the economic recession and the rise of racism which casts them as 'job burglars.'

The script of a 'migration in crisis' has been recent promoted by the International Organization for Migration (IOM) in order to address the Libyan political turmoil and its 'disseminations,' in other spaces - Tunisia and Europe - and in different domains - the humanitarian regime, security, economics. However, it is certainly not the first time that the paradigm of the crisis has been introduced by States or international agencies as a keyword encapsulating an array of political technologies of migration governance (IOM was itself put in place in the 1950s precisely to respond to the crisis produced by the two-block politics which emerged in the aftermath of the Second World War). That said, in the aftermath of the Libyan conflict and of the Arab uprisings, the catch-phrase of the crisis has been re-introduced as a multifunctional prism for framing a heterogeneous array of 'mobility disorders' - namely, practices of migration that through their 'spatial takeover'[2] trouble the 'b-ordering spaces.' But what does 'migration crisis' stand for? It is not merely a question of semantic niceties if we take into account the nuances of the formula, especially the

---

[1] In his genealogy of the variegated occurences in which the term 'crisis' has historically been used, Reinhart Koselleck shows the catch-word function of that notion and at the time its blurred meaning, covering a wide semantic range and draws on multiple domains - medecine, law, theology, philosophy of history: retracing the emergence of the word 'crisis' and of its use, the political-economic signification came out only in the late 18th Century and it still continues to encroach upon other domains. See Reinhart Koselleck, *Crisi* (Verona: Ombre Corte, 2012). Ultimately, drawing on Koselleck's analysis, it could be argued that what relates migrations and the notion of crisis is their hybrid nature, namely 'the quality of creating connections, and at the same time the necessity to connect itself to other terms.' (Koselleck, p.92)

[2] F. Sossi (ed.), *Spazi in Migrazione. Cartoline di una rivoluzione* (Verona: Ombre Corte, 2012).

swing between 'migration crisis' and 'migration IN crisis.' In referring to migration: 'a large scale, complex migration flows resulting from crisis and typically involving significant vulnerabilities for the individuals and communities affected [...] migration caught into crisis involves different categories.'[3]

Now, it's noticeable that the crisis refers on the one hand to the state of precariousness, vulnerability and restricted mobility which affect migrants crossing the borders of a third country due to war conflict and people who became 'migrants' because of a crisis, and on the other hand to the political and economic backlash as well as the security issues affecting receiving countries. Migration as a 'disordered practice of mobility' is staged as a turbulent and troubling factor in itself, triggering a state of crisis or fostering an ongoing crisis already present, irrespective of the nature of the crisis - humanitarian, economic, security and so on. Secondly, what the context of the Arab revolutions and the regenerated formula of 'migration crisis' have made visible is that migration works precisely as a magic-tenet through which the conquest of democracy and the revolution for freedom, as the 'Arab Spring' resonated in Europe, have suddenly become translated into an unfulfilled democratic revolution with unpredictable fallout for European democracies as well. 'Migration' works as a transformative catalyst for re-codifying political struggles and spatial upheavals into a source of an undetermined crisis. Migration as the space-troubling factor, migration as the degenerative force of a favourable mobility, migration as the deviation from the road to democracy, migration as a plight for the social cohesion and as a disobedient practice of movement.

The Tunisian migration cluster

While the migration crisis was coined for addressing the Libyan political turmoil and its multiple and multiplying effects, revolutionized Tunisia constitutes an equally interesting space for interrogating the formation of what I would call a 'migration cluster.' After the outbreak of the Tunisian revolution and of the Libyan conflict, Tunisia has become a space of 'complex' migrations, that is a factory and at the same time a recipient

---

[3] IOM, 'Protecting Migrants during Times of Crisis: Immediate Responses and Sustainable Strategies,' *International Dialogue on Migration 2012: Managing Migration in Crisis Situations* (2012). Available: http://www.iom.int/cms/en/sites/iom/home/ what-we-do/international-dialogue-on-migrat/protecting-migrants-during-times. html. Date Accessed September 9, 2013.

of migrants and would-be migrants, sub-Saharan refugees and asylum seekers, young 'Tunisian beggars' crossing the Mediterranean and Libyan nationals. But Tunisian citizens who left the country for Europe and the migrants who fled Libya were seen in Tunisia as two completely different phenomena: this consideration is in part true if we consider the different conditions and reasons for migrating, but at the same time it overshadows the commonalities that depend on the very mechanism of 'selected mobility' from which both these practices of migrations are excluded. In this regard, the refugee camp of Choucha, close to the Libyan border of Ras Jadir, crossed by almost 1 million of people in 2011 after the outbreak of the war conflict, has remained in the shadows in comparison to other political issues taking place in revolutionized Tunisia. Or put differently, the problem of migrants and refugees fleeing Libya was tackled in terms of the 'popular chain' of hospitality set into place by the Tunisian people.[4]

'Give us our lives back': stranded migrants out-of-place in the space-frontier of Choucha

Choucha is a tent camp in the middle of the Tunisian desert, nine kilometres from the Libyan border of Ras Jadir and more than 10 kilometres from the closest Tunisian village - Ben Guerdane. And up until the time of writing, the problem of the denied refugees and the refugees still awaiting resettlement has not arisen. These stranded people, awaiting months as if in a lottery have remained in the shade of the Tunisian political debate centred on the construction of a 'new democratic Tunisia.' The camp opened on February 26, 2011, hosting those displaced by the Libyan war, those hundreds of thousands of Libyan residents - almost all of them 'third country nationals' - who fled the conflict towards Tunisia. The number of people trapped in that space peaked at 22,000 people between March and April 2011. Then, from late summer 2011 the average of asylum seekers stranded there for the following year remained at around 4000. At the time of writing this article (March 2013) 980 people are still there, although the exact number, as I will explain later, is very difficult to establish.

---

[4] See M. Tazzioli, 'S/confinamenti degli spazi frontiera: Choucha, Zarzi, Ras Jadir' in F. Sossi (ed.), *Spazi in migratione*.

An intermezzo on the 'popular chain'

It is worth noting that Choucha camp was neither the first nor the only site that hosted Libyans and third-country nationals escaping from Libya. And, most importantly, the humanitarian organizations were not even the only actors that mobilized in response to the 'Libyan crisis' from the Tunisian side. Ben Guerdane, February 20, 2011: thousands of people cross the Ras Jadir border in order to flee Libya where three days prior the first political turmoil started. The Tunisian temporary government decides to keep the border open. But beyond the Tunisian border, no international humanitarian organization is there, in the immediate proximity of the border, and so asylum seekers move to the closest village of Ben Guerdane, whose inhabitants self-organize to host them. Considering that people continue arriving for several days before the opening of Choucha camp, it is estimated that around 1000 people are hosted by the village, through the mobilization of the 'popular chain.'

Tataouine, May 2011: the first big village coming from the other Libyan border, Dehiba, is Tataouine, in the middle of the desert and approximately 90 kilometres from the border-post. Here, around 55,000 Libyans are hosted by Tunisian families, in parallel with the activity of the UNCHR camp near Tataouine. In fact, the delay on the part of the humanitarian organizations in setting up the camp, and the preference on the part of Libyans to live with Tunisian families rather than in a camp and to not claim asylum, has meant that the majority of these Libyans fall outside the UNHCR headcount. Having been 'counted' on crossing the border, their presence on the Tunisian territory subsequently disappeared off the IOM and UNHCR radars, due to the parallel 'popular chain' in place in Tataouine, and also in Djerba where around 100,000 people, including Libyans and third-country nationals, were hosted. This popular chain worked in part as a form of local resistance against the humanitarian government - represented by UNHCR - and was then in part appropriated by that regime. An array of practices, forms of knowledge and relationships was put into place, and at the beginning this conflicted with the very different way of 'making space' carried out by UNHCR, breaking down from within the logic of 'exception' and procedural protocol pertaining to humanitarian government. Thus, as a riposte to the humanitarian chain set up by international organizations, the popular chain was mobilized by the Tunisian people. In a certain sense, it could be suggested that Tunisian citizens, who revolutionized the space of the nation State, made space for those unexpected presences - Libyan and non-Libyan migrants -without tracing it as a space of emergency. They put in place a network that aimed at reproducing as far as possible a framework of everyday life, against the suspended temporality of life in the camp. However, the relevance of the 'gifle tunisienne', as it was described in Tunisia, i.e., a 'slap' given by Tunisian people to humanitarian government, was not entirely unambivalent. For instance, the differential treatment of Libyans and non-Libyans is an element that cannot be overlooked. In Tataouine, only Libyan citizens were hosted by the popular chain. In Ben Guerdane non-Libyans were subjected to acts of racism, especially during May 2011, when citizens of Ben Guerdane burnt tents at Choucha camp, causing the death of six people, as a response to the blocking of the main road by asylum seekers protesting against UN-HCR and its slowness in processing their demands for asylum.

'We put them up, but they are not our concern': the production of sideways subjectivities and the 'humanitarian' tactic of dis-charge

At the outset the main division at Choucha among those displaced by war people was between those who decided to return to their country of origin and those who applied for asylum. Then, when UNHCR started to communicate the results of the demands asylum (after months of delays, which caused protests by asylum seekers who blocked the main road) the camp was soon split into two areas, the 'official' camp and the areas of rejected refugees. The latter were 'kindly' invited to leave Choucha as presences that were 'out of place' within a UNHCR space which takes into consideration refugees and asylum seekers but not those who 'failed the trial' of the asylum process; those, I would say, incapable of proving their exceptional status within a mechanism designed to label them as non-eligible for protection. In this regard, no document is more explicative than this: when asylum-seekers come from safe countries 'applicants are requested to rebut the presumption that the country of origin is safe with regard to their particular circumstances [...] And considering the difficulty have in proving persecution, the applicant's mere assertions of the facts can lead to the granting of asylum provided that they are credible in the sense that they lead to the full conviction of the truth, and not just probability, of circumstances causing the fear of persecution.'[5] This document makes

---

[5] UNHCR, 'Background Note on the Safe Country Concept and Refugee Statues,'

clear that would-be refugees are 'not-refugees until proved otherwise.' If such a procedure represents the general standard adopted by UNHCR all over the world, the Libyan crisis and the claims of would-be refugees brought into question the tenability of the very principles of international protection determined by the Geneva Convention. Due to the presence of more than 1.5 million migrant workers in Libya, the outbreak of the war produced an unprecedented outflow of 'third-country nationals' into Egypt and Tunisia. Now, the criteria for recognising the status of asylum emerged in an interview with the UNHCR Commission, during which people were asked 'why did you leave your country of origin?' instead of interrogating the reasons why they escaped Libya, that is their country of residence or in any case the country where they had worked for years as a migrant. The Arab revolutions have in some sense foregrounded the present untenability of the logic of asylum system and its disregard for the reality of the international labor regime which demands the movement of people all over the world. 'All of us fled from Libya, from a war' rejected refugees stated during their sit-in protest in Tunis 'and so no distinction should be made among us, between those deserving of protection and those who do not.' If at first the rejected refugees were sheltered and assisted by UNHCR, despite spatial segregation, since October 2012 no food and medical assistance has been provided to them. Moreover, those who were employed by NGOs in the camp were dismissed from work so that the only possibility of getting food comes from finding an informal job in the village of Ben Guerdane, where the rate of unemployment exceeds 30% along with the rest of Tunisia which is now experiencing economic crisis. In response to the protests of the rejected refugees and to the political denunciation of certain local and international activist groups, the UNHCR replied that 'rejected refugees are not people of our concern, so we are by no means obliged to take care of them' adding that 'in a time of crisis, we have to cut the costs for managing the camp and the assistance provided to denied refugees until October was not owed.'[6] In other words, rejected refugees do not fulfill UNHCR's criteria of 'eligibility,' namely the eligibility for getting the privileged status of refugee, as an exception to the rule within the humanitarian game of 'wait-and-bounce.' Indeed, it is a mechanism which works by leaving the majority of would-be refugees

---

July 26, 1991, EC/SCP/68. Available: http://www.refworld.org/docid/3ae68ccec.html. Date Accessed: September 9, 2013.

[6] Interview with the UNHCR commissioner in Zarzis (Tunisia), December, 30 2012.

stranded, tying them to a space and to a certain 'mobility profile' - economic migrant/refugee/vulnerable subject, determining whether they are
to be resettled or not - a profile which risks being 'revoked' at any point
by UNHCR's commissioners. 'They are people that are not our concern'
really means that 'those existences are not visible for us, and even less are
they pertinent to us; to someone else goes the task of governing them.' In
fact, rejected refugees exist precisely because humanitarian government
generates a 'marginal' production: by labelling some as 'rejected refugees,'
the politics of asylum de facto makes up 'illegal' migrants: in granting the
'privilege of asylum' to the few, the mechanism of international protection
excludes the majority as non-eligible.[7] On the other hand, the mechanism
of illegality activated and fostered by the asylum regime - through the
production of the denied refugees, namely of economic migrants - is not
recognized by the governmentality of the humanitarian:

> We do not say that denied refugees are illegal migrants. This is a
> question out of our domain of concern: we simply say that they
> cannot be protected under the criteria of the asylum system. Thus,
> we can say who they are NOT, while it's of competence of na-
> tion-States to decide upon their juridical status.

To a certain extent, this is a strategy designed to chase away those 'unplaceable' subjects, and at the same time encourages them to do so. But
on this point we must proceed with caution. The mechanism of making
some people's life of no value for governmental agencies, and the claim
that these people are 'not our concern,' nevertheless requires the ongoing
control and monitoring of their movements. In the case of Choucha, the
passports of the rejected refugees are to-date still in the hands of UNHCR
which only releases the documents on the proviso that the person return
to their country of origin. The logic of a 'layered' protection is intertwined
with a substantial limitation of mobility: a unilateral pact, set in place by
the humanitarian regime which locates an exchange of security-mobility
at its core. The control over mobility patterns is articulated in relation to
the practice of getting rid of some of the 'unplaceable' subjects. Getting
rid, I have to clarify, in the sense of letting the would-be refugees becom-

---

[7] Despite to the exceptional situation - the high number of third country nationals -
in the case of Choucha camp, most have been recognized as refugees, in opposition
to the current percentage of asylum recognition in the European Countries.

ing undetected presences within Tunisian space, encouraging them 'to find a job here, to value one's own skills as economic migrant.'[8] Therefore, on the one hand the so-called migration regime is actually composed of and fragmented into different and sometimes conflicting governmental agencies, research centres and States, each one with very specific tasks and domains of concern. On the other hand, despite UNHCR's formulation 'they are not people of our concern' - which from a legal standpoint is correct - the subjectivities they produce largely exceed their jurisdiction: put simply, the figure of the denied refugee is the result of the partitioning mechanism of the asylum, and not of migration governance at large.

The crisis of what? The free-wheeling of the sorting mechanism of migration governmentality

Returning here to the paradigm of 'migration (in) crisis,' the focus on Choucha has unfolded, revealing the slippages and the ambivalences at stake in the use of that formula. Crisis refers here to the potential turmoil and demand for resettlement in Europe in response to the presence of would-be refugees on Tunisian soil. At the same time it addresses the condition of being caught in a crisis that migrants, rejected refugees, asylum seekers, refugees who remain unresettled and a plethora of 'troubling' forms of mobility as experienced by those displaced. Nevertheless, I'm not suggesting that these *impasses* have been generated by the Libyan crisis. What I am referring to here are not exceptions to the functioning of the government of the humanitarian; and it's not in terms of violations of the rules of asylum that one could begin to tackle both the sorting out of a 'migration population' - the partition between refugees, denied refugees, economic migrants etc., - and the exclusion of some of them from the regime of protection/assistance. If we take for granted the framework of the regime of asylum and the 'moral geographies' it traces, and more broadly the migration governmentality which works 'by partitioning,' the way in which would-be refugees and migrants have been stranded, bounced or classified into migration profiles does not differ enormously from other contexts. Rather, the 'Libyan crisis' has finally exploded the untenable-ness of the country of an origin-based logic of asylum; or to be more precise, this was made visible through the protests carried out by denied refugees in the name of their common (forced) flight from Libya.

---

[8] Interview with the UNHCR's commissioner in Zarzis, December 2012.

In a certain sense, they put into place a 'politics of the governed,'[9] stressing the fact of being all subject to the mechanisms of migration governance and, at the same time, withstanding the Libyan war conflict: the claim of the remaining 200 denied refugees (officially there are 312 but many of them have 'disappeared' from UNHCR headcounts, since food distribution was stopped meant de facto that many people have become uncountable) 'we are not migrants, we are all refugees and victims' could be read in principle as a reinforcement of the longstanding discourse/logic on the distinction made between the 'beggar' migrants, who move in order to find a better life, and the forced displacement of persons fleeing a country for 'political' reasons. And in this way, such a discourse could ultimately strengthen the exclusionary logic of legitimate mobility. However, in this case the claim-protest has played out in a rather strategic way, somehow reversing and counter-acting the exclusionary logic of partitioning which underpins a politics of protection, imposing another meaning onto this. In contrast to the mechanism of *partage* and to the country-based criteria (people coming from 'safe' or 'unsafe' countries) the rejected refugees demanded resettlement away from Tunisia since all had escaped from a war. Faced with the primacy of the safe/unsafe list and the emphasis on national origins, rejected refugees imposed the law of their spatial presence - the fact of being there, when the war started, and being there along with others, who have subsequently become refugees, rejected or deportable migrants - and of their being unavoidably governed by the 'migration game of bouncing' which strands people, either fixing them in spaces or forcing them to wander without a place. Moreover, they reversed the very logic of (un)safety, demanding 'to be resettled in a safe country,' thus excluding the possibility of remaining in Tunisia via with the temporary protection status, pushed for by UNHCR.

Secondly, the 'Libyan crisis' and revolutionized Tunisia made see also how the economic and the epistemic and political crisis in migration governmentality brought to the fore and sharpened the functioning of certain mechanisms of migration government. The multiple crises exploded the unquestioned functioning of the 'partitioning machine' of the asylum system and, at some points, some of those mechanisms misfired. But where for the Tunisian migrants who had arrived in Italy in 2011 the temporary short-circuiting of the partitioning system worked to some of their advan-

---

[9] P. Chatterjee, *The Politics of the Governed. Reflections on Popular Politics in Most of the World* (New York, NY: Columbia University Press, 2004).

tages as a result of the concession of a temporary permit, if we turn our attention to the asylum seekers in Tunisia we see that the 'epistemic crisis' of migration-related governmental agencies and the confusion produced by 'complex migrations'[10] was to the detriment of would-be migrants, literally stuck inside political and juridical impasses. Let me explain this point further. The migration crisis is recognized by international agencies such as IOM, UNCPD and UNHCR as, at the same time a crisis in 'migration governmentality,' or better an epistemic crisis within the mechanism that organises people, determines juridical subjectivities and spatializes their conduct of these subjectivities. 'The difficulty of responding to a complex crisis is that a complex of mobility practices is also at play: mixed migration flows formed of people moving for diverse reasons and with different aims, generate challenges for migration management.'[11] Thus, the economic crisis which dramatically impacts on migrants' lives and further tightens already restrictive European policies of asylum and resettlement is coupled with the crisis of the 'migration partitioning mechanism.' But at a closer glance the 'partitioning log jam' of the migration regime in classifying people and in fixing their profiles is at least in part, as the governmental agencies themselves recognize, the outcome/effect of migration upheavals: practices of mobility which - in this case running parallel with the revolutionary events of the Arab uprisings and as one of their outcomes - to some degree exceeds existing partitioning criteria, and cannot fit into those existing migration profiles. What the governmental lexicon calls 'complex migration flows,' corresponds precisely to the juridical confusion generated by migration practices that were not 'expected' and whose combination of status, citizenship and country of residence makes it difficult to trace an uncontested juridical profile.

The truly 'bogus' are the governors: 'we are the part of an international affair and you must solve it'

Just after the outbreak of the Libyan war migrant workers coming from Libya momentarily upset the 'smooth' functioning of the governmental

---

[10] IOM, 'Protecting Migrants During Times of Crisis.'

[11] IOM, 'Moving to Safety: Migration Consequences of Complex Crisis,' International Dialogue on Migration 2012: Managing Migration in Crisis Situations. Available: http://www.iom.int/jahia/webdav/shared/shared/mainsite/microsites/IDM/workshops/moving-to-safety-complex-crises-2012/Chairs-Summary-EN.pdf. Date Accessed: September 9, 2013.

partitioning system. Then, as asylum seekers, they embedded their condition of governed-subjects, calling UNHCR and the European Union to account for their duties as both responsible for a war and as proponent of human rights. 'Since they govern us, they must take care of us. And they need to comply with the principles and the work they are expected to do: they should take decisions upon the rights they talk about; human rights,' while 'humanitarian forces that in principle should defend our rights mock us and strip us of those rights.'[12] Therefore, following this discourse the governors become the truly 'bogus' to be opposed and unmasked. 'We know our condition is an international affair, we are part of an international problem which concerns also Palestine and Iraq. So we don't leave the camp, we do not accept their game and we will stay here as long as the work of UNHCR remains unfinished.'[13] In fact, in Choucha the UNHCR produced various degrees of unprotection among which the denied are obviously those with no place at all, 'a nowhere as their condition of existence.'[14] Besides these, among the recognized refugees there are around 100 people who have been labelled as not eligible for resettlement outside Tunisia; people ineligible for the resettlement programs; people with legal precedents, people taking part in social disturbances and people charged with terrorism. Then, following the pre-selective screening carried out by UNHCR, nation-States interested in resettling people select the most suitable profiles among the refugees and refuse many on the grounds of 'security reasons.'[15] In this way, in Choucha some of the 'official' refugees - around 150 people according to UNHCR estimates - won't be resettled at all, despite their juridical status. At the moment, the unselected refugees are those from Arab countries, Palestine and Iraq.

The moral economy of resettlement and the secrecy of humanitarian knowledge

The complex mechanism of resettlement, as a technology for governing migration population needs to be situated within a broader moral economy of states during a time of crisis. A system of economic incentives has

---

[12] Interview with the group of rejected refugees at Choucha camp, August 2012.

[13] Interview with the group of rejected refugees at Choucha camp, December 2012.

[14] F. Sossi, *Migrare. Spazi di confinamento e Strategie di Esistenza* (Milan: Il Saggiatore, 2007).

[15] Interview with the head office of UNHCR in Zarzis.

been activated by the European Union which grants up to 6000 euros per refugee for States agreeing to resettle them.[16] Beyond Europe, countries like Brazil enter the program in order to gain recognition as democratic states on the world stage. However, the criteria that every country adopts for selecting and excluding people remain 'secret.' So, if on the one hand we might hazard a guess that skilled migrants are the most desired refugees, on the other hand taking that for granted would mean corroborating the discourse of migration governmentality which at this moment is promoting such a politics. Conversely, if in place of a cursory snapshot on Choucha camp we explore in-depth the effective functioning of the resettlement process, we realize that actually selection criteria we might assume are not in fact primary. As the refugees in Choucha have understood waiting for their turn, Canada accepts only francophone people, Portugal tends to take those refused by other countries, Denmark the vulnerable cases, and Sweden and Norway prefer women. The knowledge possessed by would-be refugees at Choucha camp involves a kind of lateral thinking here. Perfectly aware of being stranded on the international chessboard of the politics of mobility, they are nevertheless able to work out their future location via a process of deduction, observing how despite the formal criteria, the dividing up of people is really made. What is supposed to constitute a shared and standardized process, is revealed under close scrutiny to be a mechanism of 'exclusionary knowledge.' And the fact of being wise to one's rights and the formal procedures of the asylum system is not much help in this case. Despite their in-depth knowledge of the international law on protection and of the geopolitical context, the would-be refugees of Choucha must acquire a more lateral understanding of the way in which their lives are managed. Who holds their passports, how they have been profiled by different states, where their dossiers have been sent, the current list of safe/unsafe countries are all unknowns to the refugees. The list of safe and unsafe countries was established by UNHCR in the late 1980s with the explicit intention of pushing through the asylum procedure, acting a 'tactic of discharge' which jettisons a part of them as 'uncountable' and 'not of concern.'[17] The telling of 'untruths'[18] that would-

---

[16] See: http://www.resettlement.eu/journey/understanding-resettlement. Date Accessed: September 9, 2013.

[17] K. Hailbronner, 'The Concept of "Safe Country" and Expeditious Asylum Procedures: A Western European Perspective', *International Journal of Refugee Law*, 5:1 (1993).

[18] F. Fanon, *Towards the African Revolution* (New York, NY: Grove Press, 1994).

be refugees are assumed to engage in is not even 'examined' if a 'presumption of groundlessness' in their demand is fixed from the beginning due to their 'original guilt,' namely the provenance from a 'safe country.' Up against this dispossession of knowledge concerning their lives and their spatial location, it's almost impossible for denied and stranded refugees to definitively take flight from the moral geography of the asylum system and its regime of knowledge. Moreover, 'caught in crisis' and trapped in between the folds of the sorting mechanism of migration management, would-be refugees are denied the conditions of possibility for instantiating another language, a language which disengages from and gets rid of the paradigm of the asylum. Instead, they have demanded to be treated as governed subjects, trying to 'bend' the existing norms and criteria to their own purposes, claiming that international institutions are responsible for their displacement ('UNHCR and international agencies made the wrong list: we are stranded here because of the war. So, we demand Western countries take responsibility for our condition'). Caught in crisis, would-be refugees fleeing Libya have to some degree and at certain points poured the crisis on the logic of protection. However, the crisis and the inconsistency of a common asylum system impacted just on the migrants: in the Tunisian revolutionized space, the unprecedented arrival of hundred thousands of third-country nationals resulted into the production of rejected refugees as the condition for the 'exclusionary' allocation of the international protection could be maintained. Indeed, the demand for a refugee status extended to all is a claim which, by stretching the borders of the international protection ('refugee status for all coming from Libya') also challenges the present tenability of the very logic of the asylum, which relies on a downgrading partitioning rationale - economic migrants/refugees, bogus refugee/vulnerable subjects, denied asylum seeker/resettled person. Faced with the incorrigibility of these demands,[19] UNHCR has adopted what I would call a 'tactic of discharge,' producing denied refugees who actually could neither move nor remain in any place except through returning to their country of origin with the 700 euros 'offered' by IOM in exchange for their spatial fixation, allowing them to become imperceptible/undetectable presences within Tunisian space looking for informal jobs or wandering in search of shelter. In this regard, the elusiveness of numbers concerning the denied refugees in the camp (312 accord-

---

[19] N. De Genova, 'The Queer Politics of Migration: Reflections on Illegality and Incorrigibllity', *Studies in Social Justice*, 4:2 (2010).

ing to UNHCR estimations, with 200 officially 'counted' since November 2012) depends on the tactic of chasing away and discharging deployed by the humanitarian actors that de facto push some people into abandoning the camp in order to find informal jobs, move to Tunisian towns or finally returning to Libya. To discharge the many in order to care of the few, is not a new phenomenon emerging from the 'migration (in) crisis' but rather constitutes the underlying logics of the international politics of asylum. However, as I stressed above, this rationale became more visible within a space of 'crisis.' And, meanwhile, in the context of the Arab uprisings it also has resulted in a temporary disturbance and free-wheeling of the partitioning system. In the case of Libya, the 'migration (in) crisis,' unlike other historical paradigms and times of crisis, has not worked as a moment for radically reassembling power relations or for the transition to another regime of government. Rather, along with migrants, the migration regime also seems not so much in crisis but fractured and fissured from within via the opposing interests, forces and logics which are internal to its functioning.[20]

A parenthesis on the 'regime'

Drawing on 'regime analyses' on migrations,[21] it's worth reminding ourselves of Foucault's clarifications on the notion of dispositif :

> a dispositif is a thoroughly heterogeneous ensemble consisting of discourses, institutions, architectural forms, regulatory decisions, laws, administrative measures, scientific statements [...] a formation which has as its major function at a given historical moment that of responding to an urgent need. The apparatus thus has a dominant strategic function.[22]

And it's precisely in these terms that, I contend, the reference to a mi-

---

[20] Maybe the question should be posed in these terms: Is there, after all, something like a cohesive migratory regime or it is nothing but a name given to policies, discourses and techniques of bordering which frantically try to respond to migrant upheavals?

[21] S. Hess, 'Denaturalizing Migration. Theory and Methods of an Ethnographic Analysis', *Population, Space, Place*, 18:4 (2012).

[22] M. Foucault, 'The Confession of the Flesh', in *Power/Knowledge, Selected Interviews and Other Writings, 1972-1977* (London: Harvester Press, 1980), pp. 195-196

gration regime could eventually be useful. In fact, far from indicating a coherent array of politics and a shared script of government, the idea that something like a 'migration governmentality' exists is precisely what needs to be questioned. Instead, the regime in place is rather a set of more or less linked heterogeneous discourses, techniques of control and instantiations of borders which are put into place in face of the turbulence of migration. Obviously such a regime is not a mere response to a 'state of crisis,' since migration policies tend also to function by pre-empting migrant strategies; and it is not even a question of investigating a chronology of migrations and migration policies. But despite all this, the re-assemblage of the techniques of bordering, the proliferation of new systems of monitoring and the redefinition of what governing migration means, all these technologies are mobilized because migrants constantly displace and try to dodge these mechanisms. And the migration turmoil occurring at the time of the Arab uprisings has made this point glaringly visible. It suffices to dig up statements and documents released by the European Union in 2011 and 2012 to find evidence of this and to see how new 'pre-emptive' borders are envisaged in response to the 'migration crisis.'

> *The instability in certain North African countries and the Middle East led to mass influxes of persons at the Southern border of the EU [...] These developments have increased the visibility of the external border management questions, highlighting the importance of having effective systems for controlling the borders, maintaining security, managing asylum applications and implementing visa-issue processes.*[23]

Through these words, which blatantly acknowledge the 'migration crisis' as provoking a crisis in the governmental machine, the European Union has inaugurated Eu-Lisa, the new agency for the management of databases like Eurodac and Sis II, and for the control of all monitoring IT-systems. An agency that reinforces the displacement of the border before (surveillance systems in the Mediterranean and Visa mechanisms) and beyond (the digital information stored on the European database) the geopolitical line where the agency of Frontex is still working.

---

[23] EU-Lisa, 'Regulations establishing a European Agency for the operational management of large-scale IT systems in the area of freedom, security and justice' (2013). Available: http://eur-lex.europa.eu/LexUriServ/LexUriServ.do?uri=CELEX-:32011R1077:EN:NOT. Date Accessed: September 9, 2013.

The politics of presence: the refusal to stay in one's own place by taking one's own space

What the spatial upheavals of migrants highlight are the limits of a hyper-governmentality grid mobilized for reading the politics of mobility and the mechanism of protection. In fact, far from taking charge of the lives of all would-be refugees, the majority tend to be discharged even though their conduct of mobility - their displacements - continue to be monitored - as the custody of their passports by UNHCR confirms. In particular, an episode involving refugees en-route to Tunis highlights this conditioned and monitored (im)mobility very clearly. Ben Guerdane, March 26, 2013: on their way to the World Social Forum that takes place in Tunis, a group of 96 refugees from Choucha camp traveling on three buses were stopped at Ben Guerdane by the Tunisian national police. 'You are not allowed to circulate in the Tunisian territory', the policemen argue, disregarding the special permit that the refugees had obtained from the Defence Ministry to go to the Forum. They had taken the occasion of the Social Forum to make their voices heard, as the name of their blog also suggested 'Voice of Choucha',[24] and to demand the UNHCR 'finish its work', acknowledging their status as Libyan war refugees and resettling them in safe countries. After their confrontation with the police, eight of them succeeded in reaching the Tunisian capital by group taxi sneaking away from the police block. The next day, only half of the people who had been stopped by the Tunisian police managed to arrive at the Forum. There, non-resettled refugees and rejected refugees split into two groups choosing to set up two different protests: the former started a hunger strike lasting for twenty days in front of UNHCR headquarters, while the latter decided to demonstrate at the entrance to the Forum.

The decision by rejected refugees and non-resettled refugees to set up different protests as a result of the different 'mobility profiles' given to them by UNHCR, draws our attention to the ambivalences that surrounding the issue of pluralizing and differentiating migrations. In fact, if on the one hand the splitting of the Choucha group was the result of their strategic consideration that two different demands should be addressed to UNHCR, on the other hand such a decision also highlights their complicity with those categories - rejected refugees/ recognized refugees; and,

---

[24] See http://voiceofchoucha.wordpress.com/. Date Accessed: September 9, 2013.

moreover, it could be seen also as a success of migration governmentality in hampering the building of any possible alliance or common ground for struggle among migrants. In a nutshell, the epistemology of the humanitarian regime is predicated on the multiplication of mobility profiles that ultimately fragments migrant struggles. In this regard, the important task is to pluralize the migration catchphrase, stressing the heterogeneity of migrants' conditions and of their stories, should however take into consideration the strategies of *fragmenting-by-differentiation* that migration agencies appropriate. Thus, the stakes becomes a question of how to keep together the necessity to unpack the term 'migration' affirming the multiplicity of migrants' conditions whilst envisaging a pluralisation that does not work towards dividing and weakening possible common struggles by migrants stranded in the same space.

'They are not people of our concern, any more' repeated the UNHCR Officer in Zarzis 'so it's not our problem what they do with their lives. They are not vulnerable or at risk, it's their lives, we are not responsible for them and it's not our fault if they die going to Italy by boat.' The definitive closure of the camp is expected by June 2013, when all the tents will be removed leaving the rejected and the stranded refugees 'out of any concern.' But beyond any demand and public protest, the would-be refugees reversed in a less concealable and more tangible way the politics of no-space that the government of the humanitarian carried out against rejected refugees and stranded asylum seekers. In the face of encouragement to leave the camp and feel responsible for their own lives, most of the rejected refugees have chosen to remain, to stay in order to impose the law of their presence: 'they cannot but see us, they want to make us invisible but we are here,' rejected refugees stress persisting in the space of Choucha. Coming back to the first question 'what does the crisis stand for?' in the Tunisian revolutionized context and in the European space 'disturbed' and cracked by migrant upheavals, we have seen how different orders of crisis overlap and become blurred: migration crisis, migration in crisis, the crisis of the international regime of asylum, the economic crisis impacting on migrants' lives, the epistemic crisis of migration profiles. Nevertheless, what remains is the presence in Tunisian space of out-of-place subjects - the rejected and stranded refugees - to whom literally any space to move or to stay is neither granted nor conceded: by persisting in that space to the last they refuse to stay in their own place,[25] the par-

---

[25] F. Fanon, *The Wretched of the Earth* (London: Grove Books, 2007).

adoxical place of being without a 'legitimate' space to tread upon or the non-choice of returning to one's own country of origin. They refuse to stay at their own place making space for themselves standing in Tunisia, until they are resettled in Western countries. They crack the feasibility of a 'good democracy' to transit to, as conceived by European states gazing at revolutionized spaces. The 'non-democratic condition of democracy'[26] is brought into focus by the out-of-any-place denied refugees. The injunction for a 'democratic transition process' and the model of a procedural democracy become untenable and emptied by the very presence of out-of-place refugees. Their mere persistence and the impossibility for national and international actors not to see them, make us question what migrant upheavals in the Arab uprisings context impose on the exclusionary borders of democracy. There cannot but be people of concern to everybody; and the denied refugees through their spatial takeover, their persisting in Choucha and in Tunisia, demand that space is made for them and that a space in which to move is produced.

---

[26] E. Balibar, 'At the borders of citizenship. A democracy in translation?', *European Journal of Social Theory*, 13:3 (2010).

'We Are Here and We Wait'
AN INTERVIEW WITH K, S and Y

Interviewed by Federica Sossi and Martina Tazzioli, Choucha Camp,
July 2012

K: You are welcome. Interviews don't bother us, rather they support us and can bring us to something. Here at the camp we need journalists and we need to make exchanges and have information, since we have been here at the camp for one year and, you know, one year like this in a camp… Nobody among us is in high spirits. We hope to find a solution to our problem, we arrived here in March 2011, after the outbreak of the Libyan war, we got on a truck and we had many problems down the road in order to find a solution to our problems. We also have problems in our country, the Ivory Coast. Instead, we are in a refugee camp where people have been killed. And so it is unsafe and now we have been rejected by UNHCR, we have not been recognized because we are told we do not meet their criteria. We have explained to them that we are persecuted in our country and every one of us has personal problems: we explained this to them, but they told us that we don't meet UNHCR's criteria. What do they want us to do? What are the criteria that we need to meet? They have demanded we return to Libya or to our country. We are here and our dossiers have been rejected.

Q: So, you are here, and how many of you are there from the Ivory Coast?

K: We don't have the exact number but there are not many of us.

Q: Do you live in this zone of the camp?

K: Yes, we do.

Q: But this is not part of Choucha camp.

K: This zone is the area of the rejected refugees. And it was like this since the beginning. UNHCR does not recognize this zone.

Q: Have you been rejected after claiming asylum?

K: Yes, we have.

Q: And after your demand was rejected you were put in this zone outside of the camp?

K: No, we have were here before our dossiers were examined. Indeed, at the beginning there were problems between the communities in the camp, and so UNHCR told us that it would have to split the camp into different zones. So we were put here, the people from Mali, Senegal and the Ivory Coast.

Q: A little bit far from the other communities?

K: The other communities over there, Darfur, Sudan, Eritrea, Ethiopia: they have all been grouped together, and on the other side of the camp there are those who have been recognized by UNHCR as refugees, because they fall under the criteria of the Geneva Convention, and so they didn't have any problems. Somalian asylum seekers that come today are recognized as refugees.

Q: So, right at the beginning when you arrived they split the camp into those who meet the criteria, as an Ethiopian or an Eritrean, and those about whom doubts existed? And so, did they actually divide up the camp in this way?

K: Yes, they split the camp. But at the beginning, when journalists or humanitarian agencies came, to meet refugees, we were not even aware of their presence, they got out of their cars, and they used to go directly to the other area of the camp; they did not come here, and we cannot speak with journalists. But we are not revolutionary people, we are intellectuals and we can tell the truth to journalists, the truth about this camp, while those who are here in the other zone keep quiet. Instead, we tell the truth because we want defend our rights.

Q: And were all the communities out of the camp rejected by UNHCR?

K: They did not give refugee status to some communities, such as, for instance, some of the francophone peoples, including not only the Ivory Coast, but also Chad, Mali, Senegal. And we have been rejected.

Q: But this is very similar to Italy, because also in Italy if you come from the Ivory Coast sometimes you are recognized and sometimes not, while if you are Somalian you are given refugee status. So I think it's the same partitioning. A person from Senegal doesn't receive the status, nor those from Mali; or maybe now yes, because of the war, but a year ago persons from Mali did not receive it. Except if they proved they were persecuted. And maybe the division they make here is the same as elsewhere. And maybe they started to think in these terms from the beginning.

K: Yes, I know, but those who arrived in Italy and in Lampedusa from the Ivory Coast they were given the humanitarian temporary protection.

Q: It's not precisely like that, there are many refugees from the Ivory Coast coming from Libya and who are in some holding centres - although not like this camp - while their status is decided. Now many associations are demanding that in Italy asylum seekers are given at least humanitarian status. But at this time the Italian state had not decided, yet.

K: Because the problem is that those people are like us, they arrived from Libya and before the outbreak of the war refugee status was not recognized, or maybe it was recognized for those from the Ivory Coast because of the war in their country. But you see, since 2001 we were no longer in the Ivory Coast; and now UNHCR tells us that we can return to our country. But do you think that, if I could, I would be in this situation? I would have never come to Choucha.

Q: Did you have a shop in Libya?

K: Yes. A textile shop.

Q: And when the war started you needed to close the shop?

K: Yes. And if we are here in this situation, which is so volatile, they cannot tell us to come back.

Q: Did you receive different treatment in comparison to the others?

K: Yes, very different.

Q: And what about medical assistance?

S: There is no medical assistance here. But you know that all those who are in Italy have magnetic cards for medical care, even though they are not still recognized as refugees. I have many friends who arrived in Lampedusa and they have these cards, but here we don't have these. Why? It's the same entity in the world that manages all the refugees. There were donations, but here nobody takes care of you, when someone gets sick it's a big problem. And an old Senegalese man died here. The stress can kill, you know?

Q: But are the Danish Relief and the Islamic Relief here in the camp?

S: Yes. But they do not provide real assistance, and the food that they give us is not good at all. While those who are in Italy and claim asylum are very well looked after, they do not lack anything. But here the food is bad and it's not cooked. We cook the food by ourselves, in our tents. We are obliged to prepare the food by ourselves, because it is not good. The base of health is food, and when you don't eat well, you get ill. And our problem here is documents. We don't know where to go. For example, I left the Ivory Coast in 2007 and I haven't seen my family since 2007.

Q: Do you have children?

S: Yes, I'm married I have two children, they are not in the Ivory Coast, they fled the war and I also left because of the war. I have a family, two children and my sons were in Mali before the beginning of the war; now they are in a calamitous situation, when I think about all these problems I have a headache, I become crazy. And I cannot go to Mali.

Q: And you? What is your situation?

K: I've been rejected, I received the definitive result, and all those who are here in this tent have been rejected, we all filed an appeal and usually when you do that, the second time you get it. Because when you are rejected the first time, you are requested to do something supplementary.

Q: So, the appeal needs to be addressed to the same institution that rejected you, namely UNHCR...

K: Yes, to UNHCR.

Q: So, could you tell us about the procedure? Were you registered here or at the frontier?

K: The first time when we arrived, we were registered in order to get a number. We were registered once we arrived at the camp. And when we arrived here UNHCR started to register us. Many associations were at the border but they did not register us. They took all the documents and then put us into a truck and brought us here at the camp, and then UNHCR and Croissant Rouge registered us. We told them that we came from the Ivory Coast.

Q: So, you were asked if you came from the Ivory Coast and then, for this reason, they took your passports. So, this was a politics decided at the beginning... to take passports off people so that they have no right of circulation anymore and then put them into a camp. And was it the same procedure for all of you?

S: Yes, it was the same.

Q: So, they put you in a truck and they brought you here. But did they place you in sectioned-off areas?

S: No, when we arrived there were thousands of people, and so they put us all together. But then there were problems between communities. Some people were killed.

Q: In May 2011?

K: Yes. There were problems between the communities and so they decided to split the camp on the basis of the different communities. They said: we put the French communities together, all those who can understand each other together, and the other communities like Somalia, South Sudan, Sudan Darfur, Eritrea, Ethiopia, were put over there, in that area. And now we are all here, since that time there have been no more discussions and disagreements among us. We are here with Liberians, Gambians, Malians, but all of us have been rejected. We came here before being rejected.

Q: When were the procedures carried out?

K: Procedures were made step by step, and after some time the result was negative.

Q: And what you have to tell in order to undergo the procedure?

Y: Procedures are personal, and they depend on the experience you lived in your country. And every one of us has a story to tell, the story you lived but it is personal.

Q: And so you told them your personal story.

Y: Yes, I told them my story from the start to the end, my entire story.

Q: So, the first time you were interviewed did you tell them your entire story?

Y: Yes, sure. You need to tell your story in order for your story to be taken into account. But there are too many problems that took place here. And what hurts me in this whole situation is that we have been rejected. We have been recently asked to take a supplementary exam but then they need to give us the documents.

Q: So, first you did the interview and then you were asked to do a supplementary exam?

K: No, the appeal. And then we were required to take a supplementary exam and we went to Zarzis.

Q: Why?

K: Because the UNHCR office is there, and here at Choucha there were problems with the Tunisians that worked in the camp and who wanted to make demonstrations. And UNHCR feared them, they didn't work here for two months.

Q: But this problem was with the residents of Ben Guerdane.

K: Yes, with those who work in the canteen and in the warehouses. They were angry because the UNHCR office told them that the budget was over. But Tunisians want to work, and so there were many problems and many demonstrations.

Q: But when did it happen?

K: I don't remember, in April or in May 2012.

Q: And so did you go to Zarzis for your dossier?

K: Yes, I went there with him and we met the international protection, we met the director. Two weeks later, six or seven of us from the Ivory Coast were called, and we were rejected. We refuse to sign and until now we are here. He was the last person to receive an answer and now his result is negative. This is what happened.

S: And at the beginning rejected refugees were told they would be given an allowance to return to their country of origin and restart their life. 500 dollars. For restarting a better life. 500 dollars? You think that one could restart a life with children that have to go to school, you think that it's feasible with 500 dollars? You think that it's possible if you need to find a house? 500 dollars it's not money. And we were told if you want we can give you 500 dollars to restart a better life And this hurts, it hurts too much for people who have lost everything.

K: Ok, but this is not so very important. My problem is how to carry on my life. My problem is that I cannot solve the problem anywhere. How can I return to my country if people are being persecuted there? I'm 40, I'm not a child, I don't' like staying here, I'm not here because I like it, if I'm here it is because I have a problem and I' m very scared about the idea of returning to my country. My children miss me. And the same thing with my brothers. These persons must understand that if we are here we have problems; the others went back to their countries. And I think that UNHCR's people have to understand, I don't' dispute their criteria, but they must understand, it's their job. I didn't need money, I left because of the persecution and now they propose to give me money, but what I can do with money? Money against life? It's not possible. There are 30 people from the Ivory Coast who returned three last year and that have now come back because of the persecutions. All of them left again, some to Mali or to Morocco, where a visa is not required. We know the truth about the Ivory Coast, while you don't know because you are a foreigner. The current president... there are still killings and aggressions, bloodsheds, and the State is not able to protect all the population. And in this affair it's not even a question of the State. If we are told that there are 13 refugees died, the State is involved. A tuck was assaulted and 13 people died, and the State was involved.

Q: When did UNHCR tell you that you would be given 500 dollars?

K: At the beginning we were told that we could also go back to Libya, but we left Libya because of the war.

Q: And were you told that you could not stay here anymore?

S: We are told we have three choices: going back to Libya, to our country or staying in Tunisia but without refugee status.

Q: And here you have nothing, not even water?

S: No, we have water like refugees, we receive food but we lack medical assistance. But the great problem is being rejected and we do not agree. As far as medical assistance is concerned there are no big problems, the real problem is to be rejected and we have said that we don't recognize this rejection. It is like during a trial, when you are judged, and you say 'no'. We have told everything we could tell, and so they should revise our dossiers but they do not revise them. Too many things take place in a camp, now I don't' like to enter into details but there are too many things.

Q: What?

S: There is too much discrimination. There are people who went to Lampedusa, they get lost they came back here and then were recognized as refugees. We have been here for more than one year and we are rejected, while they went to Lampedusa, then to Tunisia and they were recognized as refugees. This is not normal. The Ivory Coast recognizes the international right of refugees, we have 100,000 Liberian people there. Instead we are in different countries and we are not recognized. Why? We have the same blood and we are different? It's not normal, it's not right?

Q: After the Ivory Coast where did you go?

K: I moved to Morocco, passing through Algeria. In Morocco I was caught by the police and then I went to Libya where I stayed for 4 years, while in Morocco 6 months and in Algeria too. One year in Mali.

Q: Were you in the forests close to Ceuta and Melilla? And were you repressed by the police?

K: Yes. And then I escaped from Libya because of the war.

Q: And did you have problems in Ben Guerdane?

K: It's somehow like in Libya, there are people who treat us as slaves.

Q: But are you talking about last year?

S: No, this year.

Q: So, you are saying that there is not so much difference between Libyans and the residents of Ben Guerdane?

S: No, after all Ben Guerdane is almost Libya.
Q: But Tunisians say that they have been very kind to you.

Y: Tunisians?

Q: Yes, those we spoke to. They say that the refugees at Choucha are happy.

Y: But they are defending their country. Do you believe that an Italian citizen could say that Italians are not kind people? Anyway, people in Ben Guerdane have a bad mentality... they killed us. We did not die except there.

Q: We interviewed someone in Ben Guerdane who told us that those who killed refugees in May 2011 were from the Mafia working with Libya and that they are not very beloved even in Ben Guerdane.

K: I don't think so, because there were also young people with guns, people from Ben Guerdane and there was also the Tunisian army. And also the military took part in those events. And it is still here now, in the other camp. Besides, this country is not stable. Everybody knows that, it is not stable because there were not political elections and there are demonstrations in Kasserine and as soon as there are they protest. And so who could stay here? Those who are in Zarzis have an open mind. In Zarzis you can walk in the street like the others and they don't kill you, while in Ben Guerdane they can kill you. And there is a big difference between Ben Guerdane, Djerba and Zarzis. It is a city of smuggling, they sell fuel and they exchange money, it's a city of Mafiosi and so there is no security there.

Q: Do you go there quite often?

K: Yes, because it is the closest city to the Libyan border and we have things to buy there and we can earn some money. We are not paid here, while in Italy they take 50 euros every two weeks. And in any case we need some money. Instead, here in the camp there is a mafia. Nevertheless, they had a lot of subventions for managing the camp. Angelina Jolie came here and the African Bank gave money. It's a bank for the Africans and they gave a budget for the camp, without considering all the different associations. And where does this money go? They say that the budget is now over, but associations are still here –like Islamic relief- and so they have funding, the longer they stay here the more funds they get. We are not children all of us went to school, we know our rights. President ...When you know your rights people are scared of you and those who don't know anything of their rights are those in the other part of the camp. For these reasons UNHCR doesn't want journalists to come here, while the other people of the camp, those recognized as refugees, are not able to speak, they agree to do what they are told. But this is not life; life is everyone with their own rights, human rights. So these organizations don't want the camp to close. This camp was opened as a transitory camp, but it has now been open for more than a year. And what does it mean? If it is a transitory camp, it should close, but this camp has been open for more than one year. Moreover, Tunisians who work here have to feed their families and they always succeed in getting paid, while we have to remain here but it is impossible. At times the storm comes, the phenomenon called the storm of the desert and it comes everywhere, you cannot breathe and you want to kill yourself. No, it's not a storm like today, this is nothing. What do our lives become? We are traumatized?

Q: Are there also any children here?

S: Yes, sure.

Q: But also in this zone of the camp?

S: Yes, there are families with children like the family from Chad... Women with three or four children who got sick.

Q: And do they go to school in the camp?

S: Yes. Our problems need to find a solution. This camp should be a transitory camp but everybody's problems must be resolved first.

Q: And how did you organize among yourselves? How do you go to speak with the authorities of the camp?

Y: UNHCR organizes meetings every two weeks with all the communities.

Q: And are you asked to participate in these meetings? Or as rejected are you excluded from those meetings?

Y: No, everybody has the right to participate. Every community has a representative that can participate and then he comes and reports what happened. But since there have been these meetings, nothing concrete has been done. At the last meeting they talked about human rights and of children going to Lampedusa by boat. But if they want to prevent this they need to regularize people, so that they don't have to go to Lampedusa. In Libya there is the sea and ... There are a lot of children who were rejected and so they walk to Libya and there they take a boat. In Libya there are still bombs. Libya is a country in which there were more than 3000 candidates in the political elections.

Q: I read that last month you asked UNHCR to have a meeting.

S: Yes, but they refused. And we wanted to say that the problem is that of *sans papiers,* namely of the rejected.

Q: How many?

S: Around 300, or 200 and something, it's nothing; we could all be resettled in one country. They could also send all of us to one country. There are many countries that need people, for jobs. Maybe an Eastern European country, I don't know... If they ask some country it could work. So the real problem now is about the rejected refugees.

Q: But actually, not everybody was resettled.

K: Yes, but those are the asylum seekers who do not have a status yet. Because once you are recognized you have a country of destination. Anyway, they are negotiating with Tunisia for those who do not have a place somewhere else. But we don't have the documents... and when the camp closes, there will be many problems and many deaths here. UNHCR is a very powerful organization, if they find a solution for us there won't be problems, otherwise there will be problems. And if they decide to make us leave the camp by force, such a decision will cause a lot of problems. There are vulnerable cases here, that have been definitively rejected. Someone walks with a cane and there are women with children rejected like us. How is this possible? We can walk and run but where do we go? We need to find a solution for all this. They decided that some minors could start a vocational training here. We are here and we wait, we suffer, we don't have money, we don't work, we have mobile phones and we don't know how to go on living.

Q: And, for instance, how did you get the mobile phone? Do you work in Ben Guerdane?

Y: Yes but these are informal daily jobs, you work today and then maybe you don't work for one week. Ten dinars. You become a beggar. People in Ben Guerdane exploit us because they know we are refugees and maybe they give us 30 euros, or they tell us 'work and then I give you food.'

Q: and did the residents of Ben Guerdane also come here?

Y: No, here there is only a little café and then they sell cigarettes.

Q: Are they Tunisians?

S: Yes, Tunisians from Ben Guerdane.

Q: And how much do you pay for cigarettes?

S: Here 1 dinar, in Ben Guerdane 50 centimes. Here at Choucha everything costs twice. They say that we have money. Watch out! There is a snake here!

Q: What? A snake?

S: Yes, because here there are some snakes. If you want I can show you one of them.

Q: No, no, please.

Y: Now we show you one, so that you realize in what conditions we live here. There are also scorpions here. And these are the snakes of the desert. That's the life at Choucha camp, it's not easy, this is the life at Choucha. Maybe there is a country that in the future wants to take us because all the world knows that here there are rejected refugees. We wait. Now almost every day there are people who leave the camp. Last week 75 people left for Spain and the next one to the US and the next month Germany will take 200 people and we are here. We see people leaving and we wait.

Q: How many people are living in Choucha now?

K: Around two thousand. But the camp today is empty, because many people are leaving.

Q: And are the representatives of the communities who go to UNHCR meetings elected?

K: Usually here we don't have elections. We come to an agreement amongst ourselves and we choose our leader.

Q: And then could you change?

S: Yes, but this is not the problem. There are representative of the communities that are more important than others. This is the problem. There are representatives here that are informed by UNHCR, but we are not given this information, on the situation of the camp, when people leave, everything that happens in the camp. And when we ask for information they don't tell us anything, it's not normal. Now UNHCR has nearly no one employed, but in 2011 there were around 150 people. When we arrived there were more than 150 people from UNHCR because there were a lot of people in the camp.

Q: But were they Tunisians?

Y: No, there were Tunisians but they did not decide on our dossiers. There were also people from Cameroun, Pakistan, India, US, France, Belgium.

All these people came and they interviewed us. And they decided upon our status and so everything depends on them: if they give a good note... here it is like at school... if the person said that the dossier is good, it's fine, otherwise everything is ruined. And we... I did an interview with an African person and maybe he didn't like my country. An African person conducted the interview... I did it with a person called Serge. Four hours of interviews. He asked me many questions. Then he told me now I have to study your dossier and then we give you an answer. After 8 months I still don't have an answer yet. I waited for 8 months. Usually, after the first interview the result has to come out within 2 weeks. I know the procedure, but mine lasted 8 months, this is a dictatorship, then I had the result: rejected in the first instance. I have not been rejected in a definitive way. So, I still had a chance to get the status. I filled I the document for the appeal, arguing my story once again.

Q: But did you fill out the form by yourself?

Y: Sure, I'm not a child. I argued my story and then I went to register the appeal. It was the November 7, 2011. Then, I had to get the final result instead I had to wait four months, only after UNHCR told me to do the complementary in Zarzis. I left to Zarzis with my brother to visit the director of the Civil Protection, Isabelle, she paid attention to us but she was not the person in charge. But since our dossier was very big, we stayed some time with her and I told her that I was persecuted. She asked me if my wife is in Mali. She asked me where she is and I answered that she is hosted by a family there, I also showed her the photo of my children. I took this during a demonstration in the Ivory Coast. She took the image and then made a photocopy of it, I left her office and some days after the result was negative. I say that it is not normal. I left the Ivory Coast the November 28, 2007 after the death of my Dad. He was killed and I demanded asylum in Tunisia, so I've been asylum seeker since 2007, and seniority must count, but the procedures are still in progress. I've been raided in Tunis by the police, during the period of Ben Ali. But I showed them my documents and they tore them up. Not now but before the revolution, but fortunately I had a copy in my email, but the original version was torn up. They took me under preventive arrest. There was an underground prison in Avenue Bourguiba. I found some friends there who were arrested in Lampedusa, then we were photographed. However, I didn't steal. If I could have called the UNHCR office, they would have freed me. Instead they put us in a car and brought us to the frontier, because at that time if you were (raided) arrested you would be brought here, to the frontier, walking across the desert.

Q: and did they bring you here to the frontier?

Y: Yes, at 2 in the morning and you had to walk in the desert towards Libya. And so we remained like that, at the immigration office, every morning they let us go out, giving us something to eat. After two weeks they put us in a cargo and there were 4 people. They brought us to the frontier. We arrived here and the Tunisian army was there. First, they took our things, they took my mobile phone and also my clothes and then they were told that two policemen would have brought us to the frontier and that we had to walk. But it was a little bit behind the frontier. I walked and I tell you that I saw the deaths with my own eyes, and I said to myself: 'if I have to die it's better if I walk in the desert.' And they told us 'you have five years until you can enter here again, you need to go to Libya now and if you come back we shoot you.' And they told that very seriously. 'If you enter here in a clandestine way we shoot you.' We walked, it was, I believe, November 2008, let's say end of 2008. We walked in the desert and before exiting the desert there is salt water, and in the water you don't see anything, there could be snakes, I walked like that in the water, you cross the water, we walked like that, at night, up to Libya. We were followed by wild dogs, but thank God they did not bite us. We arrived at the first Libyan village, a family welcomed us and we told them that we had been expelled and that we needed some water. The woman gave us the water and we had to change our clothes because we were dirty, then we took a taxi towards the first Libyan town, Zwara, and there we hid for a bit, until sunset and then we took a car. This is how I arrived in Libya; there I found a job in a clothes shop, called Calliop, an Italian brand. I worked there for six months, and I also went to the UNHCR office to claim asylum. I was registered in Libya and I was under the protection of UNHCR and I followed the procedure in order to have international protection. They gave me a little card. The day when I had to go to do my interview, I found that the UNHCR was closed, because the Libyan government closed it.

Q: Was the period under Gaddafi that they decided to close it?

Y: Yes. So it was not my fault, otherwise I would have already had the document as refugee. So I didn't know what to do. I remained in Libya and then the war broke out. We were obliged to escape, and this is my little story, if you want. Therefore, we ask God to help us.

Q: How was working in Libya?

Y: In Libya there was much work. But it's a country where they have their own behaviour, because all the Arabs are the same. They have all the same behaviour but it depends on the milieu where you are. If you are in the milieu where there are Arabs, they can hurt you. But there are also some of them who are kind. But the work is paid very well. In Libya we had everything; I had a house, a TV. Usually I sent at least 100 euros to my family. And here I cannot send even 10 euros.

Q: Did you have any problems with discrimination?

Y: Yes, sometimes. In my neighbourhood I had some problems with the Libyans. They treated me as black, terrorist. But I did not reply. They assaulted me; they took my mobile phone and beat me. But I told myself that this is the life, and that consequently it was not a problem. In Libya before the war there were many things like that. Libyans have a lot of money and so they are very pretentious and arrogant. So, also when you take the bus they insult you in Arabic, often they tell you not to get on the bus. And when you get on the bus you see girls with perfume. And this is a thing that you feel and that means 'dégage'. But all this it's life. This is not easy. Thanks a lot and we thank you because you had the idea to come here to meet us, with this sun and with such a hot temperature. So, thank you. I hope that God gives you the strength to do what you are doing.

Q: But our life is much simpler than yours.

S: Here we met all the journalists in the world. But what can we do? We don't have the spirit. Our spirit is elsewhere. Because the Ivory Coast is an unstable country, unsafe, there are problems with circulation and assaults and everybody has weapons. So, I tell myself, if I go back to my country there are those who were against me and that will say 'ah he has come back', and so they could kill me. This is the problem of the Ivory Coast.

This is the fear that all of us have. And this is the reason why we demand international organizations to find a country until there is the political stability that hasn't come. First of all we want to have stability in our country, and so we could be given a humanitarian status. It exists and they could give it to me. And then finding a country, a job for some years, but they don't want to do anything about that.

Q: What do you think that, as Europeans, we could demand and how we could help you?

Y: But you are not journalists?

Q: No, we aren't.

K: Anyway, you can inform the world about our situations through articles and you could do that. You can publish our complaints. Maybe the articles that you publish could be read or seen by some charity organizations. There are charity organizations in Europe that could take care of us, for instance catholic organizations that are everywhere and that could say: 'let's take those persons from there.' Some countries came here to take people, Poland for instance. An organization without any statute came here to take some people.

Q: And you said that there are around 300 persons. How many women and men?

K: I don't know exactly but for sure there are more men than women. But there are also children and old people, we are a mix.

Q: And you, what do you demand?

S: We don't need money, in the Ivory Coast I had money, I had a house, I had everything. We didn't leave our country for economic reasons but because of the persecutions. Some who try to kill you. What would you do? You escape, otherwise you die. What you could do is to launch a message that could help us, saying that we do not demand something eternal but a temporary humanitarian status, until our country is stable. We don't need money, we want to go away from here, but it doesn't matter where. We want stability and we want to work. We don't want to go to a country to drink a coffee at the café, we want a job, and in the Ivory Coast everyone has a job. All Ivoirian people have jobs, Ivoirians who are here could do everything, construction, driver or plumbing. Almost everything. Every time that there are humanitarian voluntary organizations we repeat this. We need help, our families need us, and our families could not benefit from us. My family is in Mali and I have not heard from my family for one year. And Mali is going wrong now. In Mali people are being trained then conscripted for war. I watched that on TV, and this is the same thing as in the Ivory Coast. So I would like my family to leave Mali as soon as possible, but I have not the means to do that.

Q: Did you speak with European organizations?

S: Yes, a lot. I don't know how many. We talked with Lea Baron, she is a journalist, then with Amnesty international and all the organizations that come here to meet us, so it means that they are interested in our story. Sylvie Guillaume, the socialist deputy in the European parliament came here, and she did her utmost demanding UNHCR to help us. And also the French association La Cimade, that defends immigrants, came here and we are in touch with all of them. They are trying to see what they can do. Maybe it takes some time but I think that they could do something. This is the problem. Many journalists and organizations came. And also other French and German associations came and are struggling for us.

Q: Are there any woman among you from the Ivory Coast?

Y: Yes, there was one but she left to Norway. For the rest we are all men, but some of us are married and have a family.

Q: But, for instance, when Norway came here did you understand according to what criteria they choose the people?

K: This is very interesting but we don't know. They hid many things from us. The country that comes doesn't come here, UNHCR decides and it gives the country the communities that it wants. And we are excluded from everything. For instance, Norway and Denmark came and declared they need 100 people and then UNHCR decides.

Q: Yes, I know that it's not up to you to decide. It's the country with UNHCR.

S: Yes, it's like that. There are some countries that want the rejected refugees. I don't know these countries but they need rejected refugees but UNHCR answered no, because they want to move those who have the refugee status. In this way UNHCR does not lose its reputation. If these countries came, taking those without a refugee status, then this would be published in the newspaper and it would be known that UNHCR allows people to travel without a refugee status. I assure you that there are countries that want the rejected but UNHCR refuses because it is a powerful organization. And so we are here and we wait, we are suffering, it's hot and in such a temperature it's not easy. Now there is no water anymore. Is this the first time that you come here?

Q: No, we came last year.

S: Do you see the difference? There are not so many people now.

Q: Today we have not visited the camp a lot, we came only here in your tent. We came here in August 2011.

S: But there is a huge difference in comparison to August 2011. Now when you arrive in the other zone of the camp there is almost nobody. If you count the tents, you see that they are empty, there are not so many people.

Q: Last year there were around 3000 people.

K: Yes, over the last period there were many departures. People leave every month. And I also believe that Choucha camp won't be open for long. In fact, according to the information we have, in early 2013 the camp will close. This is unavoidable, it is already signed, and I hope that they will find a solution for everybody. I've been called by UNHCR no more than one week ago, asking if I could find a solution, returning to my country or to Mali, where my sons are now. I also stated in my declaration that I cannot go to a country which borders on my country, since all those country have problems. And when I said that, they answered: 'we called you to have information, we do not oblige you, we want to know if you will accept to leave.' And I replied 'I don't want to leave.' And I told them that I cannot go to an African country where there is not stability. To Mali, to Guinea or to the Ivory Coast. If I go to these countries on the border with the Ivory Coast what could I do there? In Mali there are no jobs, and in Guinea none at all. So I left the UNHCR office. But it's up to them to find a solution. They want to find it. We are patient, we are suffering but they need to find a solution. It's a mafia, everybody knows, it's a big mafia. Their chief when he came here said to us: 'you, the Ivoirians, will be the first to find a solution. You will be helped. If there are people that must be helped these are you, because your country is not going well.' He was the high-commissioner, and if someone like that comes and speaks with you, it is somehow as if the president of the republic came and said that he gives you 500,000 Euros. And so, it's like that, we are here and we wait.

Struggles in Migration: The Phantoms of Truth
FEDERICA SOSSI

I.

I will start with some brief considerations about the way in which the space and the time of the revolutions which took place in 2011 - and in particular the Tunisian revolution - have been looked at from the space of the European representative democracy. In fact, I believe that, as other scholars have also pointed out, migrations towards Italy and Europe, as well as migrations from Libya to Tunisia in the immediate aftermath of the insurrection against Gaddafi and then following the UN authorized war, are constitutive events of the Arab revolutions.

Therefore, in this essay I will focus upon that revolutionary space looking at the events which have formed and still constitute its plot as a whole, despite the fact that they have not been seen as such, they have been hushed up, silenced, made irrelevant or imperceptible. In using the expression 'struggles in migration' I want to hint at precisely that aspect of invisibility and at this subterranean dimension, to the extent that some of the migrant struggles at large – and especially those that I will take into account here – 'act' a kind of 'migration,' that is a displacement, a break with common sense concerning what is 'political' and what is a 'political action'; and in order to be perceived as such, these struggles require the gaze to engage in the same breaking gesture.

I want to keep in the background two Kantian considerations.

The first one concerns the space of the Earth and the irony through which Kant, in the essay *Perpetual Peace*, founded the idea of a cosmopolitan law, that is of a political law which could preserve the right to hospitality, starting from the natural configuration of the earth's soil: as Kant suggested in 1795, it's because the Earth is round that human beings must re-inscribe onto the Earth's space a legislation which would hinge on the assumption that, however much we could wander, sooner or later we should all run into one another.[1]

Obviously, I leave aside the solution that Kant indicated for writing that political law. I draw on this passage from Kant just for that ironic parenthesis and for the various implications which can be glimpsed in it. Firstly, the claim of the commonality of the earth's soil. Secondly, the idea that there are ordinary practices and events – that are the necessary encounter of men - taking place irrespective of any will to political foundation. Finally, the critical gesture - this time enacted through the ironic parenthesis - through which Kant reminds any political government's will - also an ideal government - of its own limit, here marked by the reference to the configuration of the earth's space which comes before any possible legislation. Furthermore, I contend that in order to return, at least in a faint way, to that ironic suggestion and its implications today, centuries later, it is necessary to refer to a spatial upheaval enacted by revolutionary events and to an upheaval of the common sense.

The second Kantian consideration, conversely, concerns the theme of distance.

Some years after its outbreak, the French revolution returns once again, as is well known, in the pages of a philosophical text, *The Conflict of Faculties*,[2] but as neutralized in the 'hall of history,' as Lyotard puts it,[3] in which while the events of the revolution become 'facts and misdeeds' that perhaps it would be convenient not to repeat, what comes to the fore is the sentiment of the spectators who looked on without participating in those events. It is their sentiment of enthusiasm that speaks and from which we can deduce the idea of a 'progress towards the best' of humanity. Therefore, in the Kantian text the element of distance and the silencing of the actors, in addition to being hinted at in the theorization of the spectator, are the inevitable assumptions, left implicit, required to begin to theorize and for that event to start to 'speak.' Obviously, this event 'speaks' in another language than the language or the languages of the event itself.

Thus, we have here on the one hand the reference to the Earth as a

---

[1] I. Kant, *Perpetual Peace* (London: Pearson, 1975).

[2] I. Kant, *The Conflict of the Faculties* (Lincoln Mall: University of Nebraska Press, 1992).

[3] J.-F. Lyotard, *Enthusiasm. The Kantian critique of history* (Stanford, CA: Stantford University Press, 2009).

common space shared by human beings, and in order to rethink such a space today an interruption of common sense is necessary; on the other hand we have the question of distance from the events, not only with respect to seeing them but also to making them speak.

II.

This very gesture of maintaining a distance, in this case while the events were still underway, was enacted in different ways by the gaze of 'European representative democracies' and by the approach of their representatives to the revolutionary events of 2011. This gaze was further enacted in part through the discourses and practices of action that were more in tune with them, and that in some sense took the form of those events - Tahrir square, the Tunisian Kasba - reproducing that form into the European space. Nevertheless, by reproducing the form of revolutionary events in Europe, they were not attuned to the way in which the European space was itself shaken in turn by events which were part of the 'revolutionary events.'

In the face of the revolutions of 2011, it was mostly through a spatial and temporal delimitation of what was happening that the Kantian gesture of maintaining a distance, and the gesture of translation-neutralization thanks to which the events can speak was reiterated.

Something was happening in the Arab world; something that could be admired or feared, something about which one could get enthusiastic but that concerned another space than the European one. This is the shared horizon of what has been said by commentators, politicians and journalists. In this way, *a spatial distance* was enforced: here Europe - if you want with its four seasons - there, in Maghreb, Mashreq and in North Africa a 'Spring' which was close to being conquered by people.

Then, there was a double temporal delimitation. On the one hand, the 'Spring,' as well as the dates of the beginning and of the end of the revolutions - mainly of the Tunisian revolution, December 17 to January 14 - while the squares and the streets were actually still in revolt during the months of February and March, as they have not ceased to be up to now.

On the other hand, the events that were happening in that other space (Maghreb, North Africa, and so on) were traced back to dates already-known in the space from which these events were narrated and gazed upon: it was called the Tunisian 1789, 1848, 1989, etc. A kind of narrative that in the so-called post-revolutionary moment has then been translated in the sense of the 'democratic transition' which allows us to look at the present events using the yardstick of the transition in terms of its progress or setbacks.

Therefore, spatialities and temporalities are directed towards a delimitation: an horizon from which the other neutralizations are then articulated.

The Jasmine revolution, the facebook and twitter revolution, the revolution of the youth: flowers, social media and one generation implicated and exalted from time to time to entirely neutralize bodies and existences.

A problematic opposition between bread and politics, as if the 'bread,' namely the economic dimension, was not itself political as well, and as if the existences of each of us were not always shaped - willing or not - by both politics and 'bread'.

The ever-present praise of 'the end of fear,' as if the only sentiments at stake played into a binary and traditionally masculine opposition between fear and bravery, indicated a sentiment that delimited what was happening as a movement against the dictatorship. The dictator is *degagé* and freedom is gained: end of the revolution and of the teenage years. Then, there is the long period - timeless and empty of sentiment except the sentiment of the effort - monitored, accompanied and judged by Europe for its successes and failures as it enters adulthood. However silenced and always implicit, with a further glance the yardstick of comparison with a generic 'democracy' reappears even in those discourses that most sympathized with the revolutionary events. Frequently, we come across chronicles and reflections concerning what is at stake in the present, that would force us to re-read what took place in 2011: it was not a revolution but a revolt, an intifada, a pseudo-revolution or a nearly revolution, a...? A sign that in this case there is also a basis for comparison - however not an explicit one - through which the reading of the past can be reformulated from time to time, reworked in the face of new events.

I would not go as far as to argue that this grid for reading was so pervasive that it in turn also impacted on the actions of political movements. Nevertheless, what perhaps needs to be interrogated is the reason why the bodies and existences which gathered in occupied squares across Europe failed to encounter, or encountered only in a marginal way, the uncalculated bodies and the unaccounted existences of the Tunisian migrants. In fact, their newly acquired freedom was brought beyond itself when Tunisian migrants acted on it as a freedom of movement. In this way, they produced *an upheaval of European space*, acting in-between the interstices of that space more than in the squares: on the trains, in the parks, on the rails, on the islands, in the detention centres and in more or less claimed squats.

In the end, there is something quite paradoxical in this non-encounter or marginal encounter, and it seems to me that it is worth reflecting on this point. In fact, on the one hand the 'unrepresented' of the European and of the Western representative democracies were translating and re-inventing their ways of counting as a subject simply through the practice of staying in the space appropriated during the Arab revolutions. On the other hand, the Tunisian *harraga* had meanwhile burned the borders of States, as well as all obstacles that governmental migration politics imposed on their freedom of movement.[4] Moreover, they also burned every kind of cultural, spatial and political distance between the two continents, sweeping nation-States, territories, supra-national entities, islands and cities into the interstices of their action, acting, counter-acting and short-circuiting for no short amount of time the very possibility of being governed.

Maybe the linguistic invention through which some of them defined themselves when their claim to be '*here*' had assumed a more classical political form, enables us to grasp, at least in part, their upheaval and the anarchic insurrection in the face of any capture of their *pretension of presence* on the part of the governmental politics of mobility: the 'Collective of Tunisians from Lampedusa in Paris,' a kind of nominalist subversion breaking into the spatiality of the Earth, shattering centuries of history, political thought about space, belonging and the spatial inscription of the body.

But that self-definition and the collective which performed this in the Parisian squats is only one of the most traditionally 'political' moments - since there is a collective which identifies itself and lays claim by making itself visible - of a temporal and spatial spread of the Tunisian revolution towards Europe: a revolution acted out in a more interstitial and less visible way, not only by the *tunisianslampedusaparis* migrants or by the *tunisianslampedusarome, milan, bruxelles* migrants in European space but also by their families within Tunisian space. And also in this second case, that I'm going to speak about here below, I believe that what is at stake is precisely a struggle against forms of knowledge and the powers that dic-

---

[4] For a definition of '*harraga*,' see footnote 14 of Paola Gandolfi 'Spaces in Migration, Daily Life in Revolution' (this collection).

tate one of the most fundamental political laws of our contemporaneity.

III.

July 2012. The families and the mothers of the missing Tunisian migrants are still carrying signs and placards with the images of their sons around the streets of Tunis. The scene has become commonplace in Tunis and many people are accustomed to seeing it. People know that those 'photograph-women' are the mothers of the sons represented in the images: the Tunisian migrants who have 'disappeared' since March 2011, when, with some thousands of other Tunisians they left the Tunisian coasts. In this case, besides the language of the photos, on those placards there is some text, both in Arabic and in Italian, because with the mothers there is a group of Italian women - to which I belong - that has been supporting the struggle for over a year through the campaign 'From one shore to the other. Lives that matter.' One of these placards bears the text: 'We want the truth. Where are our sons?'

This was a demand resulting from the obstinacy of the mothers. Indeed, after a year of sit-ins a truth was communicated to the families; or better a half-truth, or better still some contradictory truths were communicated after the comparison of digital fingerprints on the databases of the Italian and the Tunisian Home Office had been made. In fact, one of the demands made both to the Italian and the Tunisian institutions was to exchange the fingerprints that they were holding in their databases, thus demanding that the technologies through which migration politics produce their truths, would be bent to the will to truth sought by the mothers and families.

The mothers were told by the authorities that any fingerprints taken after January 2011 had been checked on the Italian database but that no matches had been found. Then, some months later, the version of events changed slightly. An Italian vice-secretary revealed during a parliamentary interrogation that five sets of fingerprints from after January 2011 *had* been found. Nevertheless, the identities of these fingerprints remain unknown.

And it's not by chance, because two half-truths, one in contradiction with the other do not correspond to a whole truth even in the case that the latter should follow the logic of a more or less refined technological truth. But most of all, because the traces of biometric information constitute a poor and unessential truth; a truth composed of 'histories of fingerprints,' which fragment the life of a son. Yet, this is the only truth that the institutions of the two States managed to produce.

Radars, satellite systems, high resolution mobile sensors located in that narrow strait which divides the two shores of the Mediterranean followed by digital fingerprints taken at the point of disembarkation. This is the knowledge which overwhelms and shapes the existences of that part of humanity, whose mobility the migration policies of the European Union aim at governing, according to a rhetoric of absolute visibility and through practices which dematerialize the bodies in order to capture them and to make those bodies reappear as existences expropriated, at least in part, of their physicality. Histories of fingerprints and phantom subjects are produced on the Northern shore of the Mediterranean; and at the same time numerous shipwrecks have produced at sea a *metaphoric or oscillating ontology*, that is an ontology *between the existence and the non-existence* of those human beings. Disregarded and unessential lives that, lost at sea, lose at once their possibility of speech as well as the possibility of a speech about them. These lives mark the barrier of the sea not as a space of crossing but as a cut between two worlds that cannot communicate: on the Southern shore those lives existed and still exist in the memories of relatives and friends who mourn for them while the other shore asserts their constitutive non-existence.

The problem is that those mothers, with their ongoing demonstrations and protests demanded that the Italian and Tunisian institutions account for the lives of their sons. They demanded sons, lives, bodies and existences; and they demanded that those lives should not be ignored. In such a way, they broke the logics underpinning the *metaphorical ontology*, establishing again, from one shore to the other, the Sea as a space of crossing, the concreteness of the plots of lives; physical bodies that cannot be and not-be at the same time; lives that might not exist anymore, but that cannot disappear into the void, since their memory, held by those who have known them, is still alive, as non-material as it is.

If, as Butler suggests in her most recent works, it is precisely our bodily being which make us 'entangled' subjects, that is subjects constituted by others,[5] there remains 'a rest' beyond every dominant normativity according to which the subjects are more or less recognized and produced

---

[5] J. Butler, *Giving an Account of Oneself* (New York, NY: Fordham University Press, 2005); J. Butler, *Parting Ways. Jewishness and the Critique of Zionism* (New York, NY: Columbia University Press, 2012).

according to a down-grading gradualness, a *rest* which cannot be handled by any process of normativity. Everybody is worthy of grievance, or 'grievable,' this is the law brought back to the entangled plot of those existences that the mothers, through their language made of photos and images, pursued.

By acting out an *existential geography* opposed to the *metaphorical ontology* of the governmental politics of human mobility, and through the images of their sons shown in the streets of Tunis on the occasion of every official meeting between the two governments, for more than a year the mothers and the families of the missing Tunisian migrants have continued to establish their law. The sons are human beings, with their 'thickness' as existences entangled in the bodies, in the minds and in the sentiments of others, beyond every existing normativity, including that normativity which makes the sea a barrier between the existence and the non-existence of subjects; or between the fact of being there and the fact of reappearing as phantom existences, formed of fingerprints and points. The water, as this *existential geography* suggests, could drown the lives, but it cannot erase the fact that they existed within a common space; the most extended space where all of us insist, beyond the territories of States, and in respect to which the sea is only a space of conjunction.

A *geography of the Earth*, as the Earth of all people; irrespective as much of its partition into different sovereign states as of its partition into geopolitical areas, inhabited by populations, lives and existences that matter less than others, and that precisely for this reason could stay within the borders of the existences who matter, paying the price of their phantasmatic dimension. A *counter-geography* compared to that dominant normativity which is intrinsically entangled with the law of migration politics, making the existences of their sons able to be once again physical insisting in space and entangled in the lives of others, even though they are missing.

Facing the rhetoric of absolute visibility and the law of supreme immateriality produced by governmental politics of migration, the knowledge of the mothers responds, 'seizing' it and establishing their own law: the sons are sons, and the mothers want them to be reachable, irrespective of their visibility, establishing their materiality as human beings, alive or dead. It is a *dystonic law*, completely *out of the law*; a law which fixes another time and another space, which 'seizes' the law of visibility and which cannot be 'seized' by those who are accustomed to immateriality.

IV.

I talked about the phantoms of the sea, of the missing Tunisian migrants and of the struggle of the mothers and the families (which demanded that those lives are accounted for) because the language of images that the Tunisian mothers have put in play for several months between the two shores of the Mediterranean is about the combat between two forms of *power/ knowledge* concerning space, subjectivity and living.

In a lecture given in 1972 at the Collège de France, Michel Foucault proposed looking at the figure of Oedipus, staged by Sophocles in *Oedipus Rex*, as a combat between two forms of power/knowledge.[6] It is because we are within a system of thought, Foucault suggests, in which knowledge is thought mainly in terms of consciousness, that the figure of Oedipus was presented in a negative way and transformed into the hero of the unconscious. On the contrary, Oedipus according to Foucault is the one who, in the name of another knowledge - the knowledge of a subject which seeks and finds by himself - in order to govern the city, challenges the knowledge of the religious sovereign, which is based on the oracular time of divination and which imposes subjection and obliges to be heard. Therefore, Oedipus is the figure of an excess.

An excess and a challenge: these terms could perhaps describe the re-iterated gesture of Tunisian mothers against the forms of knowledge and the powers of migratory politics. Forms of knowledge and powers that dictate one of the paramount political laws of our present, namely the invention of a geography of the earth where there are subjects who belong to the space of the earth and others who do not tread on that soil. Consequently, a combat against one of most relevant nexuses of power/knowledge of our present.

In fact, the government of migration postulates that, on the basis of a normativity that is taken for granted and thus naturalized, those bodies that we are, would need legitimacy to move from one point in space to another. Such an assumption carves onto our bodies a political law, well before its concrete instantiation, which merges with the physical law of our existence.

For some of the bodies of modern history, such a political law has assumed the form of a '*territorial pact*' undergirding the pact of citizenship between the bodies and the sovereignty of nation-states, according to which the physical body came out again as the body of the citizen within

---

[6] M. Foucault, *Leçons sur la volonté de savoir* (Paris: Gallimard/Seuil, 2011).

the bounded space of the state, which in turn was inscribed not only as the territory of the state but also as a territory-soil-place-space 'belonging' to the citizen. For other bodies, that history had been inherently different, to the extent that, as Fanon pointed out, in-between the folds of the spatial insistences of the bodies, the political law of colonial domination carved out the mark of dispossession through which their place reappeared as a remainder, as a shadow, as the backstage of the space of the coloniz-er, redefining in this way the bodies of the colonized as 'improper' bod-ies, stripped of their physical dimension as well as of their mobility.[7] It is clearly also this mechanism of dispossession of the physical space of the body,[8] the permeating of political law in between the folds of its physical dimension, which underpins the manifold practices and articulations of the politics of the camps. A mechanism of dispossession acted out in new ways by the present politics of migration governance, more mobile than it was both in the space of the colony where, following Fanon, there was nevertheless a place of one's 'own' in which the colonized had to learn to stay, and in the dynamics of the camps, despite the latter being also part of the scene of the present.[9]

An excess and a challenge. This is what the Tunisian mothers and fam-ilies have produced and are still producing between the two shores of the Mediterranean, unifying the shores for a much longer time than indicat-ed by the dates of the 'Spring'; a power/knowledge of transgression com-pared to that which governs our contemporaneity. Moreover, following the analogy, this power/knowledge unlike Oedipus cannot be entrapped, since it is not the excess of a sovereign gaze aimed at governing the *polis* in a different way. Rather, their excess is precisely what gives the mothers the force of an obstinate transgression; it is the excess of women's bodies who are entangled, through their existences, their knowledge and their sentiments with the bodies of their sons, to whom they bring the sor-row and the grievance of the dispersion. Thus, a challenge to any form of government which carves out a space of the *polis*, however limited or extended this might be, starting from the already given space of the Earth

---

[7] F. Fanon, *Black Skin, White Masks* (London, Grove Press, 2008); F. Fanon, *The Wretched of the Earth* (New York, NY: Grove Press, 2005).

[8] R. Beneduce, 'Undocumented Bodies, Burned Identities: Refugees, Sans Papiers, Harraga - When Things Fall Apart', *Social Science Information*, 47 (2008).

[9] F. Sossi, *Migrare. Spazi di confinamento e strategie di esistenza* (Milan: Il Saggiatore, 2007); A. Sciurba, *Campi di forza. Percorsi confinati di migranti in Europa* (Verona: Ombre Corte, 2009).

that all of us inhabit.

In the present supranational or transnational governmental forms, the purpose of carving out a government of the *polis*, starting from the already-given space of the Earth, necessarily takes the form of its maximum extension, mapping the *polis-Earth* upon the Earth's space and following migrants' existences all over the world. In opposition to the government of human mobility in the *polis-Earth* exercised through practices of deterritorialized sovereignty, equally deterritorialized practices of mobility, or, better put, *despatialized* practices of mobility are carried out. In fact, these are the only possibilities for moving in a space 'without soil'; the very space that migration policies have carved out for those subjects that these policies cast as migrants. The 'Collective of the Tunisians from Lampedusa in Paris' is maybe one verbal invention suggesting better than others the idea of a *despatialized* mobility, a mobility which drags across states, across continents and across the borders of an island – Lampedusa - known by now as the Island of migrants. In this way, this name proposes a self-identification as subjects who try to fix their '*oscillating here*' in terms of a space of their staying.

Everybody has the right to belong to a place, and such a right belongs to everyone, irrespective of the place to which she/he belongs. This is what Judith Butler has recently suggested, seeing in the unchosen cohabitation of the Earth the very condition of our ethical and political existences.[10]

Obstinate in their *existential counter-geography*, which deeply touched the *metaphorical and oscillating* ontology of the powers/knowledge configurations of migratory policies, tackling it as a non-truth, the mothers still continue to assert their own truth, or better their knowledge/demands. Their sons, as sons of obstinate mothers, co-habit the 'Earth of all,' and their lives are worthy of mourning or of pain for their disappearance, beyond their counting in relation to the dominant normativity in which we are all entangled and irrespective of who will count and account for them.[11] A disruptive political action, even compared to the ethical and political responsibility of the unchosen earth's cohabitation that, just as any theoretical elaboration about ethics and responsibility risks producing a reflection with no effective impact on the real. Ultimately, it could

---

[10] Butler, *Parting Ways*.

[11] J. Butler, *Precarious Life. The Powers of Mourning and Violence* (London and New York, NY: Verso, 2004); J. Butler, *Frames of War* (London and New York, NY: Verso, 2009).

be objected to Butler that Eichmann had already decided who should not share the space with him, even though according to the law of the unchosen cohabitation he wouldn't have had the right to make such a decision.

Together with the sons of those obstinate mothers, instead, we all co-habit, aware or unaware of such a cohabitation. This is because through their obstinacy they establish the knowledge of the concreteness of physical bodies over the non-truths of migration policies, re-drawing the Earth as a space belonging to everybody, beyond the dominant political law of our present. And this is a political and existential practice which cannot be kept at a distance.

V.

I would like to add a final consideration, starting from a fundamental point. As a matter of fact, the knowledge of the families which is ongoing to oppose the power/knowledge of migration policies has been so obstinate because some of the mothers and the families recognized their own sons in the images of televised reports produced on the other shore of the Mediterranean. Therefore, I will focus on this first aspect that hampers one of the fundamental mechanisms of migration policies: the 'border and migration spectacle.'[12]

The production of the spectacle of migrants arriving works in turn towards a subtraction of physicality, the increase of their virtual dimension, namely making use of the virtual nature of image production to render the migrants continuously reproducible: thanks to this reproduction, migrants appear not few but many.

But, between the image and the physical body there is a distance - as Benjamin pointed out with respect to another physical body, the work of art - a distance which acts on the *here* and *then* of its presence.[13] Instead, the mothers and the families, by recognizing their sons in those images, have thus interrupted the path of the virtualization by saying 'there he is,' and so 'he must be *here* and *now*: tell me where this *here* is.' After all: 'give

---

[12] N. De Genova (2002), 'Migrant 'Illegality' and Deportability in Everyday Life', *Annual Review of Anthropology*, 31 (2002); N. De Genova, 'Border, Scene and Obscene', in T. M. Wilson, H. Donnan (eds), *A Companion to Border Studies* (Oxford: Wiley-Blackwell, 2012); P. Cutitta, *Lo spettacolo del confine. Lampedusa tra produzione e messa in scena della frontiera*, (Milano: Mimesis, 2012); F. Sossi, *Migrare. Spazi di confinamento e strategie di esistenza* (Milan: Il Saggiatore, 2007).

[13] W. Benjamin, *The work of art in the age of mechanical reproduction* (New York, NY: CreateSpace, 2010).

me my son, in his physicality of physical body/physical being, and not in his being performed as a migrant'; since as I attempted to argue above, in the condition of being a migrant you can find different degrees of *not-here*.

Actually, the claimed continuity between the image and the physical body produced something of a problem on the other shore of the Mediterranean. There, in Italy, in Europe, on the other shore of the sea, that continuity was not assumed. There from the image to the *here* claimed by the mothers, there was an absolute interruption that it still maintained. So, it is a question not only of an excess and a challenge but also of a *différend*, which is usually masked. In fact, nobody up to now had ever demanded the return of human beings in the place of 'disappeared people.'

Thus, I mobilize the notion of *différend* drawing on Lyotard here. I quote:

> The differend is the unstable state and instant of language wherein something which must be able to be put into phrases cannot be yet. This state includes silence, which is a negative phrase, but also calls upon phrases which are in principle possible. [...] What is at stake in a literature, in a philosophy, in a politics perhaps, is to bear witness to différends by finding idioms to them.[14]

However, to bear witness is perhaps too little. I would slightly shift from this position, for the simple reason that there were the mothers and the families, and not the testimony of their sons, that made me see that *différend*, forcing me to reflect on it - or better, to translate their demand into a language known to me.

So, some considerations, on the meaning of a politics of testimony. By following this route, discourses, narratives, images other than those of migration policies are produced. However, I would like to suggest various problems tied up with this production.

One among others: the risk of not deeply interrogating ourselves on the *phantom-ness* at play in the practices and in the discourses articulated by the idea of a government of the mobility of human beings.

In fact, in this way stories of migration are found and produced, as if there existed a set of stories to be narrated and subjects waiting to become language and disposed to be accompanied for becoming 'first persons';

---

[14] J.-F. Lyotard, *The Differend. Phrases in Dispute* (Minneapolis, MN: University of Minnesota Press, 1988), p.13.

these multiple 'I's who are asked to tell about themselves in order after-wards to write about them. It follows a kind of 'spectacle of migration' in opposition to 'making a spectacle' out of them, as is the case in main-stream narratives. A world of stories offered to the spectators between the space of migration policies and that of the existences, incapable of impair-ing the former in the attempt to account for narrating the latter.

Ultimately, the current 'militant' use of images, instead of breaking the magic and necessarily conservative circle of a thought which maintains its distance, risks assuming and nurturing it in another way. Besides, the idea of the spectator implies that there is a spectacle which makes itself visible and that in an event there is a certain aspect which also constitutes its essence. Thus, this idea falls into the framework of a tradition that al-ways donates - through an implicit concession - to its own theoretical and discursive gesture of narrative production the capacity to reach or to get closer to something essential.

Finally, I would say that in this way we run the risk of not deeply in-terrogating ourselves on the absence of speech and of visibility from the part of those who let themselves be spoken about and be seen, that is those we bear witness for. Why don't they speak? Or why do they speak without being heard? Why are they in part invisible even when devising their strategies for 'insisting in space'? Because generally we speak and we make ourselves visible starting from a *here and now*, and even more we narrate and we become visible starting from a *here and now*. Taking this 'here and now' in place of the persons who have been more or less deprived of them, we don't give this here and now back to them. I would add: we certainly run the risk of silencing them and making invisible the political modali-ties of their action by bringing them back into the order of our discourse, as militant as it is.

I started by pointing out the aspect of invisibility or underground-ness, in the sense that many struggles of migrants 'act' a 'migration,' a displace-ment or a break with common sense about what is political and what is po-litical action; a 'migration' of common sense that generally many migrant struggles put into place in our present. Therefore, among these struggles, due to this necessary displacement of common sense about what is polit-ical and what is political action, I let break in the struggle of the Tunisian mothers and families that counter-act migration policies. But they do that not through a discourse and even less through a discourse on migration policies, even though they are able to speak.

Instead, the action of the mothers maybe does not counter-act: rather, it acts, irrespective of any order of discourse imposing a non-order, a radical upheaval: between the virtuality of the image and the represented subject there is no difference. In this way, the mothers short-circuit not only the discourse of those politics but every possible discourse. Following them up, or trying to fully follow them up, means to try to select a limit, not only the limit of their demands, but also the limit of one's own discourse. To know that basically we will have to try to concatenate with other sentences, but that any concatenation always starts from a necessary compromise with the production of the absence and with the *phantom-ness*.

Trying not to bear witness but to be 'together' alongside them, means letting the *différend* be itself, not thinking that it could be resolved, neither through testimony nor otherwise. This point of the limit already exists: it is the idea of 'everybody's Earth' that the mothers act, acting in this way also our necessary sharing of the Earth with their sons, as disappeared as they are.

February 2013.

II. Postcards of a Revolution

Cartographic Games:
In-between the Folds of an Upheaval
FEDERICA SOSSI

Let's start from a basic fact: the 'Tunisians from Lampedusa in Paris.' They were present. And they made their presence visible, signing their statements during the May occupations as 'Tunisians from Lampedusa in Paris,' leaving signs of their presence on the web, with pictures of their banners on the buildings they occupied, with flyers demanding support or calling a march, and with a few ironic images addressed to Europe. What all these ways of making one's presence felt embody is indeed a depiction, the depiction of a presence during an action in space, a presence that occupies a space, that takes a space over, and a presence that, while announcing 'who one is' deliberately leaves marks of this being. But what would such a presence look like rendered as a cartographic representation?

We are used to maps that depict states, cities, borders, seas and continents. And maps that politically rank such depictions. The eye sees and inscribes in its 'memory' the image of such a performed spatiality which is offered up in order to be internalized and propagated. We are used to maps that tell and perform events. Maps on migrations, for instance, in the past few years, have been performing 'routes' through the use of arrow marks to signal, in European newspapers and websites, an itinerary from the 'rest' of the world to European Union countries. In this way, not only are 'routes' performed, but they are performed unilaterally: from 'elsewhere' to 'here,' the 'here' denoting the location of the eye. There are also migration counter-maps that attempt to depict something else, which attempt to visualize what usually gets untold or omitted from mainstream verbal and visual narratives about migration policies, which journalists and researchers deploy, in their role as propagator of stories and visibility. In spite of 'routes' and 'fluxes', counter-maps depict: migrants' subjectivity, patrolling activities at sea, border controls in airports - by human and non human agents -, the death tolls. In these cases, the eye keeps looking but in order to actually see it needs to linger, to take its time: the time to actually see what usually one doesn't see, the time to rid one's perceptual schema of the memory of those arrows which harness migrations and which, in turn, harness the eye itself. But the eye also needs to take its time to understand these complicated depictions, wherein the 'counter' of counter-maps aims for visibility. A challenge to hegemonic visibility, in the attempt to posit a counter-visibility.

'The Collective of Tunisians from Lampedusa in Paris,' however, posits endless problems to the sheer possibility of visibility itself, naming and 'acting on' a spatial unification. This unification is anarchic towards those perceptual and conceptual borders which have been inscribed in the grids of our eyes and minds by representations which span centuries. The Collective drags along states, continents, cities, islands, Europe, Africa, Tunisia, Italy, and France in a verbal anarchy which is acted out from within the buildings of its occupations. And, through its name, it suggests what indeed happened across the space of two continents in only a few months, continents which were separated by centuries of history, events, verbal and figural narratives, conceptualizations, as well as by a short stretch of sea. What was put in place was a sudden closeness and the bursting capacity, on the part of Tunisian migrants, to shake off the borders that migration policies inscribed onto their bodies, a capacity played by burning spatialities and temporalities, by causing the crisis not only of every possible spatial and temporal capture that these policies imply for migrants, but also the crisis of each figure or word that, despite its 'counter,' still aims to re-state and re-present them.

The map we present here is a challenge and a game. Or, to put it better, it is an attempt to spatially follow and imagine all the intricate tangles of that self-naming of 'Collective of Tunisians from Lampedusa in Paris,' in the awareness that there always remains an un-depictable 'rest' in this necessity to follow that unexpected contestation of each possible existing depiction. No longer a question of states and borders but a space of events: revolutions, departures, crossings, popular chains, fights, resistances, flights, 'insistences on space', occupations and squats. Upheavals of bodies and existences, actions and words which burst into the spaces and the times of their captures, in squares and waters, finding themselves transposed in the course of a few days from the café Relais in Zarzis, to the train station 'Quatre chemins' in

Paris, bringing in an uncanny way Tunisia and its insurrection among the streets and the parks of France and of Europe. But the map also depicts those confinement policies, border enforcement and expulsion activities, the delirious prose conjuring up new states out of thin air, all these attempts to reinstate order, to hush bodies up, to counter-act their actions, to recover the usual narratives by inventing not only a counter-insurrectional prose but also spatial obstacles to the upheaval of Tunisian migrants. These attempts coincided with various Frontex engagements, endless summits, new sites of capture, a coming and going from one Mediterranean shore to the other, in the attempt to re-map that short stretch of sea as a distance hence giving France back to France, Italy back to Italy, and leaving a bit of Europe in the debris of new borders while leaving some islands to their extra-territorial destiny. And in-between lies the sea, unaware of its complicity, the words of a few survivors, and the huge silence of many others: many, very many Tunisian migrants and refugees fleeing the Libyan war, who perished while radar and satellite technologies, Frontex patrols and NATO helicopters, airplanes, ships hovered 'contemplating' the shipwrecks. Not at all a 'shipwreck with spectator,' the metaphor of a certain European conceptual and aesthetic tradition, but endless shipwrecks with far too many spectators.

What is the cartography of this upheaval then? The 'game' we propose is an exchange which demands a double exercise of the eye: look at images and read words, by turning space into the time of the narrative and turning the time of the narrative into space. A 'game' which responds to the attempt to follow that insubordinate remainder, insubordinate to spatialities and temporalities. Each icon on the map - the map of a unified space where the sea is more solid than the land and the land refuses to reproduce borders and attempts to transform itself into the land 'of every woman and every man,' where de-bordering practices took over cities and states turning them into gardens, parks, squats, tracks - corresponds to a 'postcard,' a narrative which composes an extended caption to the map which attempts to articulate what that strange insurrectional time of 2011 was. Allow us one last game: the attempt to ripple also chronological time, demanding that in gazing at the map the eye should imagine after-moments which are located beforehand, hence displacing itself from that 'here' in order to follow those after-moments whose presents, as events, escapes depiction and narration in the past tense.

March 15, 2012

Spaces in Migration

LEGEND

- Revolution
- Departures
- Shipwrecks
- Crossings
- Popular chain
- Confinement policies and new places
- Struggles, resistances, escapes
- Border enforcement
- Expulsions
- Insistence on space
- Occupations / Squats
- Going back / returns
- New states
- Routes by train

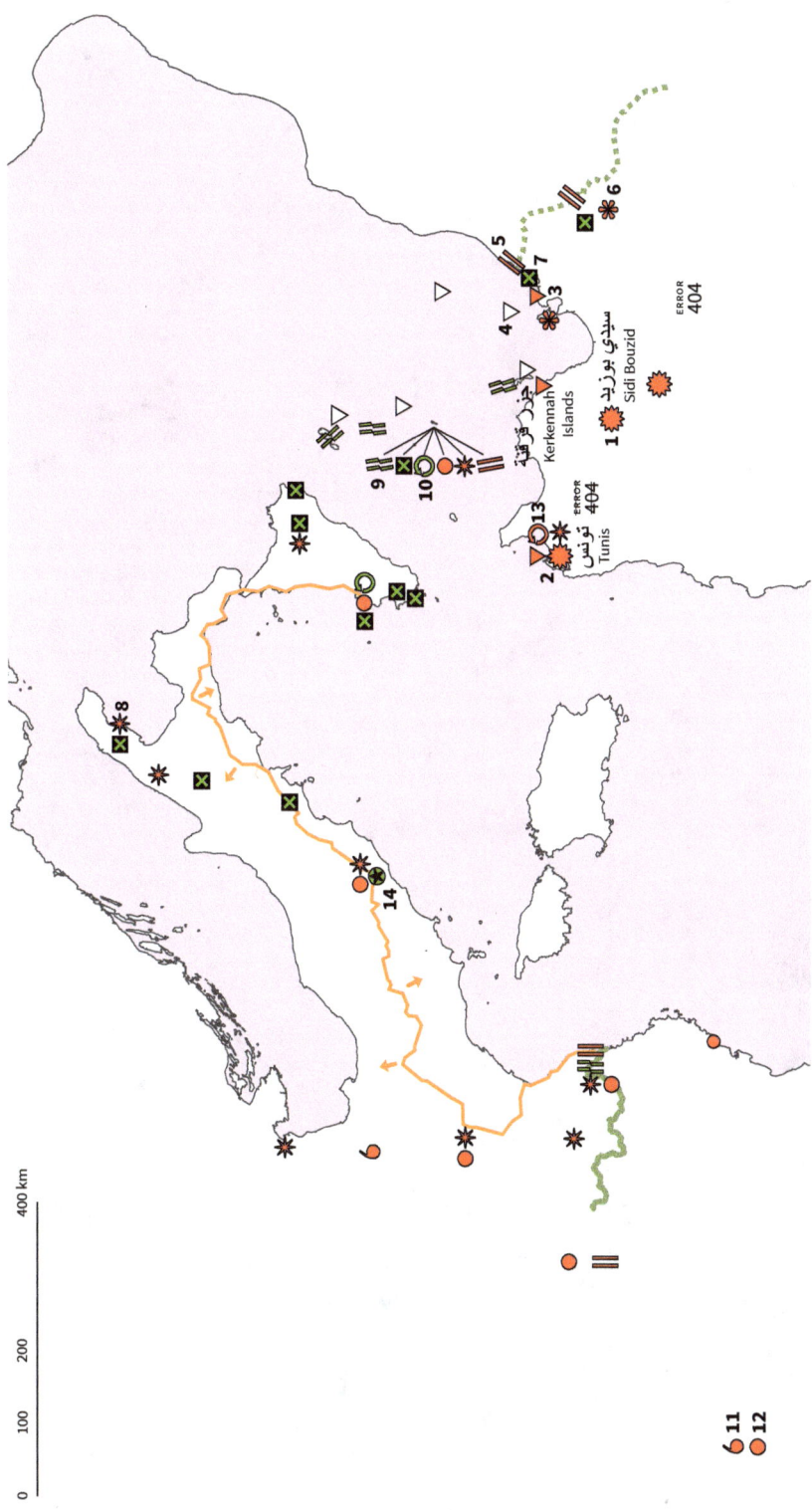

400 km

0   100   200

سيدي بوزيد

Sidi Bouzid

1

Kerkennah
Islands

جزر قرقنة

ERROR
404

تونس
Tunis

2

13

3

4

5

7

6

9

10

8

14

11

12

POSTCARDS OF A REVOLUTION
GLENDA GARELLI, FEDERICA SOSSI,
MARTINA TAZZIOLI

✺ 1. Revolution.

A specific day marks the beginning of the Tunisian revolution: it is December 17, 2010, the day when Mohamed Bouazizi, a 26-year-old street vendor, sets himself on fire across the street from the local government building in the town of Sidi Bouzid, after Tunisian authorities confiscated the merchandise he was selling. Actually, there is a 'before' and an 'after' framing the acts of immolation that have characterized the Tunisian revolution. Prior to December 17, 2010 two young Tunisian men set themselves on fire on March 3, 2010 in Monastir and on November 20, in Metlaoui. Afterwards, on December 22, 2010, another immolation follows Mohamed Bouazizi's in Sidi Bouzid: it is the immolation of Houcine Nejji, a young unemployed Tunisian, who commits suicide hanging himself from electric wires. Just a few days later, on December 26, a young Tunisian throws himself in a well, again in Sidi Bouzid. This revolution starts from the cities of central Tunisia: Kasserine, Gafsa, Menzel Bouzaiane, Sidi Bouzid, Merknassy. In the first few days, the revolution is concentrated inside Tunisia, where popular insurrections continue to multiply: on December 27, 2010, protests extend to Gafsa and Kasserine where people march in the main squares with scuffles occurring; but protests also extend out to the coast - reaching the cities of Gabès and Sousse – and also Tunis. On January 4, 2011, Mohamed Bouazizi dies and his funeral, marked on January 5, becomes the icon of the revolution.

In terms of triggers of the revolution, commentators point to the high unemployment rate, especially among young people and the lack of socio-economic opportunities associated with a dire increase in the cost of basic necessities. But already during these first days, protesters target symbols of Ben Ali's regime, the offices and headquarters of the RCD (the regime party), setting police stations on fire that, besides representing the repressive arm of power, are also emblematic of its corruption. On January 30, riots reach Monastir, where police react violently against citizens who have taken to the square to protest against unemployment and the high cost of living.

To accurately provide an account of the 'before' of the revolution one should look back to 2008, to the riots and strikes of Gafsa mine workers when police repression resulted in bloody confrontations and two people died. These riots started to produce fissures in the structures of power, following the bloody repression of student protests in 1974 and the 'bread-riots' of 1984.

On December 24, 2010 two young male protesters are killed in Menzel Bouzaian. They are the first two victims of the violent repression of the marches. A political response to these events won't happen until December 28, when Ben Ali gives an ambiguous speech, stating on the one hand that he will take protesters' claims into account but also stating that those who are protesting are just a small group of 'extremist activists.'

On January 10, the President gives a second speech promising 300,000 jobs within a short period of time and, at the same time, condemning the uprisings as 'terrorist acts.' Ben Ali's speech is delivered following two days of repressive action against protesters. Across the country, violent clashes between protesters and law enforcement agents increase and 14 civilians are killed in Kasserine, Thala and Regueb.

But already during this first stage, the revolution unfolds through networks and self-organized movements, going beyond single isolated acts or head-on confrontations between protestors and police. In Sidi Bouzid, for instance, teachers and professors form the 'Marginals Committee,' a protest coordinating unit supported by the main Tunisian union, the UGTT. In Kasserine, it is the lawyers who, for five days starting from December 24, protest putting pressure on the UGTT to fully support the ongoing struggles. The lawyers' movement reaches its peak on January 6, 2011 when the category launches a general strike. On January 3, when schools re-open after the winter break, students from middle schools also join the protests. Even the UGTT assumes a more radical position, after the increasingly violent police repressions during the first week of January (particularly in Kasserine): stepping out of the mediating role between revolutionary forces and regime's powers, now the UGTT is unambiguously on the side of the protests' claims. The change is also partially driven by internal tensions as the faction closer to the Tunisian Communist Party takes the lead in the union movement at a local level, taking part in the protests. In the meantime, immolation acts continue: on January 8, again in Sidi Bouzid, a 50-year old business owner sets himself on fire in the main square and, two days later in the same spot, a young graduate commits suicide publicly. On January 14, when Ben Ali is ousted from Tunis, a series of protests and clashes take place across the country and particularly in Sfax, Thala and Douz, where two protesters die. Clashes and riots continue throughout the country in the days which follow. On January 17, in Sfax and Sousse, Tunisian citizens vehemently contest the newly formed national unity government, for the presence of many politicians from Ben Ali's RCD. The revolutionary fervour continues way beyond January 14, which is being labeled in Europe as the Arab peoples' *storming of the Bastille*. During the month of August riots start again in the south of Tunisia and in Gabès. As a response, on September 6, the provisional government proclaims a state of national emergency. And the revolution does not cease even with the October 23, 2011 elections, in which the victory of the Islamist party Ennhada is declared, because, beyond these institutional figures, the terrain of 'political society' remains to be defined.

✳ 2. Revolution.

As was the case with the previous postcard from Sidi Bouzid, for this post-card events also revolve around a precise day: January 14, 2011, the day of Ben Ali's escape. However, reading accounts of the revolution one can observe that, in fact, in Tunis protests started before the 14th and went beyond that day as well. Moreover, turning our gaze to other crucial episodes happening in Tunis we might explore alternatives to that mainstream narrative depicting 'Arab Springs' as the awakening of a civil society calling for representative democracy - an account inscribing revolutionary movements into the predetermined path leading towards a political form already accomplished in the countries of the Northern shore of the Mediterranean.

Protests open in the capital with a march comprising about 1,000 people. The march is called in solidarity with the events of Sidi Bouzid and with the lawyers' movement who organized a sit-in across the Interior Ministry from December 27 to 31, 2010. On January 10, the day when in the rest of the country protests as well as police repressions reach boiling point, the capital is hit by violent clashes around the city's peripheries and students protest outside El Manar University which gets quickly hemmed in by the police. Ben Ali makes a last ditch attempt to stop this wave of protests which is attended so widely (by students, lawyers, teachers and professors, young unemployed people) and unfolding across the whole country: on January 12, 2011 the regime announces the liberation of all people arrested during the riots; on January 13, in his last speech, Ben Ali proclaims the freedom of the press, the end of internet censorship, and the lowering of the prices of a few food products; he also orders the police not to shoot protesters and declares that he will not run in the next elections. These promises are worth nothing in the face of an insurrection that has expanded and that the next day invades the streets of Tunis until Ben Ali is forced to leave the country. The police answer suppressing contestations that, on January 14, traverse the entire city, while the army starts to protect protesters against the police.

To defend the revolution, the next day, popular committees are formed to protect Tunis' neighborhoods. During the night, between January 13 and 14, another icon of Ben Ali's regime comes to an end: *erreur 404*, the script that tended to pop up on the screen on trying to access censored Internet pages. Censorship is banned from many internet sites, including Youtube and Dailymotion and, while during its early stages images of the revolution managed to circulate in one way or another on the web, starting from this day the use of the Internet as the tool spreading the revolutionary movement and as the means of attracting support for protests takes on a larger role. A revolution of the Internet and through the Internet: the central role of the web has been to create proximity between the spaces inside Tunisia and the spaces outside it and to create real - not virtual - spaces for practices of resistance. One example, among others, is *ZarzisTv*, the web tv started by young people in the coastal city of Zarzis and which by circulating images of the sites where the first protests were happening, contributed to the spread of insurrections across the extreme southern tip of Tunisia.

However, the revolutionary impetus did not fade with Ben Ali's escape. In fact, just three days after his flight, people take to the streets and gather in the squares again in protest against the composition of the transitional government restaging the presence of RCD ministries and which is led by Mohamed Gannouchi. On the same day, Gannouchi announces the liberation of all those imprisoned for their political views and declares freedom of information. Protests continue on January 22, on the eve of the first Kasba, a sit-in in the square of the government seat aimed at overthrowing the interim government.

An alternative narrative of the revolution to the one that media and political commentators from the Northern shore of the Mediterranean circulated would read the two Kasbas (January 23 and February 22, 2011) as two climaxes of the radicalization of the movement, moments that the discourse and the categories of representative democracy - the frames within which the 'Arab Springs' have to some extent been confined - can't quite grasp. On January 27, 2011 the first minister Mohamed Gannouchi announces the formation of a new government and the next day the square is forcefully cleared out by police. During the second Kasba (February, 22-25), when protesters demanded Gannouchi's resignation and the formation of a constituent assembly, the police kill two people. Yet, following Gannouchi's resignation, protests and contestations still continue on several occasions.

▼ 3. Departures

It is impossible to trace the exact moment when Tunisian migrants started to leave towards Europe, without looking at the arrivals in Italy. But in order to reconstruct the long chronology of departures it is necessary to also look at the other shore and to pay attention to interceptions at sea on the part of Italian authorities. At Lampedusa Island, the first arrivals are already documented on January 15, 2011, the day after the fall and flight of Ben Ali. They consist of a group of 100 people. On January 19, 2011, more people arrive at Pantelleria, Lampedusa, and Marsala. From the month of February onwards, departures become more frequent, often taking place in broad daylight, and from various areas of the Tunisian shoreline, namely small piers, beaches, and cities. Zarzis, in southern Tunisia, is the city where most people depart from. For this reason this postcard 'Departures' is sent from Zarzis, via the icon and the number that, from the map, lead to this. At first it is mainly young people from the city of Zarzis leaving; then also young people from other villages and cities from further inland. Between February 10 and 11, 1,100 migrants arrive at Lampedusa Island from Tunisia. Their arrival spurs controversy in Italy and throughout Europe. But the questioning around their departures starts on the other side of the Mediterranean, cutting across the entire Tunisian society and involving people from the places where most departures are occurring, comprising various insinuations of a betrayal of the revolution on the part of those who were leaving. It is indeed possible that among those who left first there may have been also people who were too compromised by the former regime to remain in Tunisia after the revolution. Where are they now? Rumor has it that they may have received refugee status, that they may have resettled in other European countries, and that they left Tunisia via safe crossing which brought them to very different places to Lampedusa Island. The other open question is: why did enforcement authorities allow all these departures to happen? What was the interest motivating this? The image of open borders due to the absence of police authorities in those days, i.e., the simplified image that circulated in Europe, quickly dissolves with further investigation, going to Tunisian coffee shops and paying attention to the assumptions that circulate among those who witnessed the events. Doubts and open questions persist - even if, in some interviews with the *Garde Nationale Maritime* we are shown clips of a sort of reverse 'clandestinity' featuring Garde Nationale ships, some even donated by Italy, approaching - albeit maintaining a distance - migrants on boats to tell them to turn back or, to be more precise, suggesting turning back in order not to risk their lives. In one bit of footage we saw, a corpse was laying on a guard ship and the guards were pointing at him, 'pleading with' the young men en route to Europe not to run the same risk. The day before our interviews with the Garde Nationale, at the pier in Zarzis, some young men told us how migrant boats were being approached: 'the Garde Nationale comes close and they ask us who wants to proceed with the trip and who wants to turn back. Who decides to return may board on the guard ship while the others continue the trip.' We took this as a joke and we made fun of them for this description but after interviewing the 'guardians' of the shores and of the sea we realized that there was no joke here. The phenomenon of departures, however, quickly reaches a peak and the controversy around supposed betrayal becomes ludicrous. It in fact becomes clear that there is way more at stake in people's decision to depart. Some union members in Zarzis stop talking about the betrayal of those who have left in order to prevent being called traitors themselves, someone who betrays by failing to understand the desire and the necessity behind those trips. People leave from Zarzis, Djerba, Gabès, Sfax, Mahdia, Monastir, Sousse, and Tunis. Or from the beaches of Sidi Mansour, Luza, El Kram, Chebba, El Haouria, Kelibia, and Ghar el Melhe, which are monitored less than the piers. During the entire month of March 2011, the entire Tunisian coast was taken up with preparation and departures. To give an example, we can offer data reconstructed by 'hearsay' coming from the parents of missing migrants: on March 14, 2011 five boats leave from the beaches around Sfax. Three shipwrecks are reported for that night. Estimates for departures from Zarzis reach 5,000 young residents of a city with a population of 71,000 inhabitants. Among them, a few women, who, according to the stories we listened to during the following months, were wives of Tunisians already residing in countries of the European Union returning to Tunisia to fast-track a family 'reunion,' with this trip across the sea. So people left, and left, and left. But because documentation of these departures would be required simultaneously at all the points of embarkation, we are forced to instead talk about them in terms of arrivals, if not shipwrecks or push-back operations. On April 7, 2011, two days after Italy reached an agreement with Tunisia on the repatriation of migrants, the Interior Minister Roberto Maroni, refers the following data to the Chamber: 'With regards to the situation of arrivals on the Italian shores, I report that from January 1 to April 6, 2011, 390 landings took place, coinciding with a total of 25,867 people; 23,352 people arrived at the Pelagie islands; among those, 21,519 claimed to be Tunisians and coming from a precise area in Tunisia, namely the southern area, exactly from the piers of Djerba and Zarzis, which up until the end of last year used to be patrolled by the Tunisian police and to prevent the departure of those Tunisian citizens already boarded. However, starting from the beginning of 2012, these police authorities are not there anymore.' Trips continue, even after the repatriation agreement. There are a few breaks due to weather conditions, to news about repatriations that quickly circulate in Tunisia, or to some symbolic arrests that Tunisian authorities perform in their territorial waters. On April 7, 190 migrants are intercepted and are immediately summoned before a judge. On June 13, the Italian Interior Ministry provides new data on migrants' arrivals, speaking of a continuation of the trips towards Europe even if these occur at a slower pace than in previous months. Between the Spring and Summer of 2012, migrants coming from Libya substitute those from Tunisia at Lampedusa island. 42,807 migrants arrived in Italy during the first 5 months of 2011; among them, 24,356 were from Tunisia, 4,175 from Somalia, Eritrea, and Ethiopia; 1,680 from Nigeria; 1,134 from Mali; 827 from Bangladesh; 761 from Egypt; 730 from the Ivory Coast; 713 from Afghanistan; and 530 from Pakistan. What stops departures, at least the departures which had been characterizing the 'Spring and Summer of Tunisian migrants,' is the episode of the boats used as identification and expulsion centers in the pier of Palermo, where Tunisian migrants were sequestered aboard so that authorities could proceed to repatriations directly from Palermo airport. This happens in the last week of September, after the burning of the detention center in Lampedusa, and in the aftermath of the 'lynching' of Tunisians by some of the island's residents, in which the law enforcement agents failed to intervene, caught up as they were in their duties of repression.

▽ 4. Shipwrecks.

Let's start once more from an 'impossibility'. While tallies have been kept and statistics proffered, all these numbers surely can't be more than hypothesis given the high number of undocumented shipwrecks. Some statistics indicate about 1,500 deaths in the Sicilian channel during 2011 for those who left Tunisia and Libya, whereas FortressEurope reports of 1,822 deaths, and a third source puts the total at about 2,000 deaths.[1]

Perhaps it is necessary to move away from the sea and onto the land, to look at the cemeteries and mortuaries of both site of departure and non-arrival. But all this would confirm is that the numbers of buried and unburied corpses remains unknown. On April 1, 2011, Tunisian authorities report the discovery of the bodies of 27 young men in the waters surrounding the island of Kerkennah. The men had left on March 13, March 27, and May 11, 2011. Authorities also announce that 58 corpses have been found on Tunisian beaches during April 2011.

Still, in the attempt to count shipwrecks, one could remain at sea, focusing less on those missing and more on those who caused them to disappear. Here, one is spoilt for choice over which news and data to look at: the endless fights between Italy and Malta about which pier has the competence to deal with boats adrift? Or Italy and Malta's long-standing bickering over the SAR (search and rescue) zone which achieved a new level of intensity during 'the year of the deaths'? On April 12, 2011 the United Nations High Commissioner for Refugees (UNHCR) demands that the European Union urgently put in place more effective mechanisms to rescue people in trouble at sea. 'A longstanding tradition of saving lives at sea may be at risk if it becomes an issue of contention between states as to who rescues whom,' declares Erika Feller, Assistant High Commissioner for Protection. The 'typo' accurately describes the situation: Italy and Malta's fight, in fact, is not about 'who should rescue whom'; it is about who might *not*-rescue whom.

But this longstanding tradition of saving lives had anyway already been compromised many times during previous years, with boats left adrift with survivors' bodies hanging on to tuna fish cages for days. However, should one stop at those fights, one would overlook the work of the agency Frontex and its 'interceptions' - most often a euphemism for push-back

---

[1] Geopolitics2020. Available: http://twitter.yfrog.com/user/Geopolitics2020/profile. Date Accessed: September 12, 2013.

operations - and tactics of 'dissuasion' - another euphemism to define the practices relied on by the agency in the waters belonging to the migrants' countries of origin, in this case those of Libya and Tunisia. Furthermore, to focus exclusively on the quarrel between Italy and Malta, would reduce 2011 to oblivion, overlooking those NATO forces - boats, helicopters, airplanes - enlisted to 'defend' the Libyan population in the war carried out by the Coalition of the willing, while part of that very population (taking residents, not just citizens into account) was fleeing the war by sea, 'uncontestedly' shipwrecking in front of indifferent crews. While these are often overlooked or forgotten, there are two definitive dates that are worth noting. The first lasts for days on end, the second one comprises an instant. Sixteen days were spent adrift in March 2011 by a group of migrants who left from Libya on a boat spotted by NATO forces who subsequently omitted to rescue it, letting most of its passengers, 72 people, die 'of sea', of sun, of hunger, and of thirst. On May 8, 2011 - the second date of this account - the newspaper The Guardian reports the news, following coverage from less prominent news sources and websites in previous days.

But let's stick to shipwrecks only, in isolation from the context and from those who cause them. In the Metline shipwreck, a few kilometers from Tunis, a young boy dies. On February 11, 2011, while statistics about arrivals to date and future projections are blasted around Italy, Tunisia is being asked to stop departures. A Tunisian military boat, Horria 302, rams the boat 'Raïes Ali 2', causing the death of 5 people and the disappearance of 30 others. In the days that follow, as survivors started blaming Tunisian militaries, the Navy 'gets to work' on the episode to archive it as an 'accident' for which migrants are pointed to as responsible. It is after this 'Raïes Ali 2' episode that we designate the icon *Shipwreck*.

A few days after this, Italy goes as far as to open fire on Egyptian migrants in the waters off Ragusa, Sicily, and one person gets injured. In the following days a long series of deaths. An unknown number of deaths for the March 13 and 27, 2011 shipwrecks in the waters off Sfax and for April 3, one off the Libyan coast, on April 6, 2011, close to Malta, only 47 survive out of 200 people. Unknown numbers of deaths for the April 28 shipwreck off the Libyan coast. Almost 40 people died and disappeared off Libya on May 6, 2011; possibly 300 people 'disappeared' off the Kerkennah Islands on July 2, 2011. It is at this precise moment that the United Nations High Commissioner for Refugees (UNHCR) launches a warning. According to estimates based on survivor accounts, 1,500 migrants died attempting to reach Europe from Libya and Tunisia in the course of just two months, UNHCR declares. And the list goes on. On August 1, 2011, 25 people are found dead in the hold of a fishing boat landing at Lampedusa island. On August 8, 30 people or more are found dead on a boat rescued off Lampedusa waters. The list continues as one keeps looking out to sea but this time with feet firmly on dry land. On August 4, 2011 Italian newspapers disclose an unconfirmed story. Italian authorities allegedly informed a NATO boat about a drifting ship in need of rescue before the Costal Guard of Lampedusa could intervene. NATO refused to intervene. 'If confirmed,' the Italian Foreign Affairs Minister said, 'this would be a very serious piece of news.'

During the course of the day the story is indeed partially confirmed. It is confirmed that the former Italian minister Maroni requested NATO's intervention. However, it turns out that this was not a request to rescue the boat but, rather, a request to send it back. 'It is a priority that, to meet the mandate it received, NATO should stop and push back boats to the point of departure in order to avoid all these deaths we have been witnessing,' is the 'human' discourse proclaimed by Maroni, who goes on to declare that 'NATO forces can't close their eyes and ignore the fact that they are there to protect civilians. This is a task NATO can't shirk.' Indeed, European policies have long been preoccupied with their focus on the 'all too human', at least since 2006, when the EU border agency started to intervene with 'dissuasion'/'deterrence' missions, predicated on ever-growing statistics about deaths in the Atlantic Ocean between Senegal and the Canary Islands. Returning to 2011 now and specifically to August 5, 2011. Survivors of this NATO 'not rescued-pushed back' boat provide further information through their conversations with Doctors Without Borders. About a hundred people died on that boat and their bodies were thrown in the water.

⫽ 5. Crossings.

As hard as it is to count those who died, it is equally hard to count those migrants who managed to arrive safely. Based on the idea of chronology, we should indicate the icon *Crossings* as originating from the place where the first passages took place across a state borders. Should we choose to follow this chronology, this would be the Island of Lampedusa, as crossed 'frontier'. However, this account risks unwittingly affirming the dominant European narrative. In order to turn this narrative upside-down, it is also necessary to turn temporal coordinates upside-down, hence starting the narrative from a 'subsequent' moment in order to make visible that space which, for a few months, saw the arrival and departure of people, cars, objects, food, and flags: a space of pure crossing, devoid of 'frontiers' despite the fact that this space marks the border between states as well. It is the space of Ras Ajdir and Dehiba, in the Tunisian desert at the border with Libya. These are the spaces from whence we want to start this story of crossings because it is here that millions of people converged, already in February 2011, when the Tunisian revolution began to extend to squares and cities in other Maghreb and Mashreq countries. At first people were fleeing Gaddafi's repression and then they were fleeing the 'joint' bombing by the Colonel's Army and the NATO Coalition of the Willing. These were migrants from many African and Asian countries, who, for over a decade, had constituted the 'workers army' of Gaddafi's Libya. And some of these migrants from African countries were already fleeing their countries of origin, who, while transiting in Libya en route to Europe had been stalled there because of the waiting times EU migration government policies and the Friendship agreement between Italy and the Colonel imposed upon them.

Tunisia kept the border with Libya open all the time, except for a few days when the confrontations between Libyan rebels and the forces loyal to Gaddafi moved to the borderline. This postcard of *Crossings* features images of women, men, and children: carrying packages, driving cars, transporting oil tanks, food provisions, or even nothing. After Gaddafi's fall in August 2011, this crossing turned into a counter-crossing, which witnessed Libyan families outnumbering Tunisian militaries at the border: families crossing back home, honking their cars, flying flags, gesturing the victory sign or even kissing the ground at the moment of entry into Libya. How many have crossed since February 2011? Hundreds of thousands people, who *re-revolutionized* the Tunisian space, especially in the South where Tunisian men and women were *making space* for them, those people fleeing Libya, hence giving another lesson to the entire world, even if part of the world constrained itself to the misery of a gaze, blinded by the incapacity to see beyond itself. This making space for people fleeing Libya consisted in the activity of popular committees, the young and not-so-young returning from the experience of the Kasba in Tunis, Facebook pages and radio messages to find houses, rooms to stay, and beds or mattresses, from Tunisia to the enlarged Tunisia of migrants or of Tunisian exiles all across the world. This was the spontaneous *space-making* that happened in Tunisia and that was so different from the space made by humanitarian operators, with their tents and their humanitarian kits aimed at 'humanitarian' - and not human - lives. This crossing away from repression, war, and bombings, has been photographed by a war of numbers, which were either testimony to the competences of different organizations - such as the repatriation flights organized by the International Organization of Migrations, or the management of tent camps by the United Nations High Commissioner for Refugees, or by Tunisian Half Moons or by national or international Red Cross - or to glorify one's generosity, as in the case of the revolutionary committees or of the Tunisian government itself. Numbers vary between 300,000 to 1 million, depending on who, amongst those actors indicated above, provides them and according to the ways in which *the lives crossing* kept organizing their autonomous space of crossing. At times, in fact, people were coming and going, especially Libyan men who were often crossing back across the border to join the rebel forces having made their families safe in some city, village, house or hotel in Southern Tunisia.

Other crossings, if one considers the 'border' in a traditional sense, are those of Tunisian migrants with their departures towards Europe. Lampedusa is their first step onto European soil. Ventimiglia constitutes the way to reach a Europe different to an encampment or detention center. Or it did, at least up until the Italy - Tunisia agreements mandated the repatriation for all Tunisians who had arrived after April 5, 2011 and, for those who had arrived by that date, the residence permit and the travel document for the Schengen zone, a 'valid-not-valid' permit depending on whose indications one decides to follow - i.e., the Italian, French, the EU Home Affairs Minister or Commissioner. Finally, a third crossing practice is registered towards Switzerland, when it becomes clear that, by filing an asylum claim, it is possible to stay put for a few months. But in all these cases, traditional 'borders' dissolve, as is always the case when migrants are in the act of crossing them, especially in this case when they were burned not only by the rapidity of the crossing but also by the demand and the certainty in this crossing. It would be pointless to designate the crossing icon in these crossed-not-crossed spaces, where an island is already Europe - albeit European policies rushed its transformation into a camp or segregation site; it would be pointless to designate this at Ventimiglia because, despite the re-establishment of borders that took place there, Lampedusa was already Ventimiglia, was already France, Paris, Brussels, Berlin, in a unification of spatial practices where Europe rediscovered itself as Tunisia or, more clearly put, Europe found itself equally shaken up by the Tunisian 'Spring.'

✳ 6. Popular Chain.

It was a slap in the face for the humanitarian government - referred to, in fact, as a *gifle tunisienne* - enacted by a portion of the Tunisian population when, as early as March 2011, it 'made space' for Libyans crossing the border with Tunisia in order to flee the war. A temporal slap in the face, as the popular chain started well before the arrival of 'humanitarian agencies' such as the UNHCR. But it has also been a slap in the face in terms of the way reception was practised. The hospitality provided was not that of an 'idle governmentality' over life or the issue of standardized humanitarian kits: it was a full reception that also took people's everyday needs into account. An emergency government over lives versus an ordinary government of existences, a human chain versus a humanitarian chain, so to speak, the former anticipating the latter but then finding itself coexisting alongside it, partly resisting it and partly finding itself captured by it.

The popular chain which started in March 2011 in Tataouine - an inland city in the eponymous desert situated 60 kilometers from the Dehiba border - made space for thousands of families from Libya. These reception practices were initiated by popular committees as a means of defending the revolution in the aftermath of Ben Ali's fall so as to prevent the revolutionary process being recuperated by political forces close to or in continuity with the forces of the regime.

It is a popular chain that becomes even more relevant in this story if one considers that Tataouine is not the only region where this practice of making space for Libyans emerged; for instance, on Djerba island, a human chain very similar to Tataouine's was activated. However, it is in Tataouine that almost 90% of Libyans were hosted by Tunisian families while others sought accommodations in hotels, also contributing to the compensation of economic losses that Tunisia incurred since 2011 due to the steady decrease in tourism. In Tataouine, the popular network provided accommodation and food; and when the Tataouine committees circulated the news about thousands of people from Libya on the territory, citizens of other Tunisian regions mobilized with substantial contributions, responding to the appeal launched to host Libyans from all across Tunisia.

According to estimates from the Committees, about 60,000 Libyans found a place in Tataouine, doubling its resident population. Also in Djerba a similar scale phenomenon occurred: the 100,000 resident population grew by another 100,000 people, i.e., the Libyans who found refuge in

Djerba, from April to June 2011; in the same period, eighty flights a day would leave Djerba airport to repatriate third-country nationals fleeing Libya.

However this popular chain, or, more precisely, this series of popular chains, stopped when people arriving from Libya were not Libyans anymore but 'Africans,' as Tunisians call them, i.e., Libyan residents mainly coming from sub-Saharan countries. Their presences could only find a place in the camps installed by humanitarian agencies: in Choucha, six kilometers from the Ras Ajdir border, with 22,000 presences in March 2011; in other camps in the vicinity run by Qatar and United Arab Emirates; or in the camp of Remada, towards the Dehiba border.

These complexities and ambiguities characteristic of the Tunisian popular movement can also be traced through its relationship with the humanitarian chain: the two chains - the spontaneous popular chain and the chain of humanitarian organizations - coexisted since April 2011 in the border-space of Tataouine. This coexistence was marked on the one hand by the role that the popular chain played as a source of local resistances and as a force of friction against the emergency logic deployed by the UNHCR in handling the situation. On the other hand, however, this *aide populaire* (popular assistance) allowed itself to become co-opted by the government of the humanitarian: the UNHCR ended up gaining from the popular chain, using it to get direct contact with Libyan families. Moreover, the European Union, when interpreting the outcomes of the Arab Springs using the discourse of crisis, adopted the Tunisian model and promoted 'the formation of grass root communities to assist asylum seekers.' While Italy, faced with the arrival of 25,000 Tunisian migrants, deported those who arrived after April 5 and released a temporary residence permit to those arriving earlier in the hope that they would cross over into France, and while France carried out its own interpretation of Schengen policy preventing the entry of Tunisian migrants into France, the country of Tunisia instead hosted 600,000 Libyans displaced by the war. In the tents of Choucha, however, thousands of non-Libyans were blocked and stranded by humanitarian forces while waiting to be resettled with no popular chain set in motion for them.

✖ 7. Confinement Policies and New Places.

Upheavals associated with the Arab revolutions are matched by an increase in the number of places and policies of confinement on both shores of the Mediterranean. Our mapping of this series starts from Choucha camp in Tunisia, 7 kilometers from the border with Libya, close to Ras Ajdir. This is a camp opened by the UNHCR on February 23, 2011. Thousands and thousands of people fleeing Libya were assisted in this expanse of tents, peaking at 22,000 on March 22, 2011. A transit camp turned into a parking camp for asylum seekers and refugees, which also became a death camp. In fact, after refugees blocked the road leading to Libya demanding the procedures for resettlement be sped up, some people from Ben Guardane organized a raid during the night of May 23 causing the death of four Eritrean citizens and harming twelve refugees. Choucha also functions as a suspension camp where one doesn't know what will happen but simply waits to be 'resettled' to a sort of imaginary 'elsewhere' which is unlikely to be Europe and hardly Canada or the United States, to name the resettlement places the UNHCR hinted at when 'distilling' refuge as part of its humanitarian system.

At the beginning of March 2012 more than 3,000 people dreamt of their 'elsewhere' from the tents of Choucha. Between February and March 2011, when the Libyan rebellion against Gaddafi started and then during a war waged by a coalition of willing 'in defense' of the civilian population, five more camps opened in Tunisia, along the two border zones with Libya: Ras Ajdir and Dehiba. United Arab Emirates, Qatar, and Western humanitarian operations already being run elsewhere deployed overlapping governmental technologies for fleeing populations. In deploying these technologies, these forces were assuring their future interests in the region, on both sides of the border, once the war came to an end.

In the meantime, at Lampedusa, temporary accommodations were improvised for Tunisians who started arriving towards the end of January 2011: the dock, the beach, the empty summer houses, tent camps made of cellophane or plastic bags. Confinement to the nth degree. The governmental delay in processing migrant transfers to the rest of the Italian territory provoked a forced confinement for Tunisian migrants and Lampedusa residents, a confinement which was all-too-easily seized by the media in its reports of the island's invasion by migrants.

On February 14, 2011, Italian Interior Minister Roberto Maroni, reopened the first aid and assistance center (Centro di primo soccorso e accoglienza, CPSA) of Contrada Imbriacola for adult males and the Loran former military base for unaccompanied minors and 'vulnerable subjects' - after he had talked for days of an emergency originating from what he termed 'the fall of the Maghreb wall.'

But in Lampedusa it was not a welcome reception but detention that was offered to migrants. In the former military base of Loran, minors were detained and the Contrada Imbriacola center became the site of collective expulsions - Contrada Imbriacola had served as a detention center in the past and was subsequently turned into a CPSA (first aid and assistance center), before this last transformation into detention and expulsion center. It will definitively close at the end of the summer of 2011, set on fire by migrants rioting against their seizure and against the announcement of new repatriations, while the island is declared an 'unsafe haven' after residents and police forces assaulted Tunisian migrants on September 21, 2011.

If Lampedusa was presented as camp-island under invasion, the center for asylum seekers of Mineo, in the province of Catania, was instead presented in terms of the 'made in Italy' model of European reception. Inaugurated on March 18, 2011, in the 'Villaggio degli Aranci' (Oranges Village), the center comprises a complex originally build for the U.S. Military Navy of the Sigonella aereo-naval station - the builder, the Pizzarotti company from Parma, followed the 'gated community' model when planning the 404 houses of the village. With a capacity for hosting 2,000 people, the complex was reconverted into a 'Solidarity Village' and managed first by the Red Cross and subsequently by the cooperative Sisifo, with governmental funding of 40 Euros a day provided for each asylum seeker. This 'golden prison' was actually the site of multiple forms of confinement for its 'inhabitants': geographic isolation, food poisoning, lack of cultural mediation programs, slowness in the review of the asylum claims, absence of programs to manage the second stage of refugees' reception after their exit from the center. The center hosted not only asylum claimants just arrived at Lampedusa but also those who had arrived years earlier, were living in other Italian centers, and ended up being uprooted and forced to start the whole process from scratch. As a refugee center, Mineo is indeed a 3 million Euros a month business and in fact the bid for tender became an undignified scramble.

Among the new sites for 'reception,' it is also worth mentioning the tent encampment of Manduria, in the province of Taranto, which opened on March 28, 2011. Manudria is the first of a series of temporary identification and expulsion centers that emerged in Italy in relation to the 'Northern Africa emergency.' Besides Manduria, three more centers whose profiling agendas differ yet again, emerge, i.e., the reception and identification centers (Cai, Centri di accoglienza e di identificazione) dotted around Southern Italy. We should also consider these briefly. Housed in the former Andolfato barracks in the province of Caserta, one of these structures was closed after a riot during the night of June 7 and 8, 2011. Another Cai resulting from this 'Northern Africa Emergency' is located in Chinisia, in the province of Trapani, in the area of a disused airport, with 90 tents housing 8 people each and surrounded by a fence to avoid escape. 70km from Potenza, in Palazzo San Gervasio, a 'reception' structure is improvised on a land confiscated from one of the Sacra Corona Unita bosses, a terrain surrounded by concrete walls and equipped inside with a sort of cage with nets over 5m high. The multiplication of centers' typologies and modes of confinement produces a long series. On April 21, 2011, identification and reception centers (CAI) were normatively turned into temporary identification and expulsion centers, a permutation which clarifies the eminently securitarian profile of the 'new sites' created by the 'Northern Africa emergency,' a profile that was reiterated by the Monti government, when on January 28, 2012, a public ordinance extended the Santa Maria Capua Vetere and Palazzo San Gervasio operations until December 31, 2012. Finally, in July 2011, a new identification and expulsion center opened in Milo, with 204 places, occupied almost exclusively by Tunisians.

From dry land to the sea. The Berlusconi government also instituted floating identification and expulsion centers, sort of galleons (prison ships) for the fast-tracked expulsion of Tunisian migrants. Returning to the date of September 23 when Lampedusa is declared an 'unsafe heaven' after a migrants riot and the subsequent lynching by some of Lanpedusa's residents. In that situation, 700 Tunisians were put on board three different boats: Moby Fantasy, Audacity, and Mony Vincent. Tunisian migrants were detained for weeks in these prison boats off the Palermo pier, with a measure that allows restraint without the need of validation on the part of the judge.

These spatial confinements were supplemented with a temporal confinement. The extension to 18 months of administrative detention, decided by decree on June 16, 2011 and then ratified on August 1, 2011.

✳ 8. Struggles, Resistances, Escapes.

Manduria, March 28, April 2, and July 5, 2011. Hundreds of Tunisians flee the detention center of Manduria, in the province of Taranto. It is the first big escape by those Tunisians who formed part of the revolution, after the first riots in the detention centers of Restinco (February 3, 7 and 12, 2011) and Modena (February 27), and after a hunger strike in Turin (March 1). Manduria is a symbolic place when it comes to composing a chronology of struggles, resistances and escapes that takes into account 'flight' as practice which succeeded the revolution of spaces occurring in Tunisia, acting upon the proximity of the two shores of the Mediterranean. 'The oxygen of freedom,' is how it is defined by a Tunisian guy in the processing center of Mineo who states that: 'it is the possibility to travel like everybody else. This is reason why we left.'[1] It is an intransitivity of freedom, acted upon by Tunisian migrants and which gave rise to a domino effect of events, acting as the catalyst for other struggles, and radicalizing other practices of resistance. On May 9, 2011, asylum seekers at the Mineo processing center block the state highway and start a hunger strike to protest against Territorial Commissions not processing their asylum claims. On August 1, 2011, rioting asylum seekers burst into the processing center of Bari Palese. They occupy the bypass and the railway, bringing the town to a standstill, while the police response results in fifteen injured. An insurrection of 'guerilla migrants' as the newspapers put it, also referring to the way in which events had been orchestrated. A few months later, in December, 45 asylum seekers are indicted for the events in Bari. Meanwhile, day laborers in the Apulian village of Nardò go on strike to protest against the exploitation of migrant labor in tomato plantations. The strike, which started on August 1, 2011, goes on for ten days. These revolts by migrants of the Tunisian revolution functioned as catalytic forces within Italian space. They set in motion and multiplied a sequence of struggles and resistances across Italian territory, using different modes of operation such as hunger strikes, fires, flight and self-harm. The spread of struggles reached a peak between April - after the Italian government started deporting migrants to Tunisia again on 7 April - and June, 2011. This is a period of time when flight, arson attacks and protest action fol-

---

[1] Sonia Giardina, *L'oxygène de la liberté. Dalla Tunisia al C.A.R.A. di Mineo*. Available: http://www.youtube.com/watch?v=PjEHP5czD90. Date Accessed: September 13, 2013.

lowed one another.

On May 24, 2011 more than 200 Tunisian migrants housed in the First Aid Center of Lampedusa riot, chanting: 'We want to go away from here.' They start a hunger strike against their detention that had not been legally authorized. On April 17, 2011 a group of migrants, who had been waiting for days in the streets of the town of Ventimiglia for the right moment to cross over into France, finally get on a so-called 'dignity train,' together with Italian and French antiracist groups. This train ride functioned as a kind of 'declared crossing' yet one which came up against the reimposition of national borders by French Minister of the Interior, Claude Gueant, who stopped all trains from crossing the border in both directions.

In the space of a week, migrants escape twice from the detention center of Chinisia, in the province of Trapani. The first escape takes place on May 25, 2011, less than a week after the opening of the center and the second occurs on June 1 when 44 migrants succeed in escaping. On June 27, 2011 - ten days after the extension of the maximum period of detention to 18 months is approved in Italy - a revolt breaks out in the detention center of Modena. In this context 23 migrants manage to escape. It is also in this context that the press, for the first time, makes reference to 'an external orchestration which facilitated the revolt and the escape.'

Between the end of July and the end of September, a second wave of revolts takes place. The continuation and the spread of struggles go hand in hand with their radicalization over the months. Struggles go from symbolic acts of resistance in March and April, 2011, when Tunisians climbed up onto detention centers' roofs chanting 'freedom, freedom,' to escape attempts in the same detention centers, and direct confrontation with the police, as in the case of the riot at the Ponte Galeria center (Rome, July 29-30, 2011). The week before, deportations of migrants were stopped due to revolts and frequent acts of self-harm by migrants. Many riots and escapes, in fact, took place as soon as migrants knew of an imminent deportation. This happened on August 23, 2011, when in the first aid and reception center of Pozzallo an apparent uprising of over a hundred detainees in the first aid and reception center of Pozzallo caused a diversion which allowed fifty-four to escape. After the blaze of the detention center of Lampedusa (September 20, 2011) and the guerrilla attacks against migrants triggered by Lampedusa's residents, governmental migration policies 'answered' with measures of extraterritorial detention in the form of prison ships. Successful escapes were often the result of collective strategies of action, planned in advance and acted on by large groups. Turin, September 22, 2011. Thirty migrants escape during the night, having prepared holes in the perimeter fences days earlier. And the images of the first aid and reception center of Lampedusa burning and of the riots taking place in the other Italian detention centers, all support and strengthen the idea that it is possible to struggle and fight collectively. Both the riot in Turin and the one which took place in Ponte a Galeria on September 27, 2011 when sixty Tunisians escaped, constitute a prompt response to the special agreement on repatriations signed by Italy and Tunisia on September 19, which mandated one hundred repatriations per day. But where the Italian government considered the matter concluded with this extraordinary plan for repatriation, struggles continue, and in December 2011, three other riots and escapes take place – notable among these are the escape from the detention center of Vulpitta (December 14, 2011), the riots at the detention center of Turin (December 9, 2011) and those at the detention center of Bologna (December 17-18, 2011) where migrants set various parts of the center on fire before continuing their resistance through hunger strike.

However, revolts do not occur only in an Italian context. They also spread through the space at the border of Libya and Tunisia. In May 2011, asylum seekers at the refugee camp of Choucha in Tunisia, located six kilometers from Ras Ajdir, protest by blocking the only road connecting Libya and Tunisia three times, demanding resettlement elsewhere. In the wake of the protests, residents of the nearby Tunisian town of Ben Guerdane organize a raid in the camps and kill four Eritrean migrants. Acts of violence such as the one perpetrated by the residents of Ben Guerdane are not isolated events. On February 28, 2012, the church of the camp is damaged by acts of vandalism, while the Tunisian army denies that the damage caused was intentional.

Finally, there is the resistance brought on by extreme grief. It is the struggle of mothers and families who, for months, have been beleaguering ministers, functionaries, secretaries and the appointees of European delegations visiting to sign agreements and pacts with Tunisia on the streets of the capital. They are the mothers and the families of missing Tunisian migrants, with their language of photos and the radical nature of their grief, a radicality that, from one shore to the other, suggests to us that these lives surely do matter.

⫻ 9. Border Enforcement.

Many types of borders were put in place against Tunisian migrants and asylum seekers coming from Libya by both individual European states and the EU. The beginning of the Frontex 'Hermes Operation,' on February 20, 2011, constitutes the date assigned to this icon. 'Hermes,' an operation of joint patrolling of the Sicilian Channel by EU and Italian forces, already planned for June 2011, gets put forward to February. Its initial expiry date (available for renewal) is fixed for March 31, 2011, with two million Euros allocated towards it. For border enforcement operations, Hermes deploys four planes, two boats, and two military helicopters. This equipment is provided by the six Member states taking part in the operation (Italy, France, Germany, Malta, Spain, and the Netherlands). The operation also constitutes Switzerland's debut in a Frontex operation, with the deployment of a group of experts to take part in the mission. The operation also provides for a Europol mobile office on the Island of Lampedusa to assist with 'operational analytical support,' as it is referred to on the Frontex website. However, according to antiracist associations and activists working on Lampedusa island, the agenda of the Frontex operation is rather different and consists in gathering information to identify and deport migrants.

Starting from the end of February, 2011 the Sicilian Channel is jointly patrolled by Italy and Frontex. Before that date, however, when Italy alone was responsible for managing what it termed the 'North Africa emergency,' the Sicilian Channel, had turned into a Wild West of pursuits and gunshots. On February 15, 2011, the Italian military corps Guardia di Finanza intercepts a boat with Egyptian migrants on board and, when the boat tries to escape, Guardia di Finanza takes fire, leaving the boat captain injured.

In the meantime, the Mediterranean Sea is regularly traversed by European and Italian politicians, engaged in vertiginous diplomatic activity with the interim Tunisian government, with the aim of redrawing those European overseas borders which used to be very efficiently controlled under the regime of Ben Ali before being erased by the revolution. Following a visit to Tunisia around mid-February 2011, Catherine Ashton, High Commissioner of Foreign Affairs of the European Union, announces an imminent 17 million Euros funding to the Tunisian government with another 258 million Euros anticipated for 2013. However, the journeys made by Italian politicians' to Tunis mark intense and conflicting negotiations, in the attempt to reach a bilateral agreement for managing the alleged 'immigration emergency.' The website of the Italian embassy in Tunis reports nine official visits between January 2011 and the date of the signature of the agreement, on April 5, 2011, suggesting an arduous and drawn out negotiation process. The agreement signed in Tunis by the Italian Minister of the Interior Roberto Maroni and his Tunisian counterpart Habib Essid, establishes the financial and technical aid that Italy would provide in order to train Tunisian authorities to control their coasts and prevent migrant departures. In exchange, Tunisia committed to the implementation of repatriation measures according to a streamlined procedure targeting Tunisian migrants without residence permits arriving on the Italian coasts after April 5, 2011.

Moreover, April 5, 2011 is also a very significant date, since it delineates the 'humanitarian border' that Italy imposed upon Tunisian migrants establishing a path to a temporary residency permit for humanitarian reasons for those migrants coming 'from North African countries' who entered Italy between January 1, 2011 and midnight of April 5, 2011. This permit was the result of longstanding negotiations and met with resistance from the Tunisian government with respect to the wishes of Maroni, who probably intended to send all migrants arriving in Italy since January 2011 back to Tunisia. However, this temporary permit for humanitarian reasons came with an expiry date. Issued as a six-month permit, renewable up until March 2013, it was granted only if claimed within eight days from the day of the publication of the decree. But there was always another border blocking Tunisian migrants once they had got to Europe and were holding in their pockets both the temporary residence permit and the travel title valid for the Schengen, which the Italian permit provided for them.

The other big chapter of border enforcement operations involves the story of the border between Italy and France. French authorities engaged in intense raids preventing Tunisian migrants from entering France, pushing them back to Italy. On March 2, 2011 the new Interior Minister, Claude Guéant, outlines, after the arrest of about twenty migrants at the Italian border, his vision of the Arab Spring in relation to the European borders: 'the quest for freedom that manifested on the Southern shore of the Mediterranean, presents France with two sets of responsibilities: guiding these peoples towards real democracy but also preventing uncontrolled waves of migration.' Indeed, two days later, the Minister asked Italian authorities if they would retain Tunisian migrants who were trying to get into France on Italian territory, contending that the migration of these Tunisians was an economic migration and that French authorities were required to stop it. A requirement expressed through the re-establishment of massive controls at the borders with another EU member state, Italy, which produced the interruption of the regime of free circulation between signatory states of the Schengen Agreement. According to a note from the French Home Affairs Ministry, between February 23, 2011 and March 28, 2011, French authorities blocked 2,800 Tunisian migrants coming from Italy and, out of these, 1,800 were pushed back to Italy.

But these borders which were on full display when they were 'following' Tunisian migrants and trying to prevent their arrivals through Frontex operations in the Sicilian channel, through bilateral agreements between Italy and Tunisia, and through raids and push-back operations at the Italy-France border), were instead vanishing and fuzzy when it started to be a question of establishing the competence of search and rescue interventions for helping migrant boats in distress at sea. The long-standing diatribe between Malta and Italy about the borders of the Search and Rescue (SAR) zone was indeed reactivated in the case of migrants coming from the Southern shore of the Mediterranean, with the usual conflicts over the jurisdiction of the rescue. Indeed, on many occasions the Italian Minister of the Foreign Affairs, Franco Frattini, protested or asked the Italian ambassador in Malta to protest against Maltese authorities for their failure to rescue boats in distress at sea in Malta's SAR zone. While Italian and Maltese authorities were fighting about the borders of their respective SAR zones, Tunisian migrants and migrants coming from the Libyan conflict were on those boasts, dying or at risk of dying at sea.

○ 10. Expulsions.

We chose the island of Lampedusa as the symbolic site for this postcard because the first deportation flight takes off from here, on April 7, 2011, carrying 30 Tunisian migrants. The deportation happens two days after an agreement was signed between Italy and the provisional Tunisian government that at the end of March countered Italy's intention to deport all Tunisian migrants who arrived in Lampedusa at the beginning of 2011. According to the agreement, Tunisian migrants arriving in Italy by April 5, 2011 could apply for a temporary residence permit of six months, while those who arrived after that date had to be deported 'in a straightforward way and according to a streamlined procedure,' that is to say relying only on the identification of the consular authorities. But the choice of the place of Lampedusa in these 'postcards of the revolution' also alludes to the push back operation carried out by the Italian Military Navy, just a few miles from the coastline of Lampedusa, with the collaboration of the Tunisian Military Navy. 104 migrants were on the boat that gets pushed back, in clear violation of the principle of *non-refoulement* sanctioned by the Geneva Convention and by the European Court of Human Rights.

However, between April 7 and August 21, 2011 the deportation process doesn't go on unimpeded and faces a number of interruptions. If during the month of April deportations seem a regular occurrence, with an average frequency of one flight per week from Lampedusa back to Tunis, on May 9, 2011, the flight taking off from Rome and headed to Tunis is prevented from landing by Tunisian authorities. The next day two deportation flights scheduled to take off from Lampedusa are cancelled. On May 17, 2011, the Italian government suspends deportations scheduled to depart from the airport of Palermo. The block goes on until June 3, 2011.

During the month of September, 2011 the mechanism misfires again. On September 16, a deportation flight that should have left from Palermo is blocked, while the flight departed from Milan disembarks with only 30 Tunisian citizens of a yet larger group - according to the Tunisian government this number corresponded to the maximum cap of permitted daily deportations. Tunisia resists pressure coming from Italy, despite having signed a special deportation plan, mandating, over the course of three weeks, a total of one hundred deportations per day for five days a week. The agreement was actually signed on September 12, 2011 by the Italian minister Roberto Maroni but was only made official on September 19.

More specifically, it is after the fire at the detention center of Lampedusa (September 20, 2011)[1] that deportations start to fail and Maroni declares that the agreement with Tunisia has fallen through. The riot in Lampedusa was indeed triggered by news concerning this deportation agreement reaching migrants detained in the center. However, the Italian government stared deportation towards Tunisia quickly, right after engaging in extra-territorial detention measures, establishing prison-boats off the shore of Palermo. On September 23, 2011, 365 Tunisian citizens are deported. The total number reaches 605 in just three days, and in a week all Tunisian migrants detained on prison-boats are deported or, after further waiting onboard, are then transferred to detention centers on the mainland. This special deportation plan is officially declared as completed by the Italian government on October 25, 2011 with the last 50 Tunisians deported from Palermo airport. The number of expulsions of Tunisian migrants reached 1,490 after the signing of the agreement, and a total of 3,385 migrants were deported to Tunisia between April 7, 2011 and the end of October 2011.

---

[1] See postcard 8. 'Struggles, Resistances, Escapes'

⬤ 11. Insistence on Space.

What date and which place best represent the notion of an 'Insistence on Space'? The insistence on space occurs at the moment of escape. It occurs when you get together with others in train stations, without a ticket; when you are blocked somewhere because ticket inspectors tell you to get off the train; when you go to the capital or some town or other in Italy to check out the atmosphere there; when you move on, assuming you have the option to do so. Or, the insistence on space occurs if there is someone who is waiting for you in France or in some other European country and when, as often happens, you realize you are being pushed back or that it is not so easy to insist on a space because Europe is not a smooth space and Schengen is not a country. You insist on space when you run out of money and you don't know what to do. Insistence on a space where you may have a coffee, eat a sandwich, bathe, where you may find a mattress to sleep on instead of sleeping at the station, in a public garden or on the beach. But you insist on space also after the storm has passed, when the spotlights have been turned off and the struggles to occupy a place are over, when there is no longer someone to host you; when more or less close relatives or friends who were not waiting for you no longer know what to do with you and how to manage the fights with their husbands or wives due to your presence. You insist, then, in a less visible way, in small groups or only with certain friends. Insistences on space often take place by chance, through the grapevine. You are in Milan and you come back to Rome only because someone on the phone tells you to go there; you are in Bologna and you go to Ventimiglia, then you come back to some public garden in Bologna because at the police headquarters in Ventimiglia you are not given the residence permit. You stay on the beach for a few days, or in a garden, in the square in front of the station, in a squat with only the most trustworthy of travelling companions. You spend a number of weeks in Paris. But generally you stay in the street. This much is certain and often it's not even easy to organize that. You start to get hungry, you smell and you only have one pair of jeans to wear. You never take your shoes off and your feet hurt. You call home, not too often, to let them know you are still alive but you do not speak of your insistence on space, and sometimes you start to think about returning. You even go as far as to insist on consulate offices to try to work out how to get home. But you burnt a border when you left on a boat, one that won't allow you to burn it again on the return journey.

Where does this 'Insistence on Space' begin? What space of insistence requires annotating on the map? Rome, Palermo, Milan, stations, gardens, mosques, Paris, Ventimiglia, Marsiglia. We do not actually choose cities but we choose those places downtown that only those who insisted on space for a longer time, who refused to budge, got to know. Those who insisted on space for a shorter period, only got to know stations and gardens on the outskirts, various canteens or places in which to get changed, assuming these were not too difficult to find. To mark this icon 'insistence on space' on the map a number has been assigned to the city of Paris. We remain aware however that there were other streetabodes in numerous other Italian and French cities, as well as in the cities of other European countries. For some of those who insist, these places continue to be their streetabodes. One only has to cast a glance about the subway to realize that those three or four guys wearing light jackets on a winter night are Tunisian migrants heading to some dilapidated shelter. It is Paris, but not exactly Paris: rather, it is the grass and the paths of the Parc de la Villette, where, as early as March and April 2011, the insistence on space was the most pronounced. It was here where people articulated their strategies for existence, dodging raids, joining forces with associations and other established collectives as well as inventing their own.

🔴 12. Occupations / Squats.

« *Le Collectif des Tunisiens de Lampedusa à Paris occupe depuis ce 1er mai à minuit l'immeuble appartenant à la mairie de Paris se situant au 51 avenue Simon Bolivar à Paris 19ème* ». [The Collective of Tunisians from Lampedusa in Paris has been occupying the building of the municipality of Paris, located in 51 avenue Simon Bolivar in Paris 19th neighborhood since May 1]. It is May 2, 2011 and this statement circulates on the websites of various French organizations, on social networks and on the mailing lists of different networks and associations. This is the way Tunisian migrants start to identify themselves in terms of the 'Collective of Tunisians from Lampedusa in Paris,' a strange self-identification that provides collective terminology for both a citizenship and spaces of crossing and residence, regardless of their differences; a claim, in a sense, to a 'European Spring' for their existences. 'A place of living together and self-organizing.' A place for everyone. This is what the Tunisians from Lampedusa in Paris demand in their first statement, after their occupation of the building in 51 Avenue Simon Bolivar on May 1, 2011. After the first raid by French police, about 250 people moved from Parc de la Villette, making their presence visible. Such a presence is described and affirmed at the end of their political statement. 'We live in the street, we go 24, sometimes 36, hours without sleeping, we are scared, cold and hungry and we lack of all the basic things needed for an ordinary life. But despite these conditions we remain worthy.' 'We will stay here until a satisfying solution is offered to us. We demand the necessary documents to circulate and live freely.' Yet in actual fact, they only ended up staying on Avenue Simon Bolivar for two days before being evicted by force by the police which led to a nomadic existence across Paris, occupying buildings on the hills of Belleville: the college in Rue de la Fontaine-au-roi; a building in rue Bourdon, in Rue Bichat and near to the Tunisian embassy; the villa in Rue Botzaris, the French symbol of the dictatorship of Ben Ali, seat of the RCD (*Rassemblement constitutionnel démocratique*), the site of torture and an archive of many documents of the actions performed by the dictatorial apparatus. Then, June 16, 2011 and the final eviction arrives, followed by the nights spent at the Parc des Buttes Chaumont by those who had not found other solutions, and the dissolution of the movement. Over the course of six weeks, the 'Tunisians from Lampedusa in Paris' pursued their demand for *karama* [dignity] in the streets of Paris, surprised not to find themselves in the country of rights and freedom, and offended by the ways in which they were depicted by the mass-media and local authorities: as outlawed migrants, manipulated by a group of French anarchists - so the narrative went - hence deprived of their autonomy and awareness. They responded seriously in their statements where they referred to themselves as 'the sons of the revolution' and 'mature and aware adults.' They also answered with irony on banners at various demonstrations: 'we made the democratic revolution,' 'we are here to help you do the same thing.' After Paris, Pauda, in Italy, where Tunisian migrants occupy the courtyard of a school from the May 24 to May 28, 2011, claiming this time a more institutional 'right to asylum,' playing with municipal and governmental decrees which had centralized the mechanism for asylum, placing it under the care of Civil Protection. But squats and occupations constitute a spatial takeover that cannot be limited to between the esplanades and the hills of Paris or in the courtyards of schools. This takeover proliferated this time with less noise, taking place within the folds of invisibility. It became visible again during the last few days of the summer of 2011. Here it was a case of tearing up the space, when in a squat in Pantin, in the area of Seine-Saint-Denis, in the morning of September 28 the bodies of six migrants - two Egyptians and four Tunisians - are found burned. The Tunisians had set off from the region of Tataouine, on the border with Libya, going through Lampedusa before finally arriving in Paris. They had been there for all of twenty days, with friends, before being burnt to death in the country of rights and freedom.

↻ 13. Going back, Returns.

February 2012. Data can be highly sensitive. Numbers can get offended, hurt even, if they feel they are being talked about, or discover they are being used in a book. Sensitive to the extent that it is perhaps better to avoid upsetting them at all. It is easier not to gather them together or to claim not to have done so. Better to give those demanding them different, less easily offended numbers, re-routing their calls so they don't get spread around thoughtlessly. Sometimes those wanting to find out some data are extremely obstinate, visiting the right offices where employees seem surprised to be asked such imposing questions about this data, denying it has ever crossed their minds to ask the same questions during the course of their day-to-day work as state functionaries.

But let's try to impose some order here. This icon starts from a legend. Late in 2011, a story was circulating about Tunisian migrants leaving Europe to go back to Tunisia, going back of their own free will. Actually, what is meant by 'will' here should be thoroughly investigated and only after having defined this, might it be possible to understand if the return of the Tunisian migrants was really a question of free will at all. But this would imply writing a philosophical essay, while in this context we want to write a 'postcard', two or three pages, no more. But the problem is that we don't know exactly what to write since it took us about 15 days of unsuccessful research in order to locate any such data. After endless phone calls, we then asked Hamadi Zribi, a friend of ours who lives in Tunis to help us ... as a result he made a series of useless 'pilgrimages' to different government offices. There was nothing to be done, there was no data. Or perhaps such data does, in fact, exist but is carefully protected, sheltered from us.

Therefore, the legend of the returns will remain just that, a legend. We cannot say if the returns were but a few or considerable, since the only number we have for certain, one that is perhaps less sensitive than the others, is the number of Tunisian migrants who have now gone back to Tunisia from Italy. This was 490 in 2011, we are assured by the Tunisian embassy in Rome. 'Only a few of them,' a council member declares on the telephone, and the legend starts to crumble. But how many Tunisian migrants have gone back to Tunisia from France, from Belgium, from Germany and from Switzerland? The Tunisian embassy in France claims that the question should be addressed to the respective general consulates of these countries. We tried with the consulate in Paris, and realized it would have been useless to carry on with the others.

However, searching on the web one might stumble across a piece of news featured in a number of newspapers at the end of September 2011 after the fire of Pantin. Some of the six migrants, four Tunisian and two Egyptians who died in the flames, had been offered the program of humanitarian return (ARH) and they had refused. A few more 'clicks' on the Internet yield up the reason behind that refusal. 300 Euros is the sum the OFII (*Office français de l'immigration et de l'intégration*, the French Office for Immigration and Integration) allocated for that program.

Some further effort in front of the screen enables us to fully understand what this program is really about. In France, since June 2011, the 'voluntary' returns of Tunisians became 'humanitarian' returns. Quite an odd semantic shift, don't you think? Especially if we consider that only two months before, in Ventimiglia, Sarkozy and Guéant used the French borders with Italy to produce a ricochet effect upon Italy and its release of a temporary permit granted for humanitarian reasons to Tunisian migrants. An oddity which, in any case, saved France 1,700 Euros per *humanitarian flight* since instead of paying the 2,000 Euros fixed by the Voluntary Return program (ARV) for each voluntary returnee, France now pays 300 Euros for each 'humanitarian' return.

Tunisians who arrived in Paris in mid-July, 2011, received the generous help of the Mayor who added a 700 Euros, paid by the municipality, to the 300 Euros granted by the OFII. But 700 Euros was not handed out to everybody: only to the few hundred migrants who found accommodation in the *foyers* of the capital and who, on August 31, 2011, were given an eviction order by Mayor Delanoë himself.

This data was provided by the OFII in January 2013. It is quite useless to try to push on. So, let's return to Italy and to the 490 Tunisian migrants who left the country to return 'home'. Amongst these, there are certainly also migrants who form part of the Rivan program (Voluntary Assisted Return to North Africa) conceived ad hoc by the International Organization for Migration (IOM). Indeed, on May 6, 2011 IOM had already declared that they had crafted a specific intervention program for Tunisian migrants, 'necessary due to the many demands to return to the homeland which have arrived in the past few days from the Italian authorities.' In its statement, IOM guarantees that funding for the program will come from the European Repatriation Fund and, before describing the magnificence of the program - individual counselling services and a return orientation, organization of the transfer, assistance with the delivery of travel documents, cover of room and board costs in Rome the day before leaving and assistance by IOM staff at the airport - declared through the voice of Jose Angel Oropeza, the director of the IOM coordination office for the Mediterranean, that 'so far, we have more than 30 cases.' More than 30 cases? A large amount, about which is it hard to be specific so authorities opt for imprecision with the expression 'more' which allows then Oropeza to proceed: 'and so we are right to estimate that the quota of 50 people will be reached very soon, due to the increasing influx of north African migrants in our offices in Rome over the past few days.' Hence, no more than 50 people, among the 490 persons who left Italy could benefit from the huge amount established to add a dash of spontaneity to their will: 200 Euros. Ready to go, people go back. In the same way they left. Above all, with the same spirit. This is what IOM guarantees, since IOM knows migrants, and more than anything it knows their will, without needing philosophical essays on the meaning of the word, as long as it organizes 'voluntary returns' on an international scale, it knows that 'the return request comes from the fact that migrants consider that their migratory experience has come to an end and they do not intend to stay in Italy.' The statement finishes like this, not very wise considering the sense of self-parody it inspires. May 6, 2011. After some weeks spent out in the cold in Lampedusa, - and before spending a few days in detention on the island - after crossing on the continent for detentions, escapes or riots in a camp, who wouldn't want to consider their temporary migratory experience as over? And 'temporary' means, above all, that people are aware that the experience can be repeated. All that is required is a visit to the individual counselling service of IOM, accepting 200 Euros, going back to Tunisia, forgetting one's own individuality before rediscovering the collective dimension of yet another revolution, saving up 1000 Euros for the boat trip, seeing Italy appear on the horizon once more before an excursion to a different set of detention centers not visited as part of the previous 'migratory experience'. It's worthless to add that the program, renewed in 2012, is envisaged only for migrants endowed with the temporary residence permit and who are inside a 'hosting structure managed by the organization appointed for managing the migration emergency'; it's worthless to add that a statement signed by Franco Gabrielli, head of the department of the National Civil Protection, let it be known that up until now the voluntary repatriation has not produced 'the expected results.' It's worthless to add, moving to France, that in 2010 the OSCAR archive was created for the humanitarian return compiling biometric data of the migrants who benefit from the program in order to avoid frauds. But what about numbers? Let's leave them to their sensitivity. Whether the migrants who returned - people not numbers - are few or many, they nonetheless help us to grasp the sense of dejection coming from their delusion.

✦ 14. New States.

In order to oppose the spatial upheavals generated by the Uprisings in the Arab world, Italy has also 'produced' new States, placed in odd invented geographies justifying these with a dubious logic. We annotate this icon as the final in the series due to the impossibility of fixing as chronological moment this time of delirium. We describe these new states from the standpoint of this Italian madness as it declares a 'state of humanitarian emergency on the Northern Africa territory, to allow an efficient contrast of the exceptional inflow of non-European citizens on the national [i.e., Italian] territory.' The state of emergency is declared on April 7, 2011 by Prime Minister's decree. It is from Rome, from the site of the Italian government, that a state of emergency 'on the Northern Africa territory' is declared and through a formula that combines the vagueness of the gaze from Rome upon the Southern shore of the Mediterranean (e.g. a 'Northern African territory' the components of which are never specified) and the neo-colonial expansion of Rome into 'Northern Africa.' But on what basis should Rome have jurisdiction in Northern Africa? And what is the humanitarian logic to be found in a decree that is finalized in order to guarantee the 'efficient contrast' of non-European citizens' access to Italy?

The state located in 'Northern Africa territories' or 'territory' is actually the second state issued by Italy. Before it came the declaration of February 12, 2011 of the 'state of humanitarian emergency on national [Italian] territory due to the exceptional inflow of citizens from Countries of Northern Africa.' A matter of Italian jurisdiction, in this case - Rome declares a state of emergency on Italian soil - that comes with more detail about the geographical area at the origin of the crisis, that in fact is specified as 'Countries of Northern Africa of the Mediterranean shore, and in particular of the Maghreb area and Egypt.'

This uncanny geographical vagueness matched by a colonial expansionism is reaffirmed on August 3, 2011 when another Prime Minister issues the second new 'Italian-African' state. The decree, in fact, mandates 'the extension of the declaration of the state of emergency [...] to other Countries of the African continent.' This Italian territoriality issuing states outside its national borders, in 'Northern Africa,' and then in 'the other states of the African continent' is really a scattered and confused territoriality, an aterritoriality of conquest. So how far does this Italian territoriality extend within Africa? What are the 'other Countries' beyond those already designated as 'Countries of Northern Africa' included within this new state? The uncanny designation of 'African continent' suggests an Italian range of action which got out of control. When on October 6, 2011 the 'state of emergency' is extended to December 31, 2012, Italy, North Africa and other countries of the African continent find themselves unwittingly absorbed into the common destiny of a counter-unified space.

www.ingramcontent.com/pod-product-compliance
Lightning Source LLC
Chambersburg PA
CBHW071739270326
41928CB00013B/2738